MOON ROCKS AND MINERALS

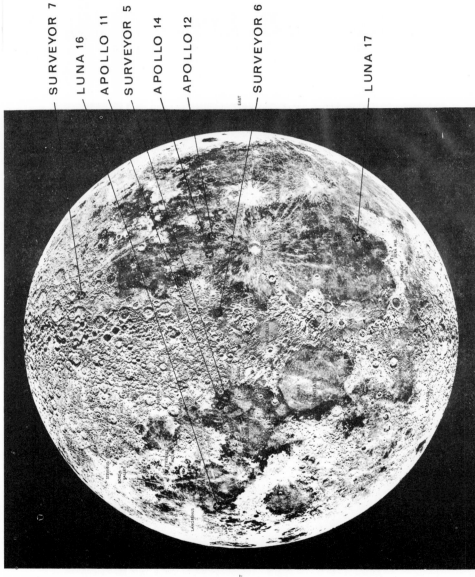

SURVEYOR 7

LUNA 16

APOLLO 11

SURVEYOR 5

APOLLO 14

APOLLO 12

SURVEYOR 6

LUNA 17

SOUTH

NORTH

EAST

WEST

Composite photograph of first and last quarters of the moon. Reprinted by permission of Yale University Press from *The Planets*, by Harold C. Urey. Photograph courtesy Lick Observatory.

MOON ROCKS AND MINERALS

Scientific Results of the Study of the Apollo 11 Lunar Samples
with Preliminary Data on Apollo 12 Samples

Professor Alfred A. Levinson
Department of Geology
The University of Calgary
Calgary, Alberta, Canada

and

Dr. S. Ross Taylor
Department of Geophysics and Geochemistry
Australian National University
Canberra, Australia

PERGAMON PRESS

New York • Toronto • Oxford • Sydney • Braunschweig

PERGAMON PRESS INC.
Maxwell House, Fairview Park, Elmsford, N.Y. 10523

PERGAMON OF CANADA LTD.
207 Queen's Quay West, Toronto 117, Ontario

PERGAMON PRESS LTD.
Headington Hill Hall, Oxford

PERGAMON PRESS (AUST.) PTY. LTD.
Rushcutters Bay, Sydney, N.S.W.

VIEWEG & SOHN GmbH
Burgplatz 1, Braunschweig

08 016669 5

DEDICATED TO

our understanding wives and children

Gail

Edward and Allyson

———————

Noël

Susanna, Judith and Helen

CONTENTS

Top: Type A: basalt; a fine-grained igneous rock (hand-specimen). Ilmenite and glass line vesicles. Specimen is 2.3 cm. across and is a chip from rock 10022.

Bottom: Thin section of the same rock as above illustrating fine-grained nature. Minerals are: black = ilmenite; white and grey = plagioclase (feldspar); red, yellow and blue = pyroxene. Vesicle appears in upper left hand corner. Width of field = 4 mm.

PLATE 1.

Top: Type B: gabbro; a medium-grained igneous rock (hand specimen). Note white areas which are plagioclase, and darker pyroxene. Grain size is about 1 mm. Larger specimen is about 5 cm. across. Rock 10044.

Bottom: Thin section of type B rock (sample 10047) illustrating coarser (medium-grained) texture in comparison with Type A (Plate 1). Minerals are: black = ilmenite; white and grey = plagioclase; red, yellow and blue = pyroxene. Width of field = 4 mm.

PLATE 2.

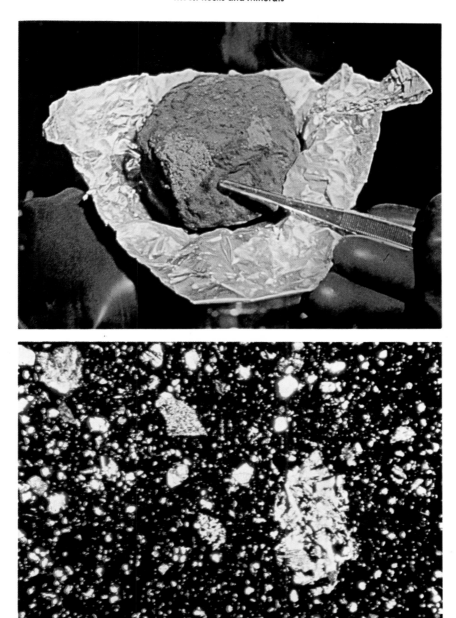

Top: Type C: breccia; an agglomeration of Types A and B igneous rocks, mineral particles, glassy spherules, etc., (hand-specimen). Note the two large rock fragments within the breccia. Specimen is 7.5 cm. across. Rock 10046.

Bottom: Thin section of Type C rock (sample 10019). Matrix is glass (dark) with small crystal fragments (multi-colors). Large fragments are igneous rocks and minerals. Width of field = 4 mm.

PLATE 3.

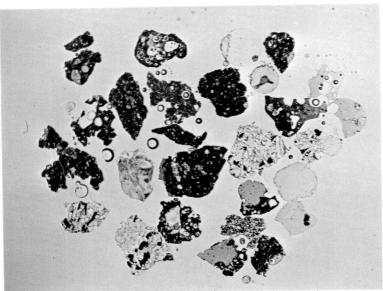

Top: Assortment of rock particles in the 1-3 mm. size range, from the lunar soil (Type D material). Particles were chosen to illustrate the various rock types encountered, and are not present in representative numbers. Microscopic view with millimeter scale at lower right.

Bottom: Thin section of same particles arranged as nearly as possible in the same positions and orientations. (One spherule is missing from the thin section.) Note orange color characteristic of most lunar glass. (Magnification 10X)

PLATE 4.

Top: Lunar soil (Type D material), with millimeter scale. Soil has been sieved to remove most very fine material (less than 1 mm.), but is otherwise untreated. Fine dust still coats the coarser grains and partly masks their character.

Bottom: Thin section of anorthositic gabbro which is found only in the lunar soils (Type D). This rock is unlike any other Apollo 11 igneous rocks and is believed to have been blown in from the lunar highlands. Minerals are: blue-grey = anorthite; brownish-orange = pigeonite; purplish = olivine (small; within anorthite). Crossed nicols. Width of field is 2 mm.

PLATE 5.

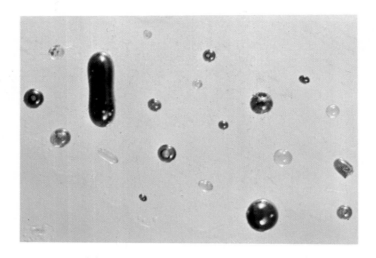

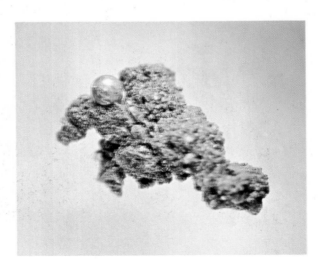

Top: Glass spheres and dumbbells from lunar fines (sample 10084). The composition ranges from anorthite glass (colorless) through variable fused mixtures of anorthite, pyroxene and ilmenite. The color trends toward dark brown with increasing content of FeO and TiO_2. Size of large dumbbell approximately 0.75 mm.

Bottom: Hardened (indurated) fragment of lunar fines, about 2.2 mm. in length containing several glass spheres.

PLATE 6.

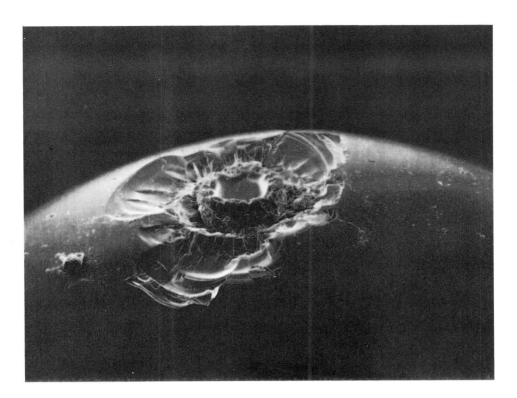

Top: Hypervelocity impact crater, with surrounding chipped (spalled) zone, on a small dark brown glass sphere from the lunar fines. Small craters of this type are believed to have been formed by micrometeorites. Diameter of inner rimmed crater is 0.06 mm. Photograph taken with scanning electron microscope (in black and white).

Bottom: Pyroxferroite, $(Fe_{0.85}Ca_{0.15})SiO_3$, a new mineral from Tranquillity Base, Moon. *Left:* a crystal of pyroxferroite (slightly out of focus), approximately 0.5 mm. in width, showing crystal faces (from rock 10047). *Right:* Thin section showing pyroxferroite (triangular white area at center) within pyroxene crystals (red and yellow). Plagioclase crystals (gray) are also visible. Crossed nicols. Width of field = 0.04 mm.

PLATE 7.

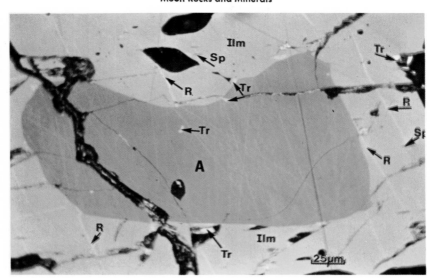

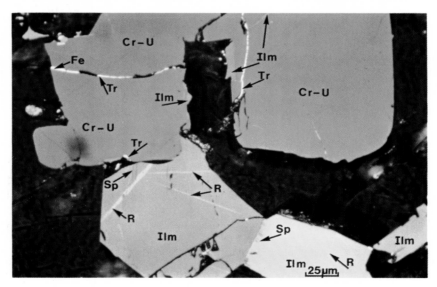

Top: Armalcolite (A), a new mineral from Tranquillity Base, Moon as seen in reflected light in thin-polished section (oil immersion-plane polarized light). Rock 10017. Generalized formula is $(Fe_{0.5}Mg_{0.5})Ti_2O_5$. Armalcolite is mantled by overgrowth of ilmenite (Ilm). Exsolution lamellae of rutile (R) and spinel (Sp) occur within ilmenite; associated blebs of troilite (Tr) are also present. Fine polishing scratches are restricted to armalcolite indicating it is softer than ilmenite.

Bottom: Large grains of a new mineral variety, chromian-ulvöspinel (Cr–U) seen under same conditions as above. Rock 10020. Cracks within this mineral are filled with metallic iron (Fe) and troilite (Tr). Ilmenite (Ilm), exsolution lamellae of rutile (R) and lenses of spinel (Sp) are also present. (This mineral variety, and armalcolite, will be various shades of gray when not viewed by oil immersion methods).

PLATE 8.

PREFACE

Few events of the twentieth century have aroused as much scientific and general interest as the Apollo lunar flights. The Apollo 11 lunar landing, sample collection and return to Earth were watched by countless millions throughout the world who saw the accomplishment of its primary purpose — the landing of men on the moon and their safe return to Earth. Yet when we realize that one of the foremost secondary aims of the Apollo program is the gathering and dissemination of scientific information from lunar samples, we also realize that this information is not readily available in an easily understandable form. The layman, as well as the scientist in any field other than those directly related to the certain areas of geochemistry, cosmochemistry, mineralogy or geophysics, are likely to find the scientific results confusing and written in very technical language. The purpose of this book is to disseminate, in as simple a manner as possible, the important findings which have resulted from the first study of the Apollo 11 lunar rocks. The need for such a book became apparent to us during discussions with colleagues specializing in other areas of science at which time the lack of understanding of both the nature of the studies and the results of the findings were all too evident. Further, perhaps when we remember that approximately 24 billion dollars had been spent on the Apollo program before the first rock was returned ($500,000,000 per pound), the dissemination of this information to a general audience is essential.

There are several sources from which we could draw our material. For example, the National Aeronautics and Space Administration (NASA) Lunar Sample Preliminary Examination Team published the results of their six-week examination of the Apollo 11 rocks in *Science* (vol. 165, pp. 1211-1227) in September, 1969. This initial report is of limited value for our purposes, for its main function was only to collect enough information about the lunar samples to ensure intelligent distribution to the approximately 150 Principal Investigators and their 400 associates throughout the world (in nine countries) who were to perform very detailed and specific studies for NASA and the scientific community. We have drawn almost exclusively upon the proceedings of the Apollo 11 Lunar Science Conference which was held on January 5-8, 1970 in Houston, Texas under NASA sponsorship. At this historic meeting the scientific results obtained by the 150 Principal Investigators and their associates were presented. Most of these scientists had received their lunar samples about three months earlier and prepared short papers describing their results. The initial reports were limited to 1800 words (or equivalent in figures, illustrations and tables) and were published in *Science* (vol. 167, pp. 449-784) on January 30, 1970. It will be immediately evident that such short articles are not likely to give more than the highlights of each project and, therefore, do not give us the necessary depth for our projected discussion of the first non-meteoritic extra-terrestrial specimens.

There is another reference source — a source in which the same Principal Investigators and their associates presented their more comprehensive and detailed articles based on their findings after three months of study, plus additional deliberation and writings in the interim period January 8-30, 1970. This source is the *"Proceedings of the Apollo 11 Lunar Science Conference,"* a 2500 page supplement of the journal *Geochimica et Cosmochimica Acta* (Latinized translation of "Geochemistry and Cosmochemistry Transactions"). This journal is the official publication of both The Geochemical Society and The Meteoritical Society and is regarded as the leading international technical journal devoted exclusively to geochemistry and cosmochemistry.

We have chosen to use the 180 technical papers of the *Proceedings* as the basis of our attempt to reduce the approximately 1,250,000 words (or equivalent in illustrations) written about the Apollo 11 rocks to about 50,000. It is our aim to consider only the subjects covered in the *Proceedings*, all based upon projects approved and supported in various ways by NASA. The broad subject areas are:

1. Mineralogy and Petrology
2. Chemical and Isotope Analyses
3. Physical Properties
4. Bioscience and Organic Geochemistry

The reader will find that we do not stray from our chosen subject, an *understanding* of the Apollo 11 rocks, with digressions into the engineering aspects of the flight, quarantine of the rocks, biographies of the astronauts, astronomical aspects, etc. We do, however, mention the origin of the moon, and a few other speculative topics, but only insofar as the chemical data or physical properties emanating from the *Proceedings* justify it. Nor do we discuss the Apollo 12 results (*Science*, vol. 167, pp. 1325-1339, 1970) in more than a cursory way as detailed information on these rocks was not available at the time of our preparation of this book.

Considering the voluminous literature now available, it must be borne in mind that it is not realistic to attempt to identify all scientists who have reached identical conclusions, or obtained similar data; those whom we mention by name are more in the way of examples, rather than an attempt to assign credit or priority. Further, because of the large numbers of individuals working on identical projects, and combining their efforts into a single report (one article has 18 co-authors), we have chosen to mention only the first or senior author of each research group. And, finally, we would like to stress that the data and interpretations presented herein represent the state of knowledge available to us as of April 30, 1970 and are subject to modification or re-interpretation at any time.

ALFRED A. LEVINSON   and   S. ROSS TAYLOR
Calgary, Alberta, Canada   *Canberra, A.C.T., Australia*

August, 1970

ACKNOWLEDGMENTS

We wish to acknowledge the assistance of many individuals in various aspects of the preparation of this book. Special thanks go to Mr. S.W. Reeder (Canada Inland Waters Branch) who pointed out to us the need for a simplified book covering the Apollo 11 Lunar Science Conference, and to Professors P. Bayliss and J.W. Nicholls (University of Calgary) who critically read the first half of the book.

During the past year we have had numerous discussions about the lunar samples and the origin of the moon with many workers in the field. It is impossible to acknowledge the many people individually but we wish to thank them collectively. One of us (S.R.T.) wishes to pay a special tribute to fellow members of the Lunar Sample Preliminary Examination Team (LSPET) for many stimulating discussions, and for much good company. Particular thanks are due to Dr. Robin Brett, (Chief, Geochemistry Branch, NASA Manned Spacecraft Center, Houston, Texas) and to the staff of the Lunar Science Institute, Houston, Texas for hospitality during a unique and exciting period. The chapter, "Bioscience and Organic Matter", is largely the work of Professor Gordon W. Hodgson (University of Calgary) but we take full responsibility for its contents. Mrs. Patricia R. O'Hara (Calgary), and Mrs. R. Worden and Mrs. C. Pedersen (Canberra), kindly typed the manuscript.

Throughout this book we have used figures (line drawings and photographs) as well as color plates, which appear in the *Proceedings Of The Apollo 11 Lunar Science Conference*, published by Pergamon Press (1970). We express our thanks not only to the publisher but also to all the lunar sample scientists whose illustrations we have used, and whose studies form the basis for this book. Credits and our appreciation for the color plates are as follows:

Plate 1   *Top*: NASA photograph S-69-41895; *Bottom*: NASA photograph S-69-50428.

Plate 2   *Top*: NASA photograph S-69-52038; *Bottom*: NASA photograph S-69-50419.

1

INTRODUCTION

Many years of thought and planning were spent on the scientific, as well as the engineering, aspects of the Apollo 11 mission to the moon. Scientists and engineers alike were well aware that the first astronauts' stay on the moon would be quite limited and their extravehicular activities would be in the order of two hours. The astronauts had been given intensive courses in geology, with particular attention to the types of rocks, landscapes and soils they would likely find on their landing. Emphasis was placed on the recognition of various types of rocks, rock textures and other characteristics so that they could promptly recognize representative and unusual rocks from the landing area. For their part, the scientists were prepared to subject the returned rocks and soil to every known chemical, mineralogical, physical and biological test in order to gain as much information as possible from the limited amount of material expected. Based on the findings from the Apollo 11 rocks, modifications in plans for future Apollo missions would likely be necessary.

Scientists from all over the world were invited to submit proposals to the National Aeronautics and Space Administration (NASA) covering such points as how they would proceed to study samples should they be successfully returned, what information they would hope to find, and the quantity of material they would like (and how little they could actually get along with!). From these proposals NASA selected approximately 150 groups of scientific investigators from nine countries (the United States, Great Britain, Canada, Germany, Switzerland, Finland, Belgium, Australia and Japan), each of which was headed by a leader known as the Principal Investigator (P.I.). A few of the groups consisted of only the P.I., but most had several Coinvestigators (known as Co-I's.); on one project there were 18 Co-investigators. The sum total of all Principal and Co-investigators (plus some associates not officially classified) who worked on the Apollo 11 rocks, is about 550, and this figure does not include the multitude in various technician and support categories. The list of scientists contains the names of two Nobel Laureates in chemistry, Professors Urey and Calvin, as well as some of today's most active and productive scientists in geology, geochemistry and geophysics. There was a deliberate attempt to have overlap of projects to ensure that nothing of significance was missed. A surprisingly large number of the scientists are in their 30's; only a small percentage are over 50 years of age.

The scientific projects, for the sake of administration, have been grouped into four broad general categories:

1. Mineralogy and Petrology: this group of about 45 projects is concerned with all aspects of the identification, composition, origin and classification of the minerals and rocks found in the lunar rocks and soils. Included in this category are shock studies to determine changes brought about by meteoritic and other types of impact, electron microscopy to illustrate various textures under extremely high magnification, and so forth.

2. Chemical and Isotope Analyses: this group of about 65 projects is generally concerned with all aspects of the composition of the entire lunar rock (as opposed to individual minerals), including elements present in extremely small quantities ("trace" elements) as well as the major elements, rare (noble) gases, short-lived cosmic-ray induced elements (nuclides), and radiation effects. An especially important type of study in this category is concerned with the abundance of the various chemical isotopes found in the rocks and soils. Isotope studies are divided into several types: (a) radiogenic isotopes, such as those of uranium, from which the *age* of the lunar rocks can be determined, and (b) stable isotopes, such as carbon and oxygen, from which indications of the geological *processes* operative on the moon may be determined.

3. Bioscience and Organic Geochemistry: one of the most fascinating of all scientific prospects has been whether or not life ever existed on the moon. and especially if there might be some low form of life there at present. Eighteen studies, using the most sophisticated of analytical equipment, were designed for this purpose. Contamination of the lunar samples with organisms on Earth (or transported by the astronauts and the spacecraft) was a major problem and extremely elaborate procedures were arranged to minimize this possibility.

4. Physical Properties and Measurements: the approximately 40 projects in this group are concerned with studies of residual magnetism, thermoluminescence, soil mechanics, and so forth, from which various types of evidence indicative of past history as well as present lunar conditions may be gleaned.

The Apollo 11 landing on the moon took place on July 20, 1969 at 3:17:40 p.m. E.S.T. at the southern edge of Mare Tranquillitatis. The site is now known as Tranquillity Base and is just north of the lunar equator (Fig. 1-1). The samples were collected by astronauts Neil Armstrong and Edwin

Aldrin in approximately two hours of extravehicular activity during which time they also took photographs and conducted various scientific experiments. The astronauts and samples returned (the latter in vacuum) to Earth and then immediately went to the Lunar Receiving Laboratory at the NASA Manned Spacecraft Center in Houston, Texas on July 25, 1969 where all were placed in quarantine — 21 days for the astronauts and 50 days for the samples. During the quarantine period the samples were subject to intensive physical, chemical, mineralogical, and biological study by the Lunar Sample Preliminary Examination Team (LSPET) behind and through specially constructed biological barriers.

Fig. 1-1. Location of Tranquillity Base, the landing site of Apollo 11. LM = Lunar Module, the spacecraft that landed on the moon. (NASA photograph S-68-23916.)

The purpose of the quarantine was to establish beyond any doubt the fact that no pathogenic catastrophes would result from a mixing of the lunar ecology with that on Earth. The quarantine period gave the approximately 30 members of LSPET time to make their various examinations, the primary purpose of which was to collect enough information about the lunar samples so that the samples could be distributed in an intelligent manner to the NASA-selected 150 Principal Investigators and their 400 Co-Investigators. These preliminary results obtained during the quarantine period served as the basis of sample distribution and also as the starting point for most of the scientific investigations.

Because the LSPET report (*Science*, vol. 165, pp. 1211-1227, September 19, 1969) contains the basic facts, terminology, concepts and preliminary

Fig. 1-2. Location of Lunar Module (LM) on the lunar surface and its relation to West Crater. (NASA photograph.)

Fig. 1-3. Coarse ejecta ray from West Crater, which may have contributed material to the Apollo 11 (Tranquillity Base) samples. Large boulders in the ray are 1½ – 2 meters in size. The tripod in foreground is about 1 meter high. (NASA photograph AS11-37-5468.)

rock classifications which served as the starting point for the scientists whose papers form the basis of this book, it is chronologically appropriate in this Introduction to summarize the major facts and findings available to the Principal Investigators when they started their lunar studies generally between late September and early October, 1969.

The Apollo 11 module landed in the southwestern part of Mare Tranquillitatis (Fig. 1-1) at latitude 0.67°N, longitude 23.49°E, which is approximately 10 km. southwest of the crater Sabine D. Unmanned lunar probes had previously landed in the general vicinity (Surveyor 5 about 25 km. to the northwest and Ranger 8 about 68 km. to the northeast), hence at least some information on this area of the moon was available. This part of Mare Tranquillitatis exhibits two ray systems; several faint rays emanate from Theophilus (320 km. to the southeast), and a more prominent ray is found 15 km. to the west whose origin has been suggested as being either the crater Alfraganus (160 km. to the southwest) or Tycho (1500 km. to the southwest). The landing site lies between major ray systems, but it has been considered likely that some material related to them, and other distant sources, is probably at the landing site primarily in the soils. There are also many pits and smaller craters in the vicinity of Tranquillity Base which range from a few centimeters to 200 meters in diameter. A crater known as West crater, about 400 meters east of the landing site, is 180 meters in diameter and 30 meters deep and is the largest sharply-defined crater in the vicinity (Fig. 1-2). It has a raised rim and its blocky ejecta spreads out symmetrically about 250 meters around the crater, and also as rays which may have contributed material to the collection area (Fig. 1-3). Several other small broad craters are in the vicinity of the landing site (Fig. 1-4). All those examined

Fig. 1-4. Unnamed broad crater, 33 meters in diameter, about 60 meters east of the Lunar Module. Note broken bedrock exposed in the bottom of the crater. (NASA photograph.)

by the astronauts were shallow and appeared to be excavated in the regolith, hence lunar bedrock was not definitely observed, but is probably represented in the Apollo 11 rocks. Subsequent evidence suggests bedrock may be as close as 3-6 meters to the surface.

The important point to be realized from the above brief description is that the Apollo 11 landing site is heavily strewn with rocky debris, is pockmarked with small pits and craters, and, as no bedrock was definitely established, all samples are from the regolith (loose surface material). Although the samples collected at Tranquillity Base predominantly consist of mare material, the presence of meteoritic material must not be overlooked owing to the large number of pits and craters, which are of impact origin. Further, the proximity of major rays suggested to many investigating groups that some material from as far as Tycho might be expected, particularly as a component of the soils. The soils would be expected to yield the greatest variation in data because of their multiple source origin.

Mare Tranquillitatis itself is part of the dark plains characteristic of the side of the moon facing the Earth. It is irregular in form (as contrasted to the ringed maria) and is not characterized by a mascon (positive gravity anomaly). The Apollo 12 landing and collection area in the Sea of Storms (about 1400 km. to the west) is similar in many ways to that of Apollo 11. Further, based on preliminary information, Apollo 12 rocks are similar to those described in this book. Some of the major differences include the facts that the Apollo 12 rocks are some hundreds of millions of years younger, show greater variation in abundances of minerals and textures, contain considerably less solar wind material, and the regolith at the Apollo 12 site is only about one-half as thick as that at Tranquillity Base.

The Apollo 11 mission returned about 21.5 kg. (47.3 lb.) of lunar samples most of which have been used for scientific study or are preserved (under controlled storage conditions) for later study. About one-third of the total (15 lb.) has been distributed for the studies which are reported here, and of this about 4.5 lb. are believed to be totally consumed or destroyed in the studies; scientists are required to maintain detailed records on the disposition of each specimen and are responsible for the safety of their samples. A total of 900 gm. (2 lb.) is available for display in the United States and other countries, and, as of February 1970, President Nixon had distributed 10 gm. in the form of 200 specimens of about 50 mg. each. Biological testing during the quarantine consumed 700 gm. (about 1.5 lb.).

2

THE ROCKS AND SOILS

The lunar samples have been divided into four "Types": three are rocks and one is the fines (soil):

1. Type A: basalt, a fine-grained vesicular crystalline, igneous rock (Plate 1 in color frontispiece).
2. Type B: gabbro or microgabbro, a medium-grained vuggy crystalline, igneous rock (Plate 2 in color frontispiece).
3. Type C: breccia or microbreccia, which is an agglomeration of the lunar igneous rocks, mineral particles, together with glassy spherules, and other materials in the soils (Plate 3 in color frontispiece).
4. Type D: fines or soil (Plates 4, 5 and 6 in color frontispiece).

The term rock is arbitrarily used for a specimen larger than 1 cm., and fines or soil (Type D) for all smaller fragments, regardless of their mineralogical or petrological nature. The distinction between Type A (basalt) and B (gabbro) rocks has been arbitrarily set at a grain size of 0.5 mm. It should be emphasized that a gradational textural and compositional series probably exists between Type A and Type B rocks and, as a result, several rocks of intermediate characteristics are known which are referred to as Type AB (Table 2-1). The classification of Types A, B, C and D was a preliminary classification made early in the initial study of the lunar samples by the preliminary examination group (LSPET). It has proved to be quite workable and most scientists continue to use it at least as a first approximation, although some do so reluctantly as the distinction between basalt and gabbro on Earth simply on the basis of grain size is not entirely accurate. The success of the classification, which is based on textural considerations, may be attributed to the fact that the mineral composition of each rock is similar. The most important and abundant minerals are pyroxene, feldspar and ilmenite which together constitute at least 90% of the Type A and B rocks although their relative proportions vary from rock to rock, as well as within individual rocks. Chemical distinctions between Types A and B rocks, based on the abundance of potassium and a few other elements, are discussed in detail in Chapter 4.

Table 2-1. The Apollo 11 Rocks.

Sample #	Weight (gm.)	Type	General Rock Classification
10003	225	B	gabbro, medium-grained, vuggy, subophitic
10017	975	A	olivine basalt; very fine-grained, vesicular to vuggy, poikilitic
10018	215	C	breccia
10019	295	C	breccia
10020	425	A	olivine basalt; fine-grained, vesicular to vuggy, ophitic
10021	255	C	breccia
10022	95	A	olivine basalt; fine-grained, vesicular, subophitic
10023	65	C	breccia
10024	70	B	cristobalite gabbro; medium-grained, vuggy
10044	250	B	cristobalite gabbro; coarse-grained, ophitic
10045	245	AB	olivine basalt; fine-grained, vuggy to vesicular, ophitic
10046	665	C	breccia
10047	190	B	cristobalite gabbro; coarse-grained, vuggy, ophitic
10048	580	C	breccia
10049	195	A	granular basalt; very fine-grained, vesicular to vuggy
10050	115	AB	cristobalite gabbro; coarse-grained, vuggy, ophitic
10056	185	C	breccia
10057	920	A	granular basalt; fine-grained, vesicular to vuggy
10058	280	B	cristobalite gabbro; medium-grained, vuggy, ophitic
10059	190	C	breccia
10060	725	C	breccia
10061	350	C	breccia
10062	80	B	olivine gabbro; coarse-grained, vuggy, ophitic
10063	150	C	breccia
10064	65	C	breccia
10065	350	C	breccia
10066	45	C	breccia
10067	70	C	breccia
10068	215	C	breccia
10069	120	A	granular basalt aggregate; very fine-grained, vuggy to vesicular
10070	70	C	breccia
10071	195	AB	plumose basalt aggregate; very fine-grained, vesicular to vuggy
10072	445	A	olivine basalt; fine-grained, vesicular to vuggy, subophitic
10073	125	C	breccia
10074	60	C	breccia

Table 2-1 *(Continued)*

Sample #	Weight (gm.)	Type	General Rock Classification
10075	55	C	breccia
10084	} 12, 486	D	fines (soil, dust)
10085		D	fines (soil, dust)

Notes:

1. Missing numbers (for example, 10001, 10002, 10004) are samples used for biological or other types of testing at the Lunar Receiving Laboratory, Houston; some samples have never been distributed, etc. All Apollo 11 rock numbers begin with "100."
2. All rocks returned on the Apollo 11 mission greater than 50 gm. are listed in the above table.
3. In technical and scientific reports, chips or subsamples are indicated with an additional number following the five-digit number; for example 10057-23 (chip 23 from sample 10057).
4. The "Type" (A, B, AB, C, or D) is based on the original classification by the Lunar Samples Preliminary Examination Team (LSPET); this classification is still widely used (see text). However, based on chemical characteristics the following five rocks would be classified differently as follows: 10020 = B; 10024 = A; 10045 = B; 10050 = B, 10071 = A.
5. The "General Rock Classification" is based on the study of Schmitt, Lofgren, Swann and Simmons (NASA Manned Spacecraft Center, Houston).

Color photographs illustrating the different types of rocks are presented in the frontispiece (color plate section). The illustrations are arranged so that the reader may see a hand specimen (Plates 1, 2, 3, 4; top) and a corresponding thin section (Plates 1, 2, 3, 4; bottom) for each type. It is evident from the hand specimens of Type A (Plate 1, top) and Type B (Plate 2, top) that the grain size distinction is not easily recognizable, but in the thin-sections (Plates 1 and 2, bottom), the distinction is clear. There are cases, however, in which different portions of a rock (Fig. 2-1) will have distinctly different grain sizes, but this is not a particularly common feature.

The igneous rocks, as well as breccias (Type C) are generally rounded, at least those surfaces which have been exposed (Fig. 2-2). The rounded surfaces indicate that erosion processes of some type are operative on the moon; this subject is discussed in greater detail later. In many cases, the exact location and positioning of a rock collected by the astronauts is known, as is illustrated in Fig. 2-3. The relative positions of several other individual samples are illustrated in Fig. 2-4.

A selection of hand specimens of rocks, along with thin sections from the same rock, are presented in Figs. 2-5 through 2-8; note that different scales (magnification) are used. The purpose of this black and white selection is to present to the reader in one place the over-all impression of the lunar rocks, their appearance in thin section, and other details of interest. For those familiar with rocks and minerals, it will be immediately evident that the lunar rocks illustrated in Figs. 2-5 through 2-7 have textures, minerals, physical appearance and so forth, similar to basalts and gabbros found on Earth. There are, however, characteristic differences in chemistry, such as high contents of titanium and ferrous iron discussed below, which have given rise to the occasional use of such terms as titanium (or ilmenite) basalt, or ferrobasalt. Some of the more common textures found in the lunar crystalline

Fig. 2-1. Photomicrograph of lunar basalt (Type A, number 10071) showing textural differences between two areas of the rock. The black mineral is ilmenite; note radiating habit of the ilmenite in the upper half of the figure. Lighter colored minerals are chiefly pyroxene and feldspar. (NASA photograph S-70-26820.)

Fig 2-2. Rock sample with rounded top and angular underside. The rounding indicates that some type of erosion process is operative on the moon.

a

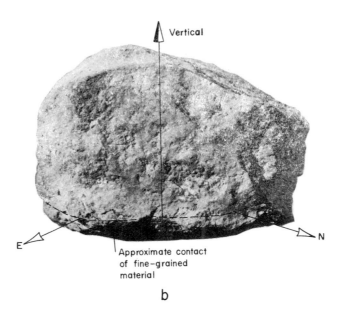

b

Fig. 2-3. (a) Rock 10046 as it appeared on the lunar surface before sampling. (b) Same rock with coordinates showing lunar orientation.

(Type A and B) rocks are listed below; all of these textures have been observed in terrestrial igneous rocks.

a. granular texture (Fig. 2-9): composed of nearly equidimensional mineral grains;

b. ophitic texture (Fig. 2-10; also 2-7): composed of elongated, feldspar crystals embedded in pyroxene or olivine;

c. subophitic texture (Fig. 2-11; also 2-6): similar to ophitic texture, but the size difference between the feldspar and pyroxene crystals is not as great;

d. poikioblastic texture (Fig. 2-12): occurrence of small granular crystals irregularly scattered in a larger crystal of another mineral;

e. plumose texture (Fig. 2-1): a radiating arrangement of crystals.

Fig. 2-4. The positions of rocks 10022, 10023, 10028 and 10032 before sampling. (NASA photograph AS11-39-5777.)

The crystalline rocks (Type A and B) are volcanic in origin. Volcanic means either a lava (surface) flow or near-surface intrusive. There are two principal mechanisms which have been proposed for the generation of igneous rocks of the maria: (a) volcanism triggered by meteorite impact and (b) volcanism in the terrestrial sense. Further discussion of these possibilities is presented in later sections but it suffices to say that the rocks have igneous textures, cavities, and mineral assemblages characteristic of terrestrial igneous rocks, which suggests that crystallization took place from melts by processes analogous to the crystallization of terrestrial rocks.

Fig. 2-5. Very fine-grained olivine basalt. Rock 10017 (Type A). Top: rock specimen (NASA photograph S-69-47560). Bottom: thin section (Lunar Receiving Laboratory photograph). Following description is after Schmitt (NASA Manned Spacecraft Center, Houston).

Size: 10 × 11 × 7.5 cm. Weight: 975 gm. Color: medium gray.

Shape: rounded to subrounded with one flat surface, hemispherical.

Fractures: very few fractures parallel to surface; hard coherent rock.

Pits & Glass: pits with glass linings are sparse, white halos remain and are 1–3 mm. dia., no glass splash. The glass in the pits can be flaked off easily. Speckled white on rounded surfaces.

Texture: very fine-grained, vesicular to vuggy, subophitic to granular; vesicles are smooth walled with no filling or late stage reaction products; cavities or vugs are 1–3 mm., usually elongate but not orientated; one large phenocryst of olivine, rectangular shape, not resorbed.

Mineralogy: pyroxene: 45–50%, dark brown, ~0.1 mm.; plagioclase: 30–35%, clear to chalky white, ~0.4 mm.; ilmenite: 15–20%, submetallic, ~0.1 mm.; olivine: <1%, medium yellow green; 1 phenocryst 5 mm. × 2 mm.

0   1
Centimeters

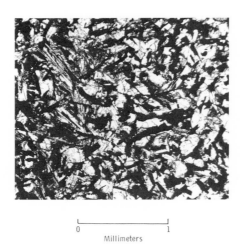

0   1
Millimeters

Fig. 2-6. Fine-grained olivine basalt. Rock 10022 (Type A). Top: rock specimen (NASA photograph S-69-45523). Bottom: thin section (NASA photograph S-69-47908). Following description is after Schmitt (NASA Manned Spacecraft Center, Houston). Another view of this rock may be seen in the color frontispiece (Plate 1).

SIZE: 6 x 4 x 3 cm. WEIGHT: 96 gm. DENSITY: 3.3 gm./cm.³. COLOR: dark gray.

SHAPE: irregularly subrounded with angular protuberances, elongate.

FRACTURES: microcracks with many orientations, glass (?) and white to chalky feldspar occur along some of these cracks.

PITS & GLASS: shallow pits with white halos and glass centers randomly distributed, concentric exfoliation in halos; small crusts of glass also randomly distributed, glass varicolored with botryoidal surface.

TEXTURE: fine-grained, vesicular, subophitic; vesicles are spherical to ovate, 2–3 per cm.², no vapor phase or late stage vesicle filling, glittery submetallic lining in vesicles; no vugs.

MINERALOGY: plagioclase: 20%, clear to white, chalky on surface near pits; clinopyroxene: 50%, dark brown sometimes honey brown; ilmenite: 30%, submetallic.

0   1   2
Centimeters

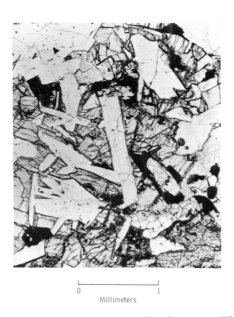

0   1
Millimeters

Fig. 2-7. Coarse-grained cristobalite gabbro. Rock 10047 (Type B). Top: rock specimen (NASA photograph S-69-45633). Bottom: thin section (NASA photograph S-69-47907). Following description is after Schmitt (NASA Manned Spacecraft Center, Houston).

SIZE: 7 × 4 × 3 cm. WEIGHT: 191 gm. DENSITY: 3.3 gm./cm.³. COLOR: light gray (salt and pepper).
SHAPE: generally subangular with one rounded side.
FRACTURES: numerous fractures; rock is crumbly or friable.
PITS & GLASS: pits are not readily visible, usually only white halo visible, rare glass centers present; dust has adhered in irregular pattern (welded?).
TEXTURE: coarse-grained, vuggy, ophitic; grain size up to 2 mm.; irregular vugs up to 6 mm. appear to be concentrated near surface of rock, not as plentiful on freshly broken surface.
MINERALOGY: plagioclase: 50%, clear to gray, lath shaped, 0.5–1 mm.; pyroxene: 30%, honey brown, translucent, ~1 mm.; ilmenite: 20%, submetallic, 1–3 mm.; cristobalite observed.

0 1 2 3 4
Centimeters

0   1   2
Millimeters

Fig. 2-8. Breccia (Type C). Rock 10046. Top: rock specimen (NASA photograph S-69-45657). Bottom: thin section (NASA photograph S-69-59843). Following description is after Schmitt (NASA Manned Spacecraft Center, Houston).
Another view of this rock may be seen in color in the frontispiece (Plate 3).

SIZE: 10 × 7.5 × 8 cm. WEIGHT: 663 gm. DENSITY: bulk 2.45 gm./cm.^{3}. COLOR: dark gray.
SHAPE: equidimensional and rounded with two flat sides.
FRACTURES: numerous fractures, many throughgoing, rock is not well-indurated and friable.
PITS & GLASS: highly pitted on two rounded surfaces, other four sides have a low density of
    pits, largest pit 3 mm., pits especially rich in beaded glass, but glass splashes are uncommon.
TEXTURE: fragmental rock with fine-grained matrix enclosing angular rock and mineral frag-
    ments; one highly vesicular fragment, 2 cm.; one large glass sphere, 5–6 mm. dia.
MINERALOGY: feldspar and other mineral fragments identified.

THE CRYSTALLINE ROCKS (TYPE A AND B)

Texturally, Type A rocks are fine-grained, vesicular (spherical, smooth-walled cavities) crystalline igneous rocks (Figs. 2-5 and 2-6; Plate 1). They are dark gray to black, generally subophitic in texture, and have a density of about 3.4 gm./cm.^{3} Vesicles are generally from 1-3 mm. in diameter and are usually spherical, although coalescence has modified the shape and enlarged some vesicles. Vesicles in these rocks are often faced with brilliant reflecting crystals from the groundmass, but no crystals project into the vesicles. However, there are some vugs, irregular in shape as opposed to the spherical nature of the vesicles, and into these some accessory and groundmass minerals do project. Vugs are more characteristic of Type B rocks.

The average mineralogy of Type A specimens is (Table 3-2): clinopyroxene, 53%; plagioclase, 27%; ilmenite, 13%; other phases including olivine, 7% (the figures reflect an adjustment for 15% void space). Noteworthy is the small amount of olivine. Type A rocks, except for their high Ti and Fe^{+2} contents, are similar to terrestrial olivine basalts. There are ten Type A (or AB) rocks (Table 2-1) with similar chemical and mineralogical characteristics, except that their olivine content varies from zero to almost 7%.

Type B rocks are medium- to coarse-grained, vuggy (irregularly shaped; rough-walled cavities) crystalline igneous rocks and are dark brownish-gray to almost black in color, with a speckled aspect as a result of some large well-developed crystals (Fig. 2-7; Plate 2). Their density is about 3.2 gm./cm.^{3} Cavities (vugs) are irregular in shape and the texture is generally ophitic. This type of rock is often referred to as a microgabbro (occasionally as diabase) especially for those specimens with grain sizes close to 0.5 mm. Grain size generally varies from 0.5-3.0 mm., although some very coarse rocks may have slightly larger grain size.

The average mineralogy of Type B specimens is (Table 3-2): clinopyroxene, 46%; plagioclase, 31%; ilmenite, 11%; cristobalite, 5%; and others, 7%. Olivine is absent. The larger crystals in the rock project into the vugs, including the new lunar mineral, pyroxferroite.

As indicated above, a possible textural-mineralogical (and also chemical) series exists between Type A and B rocks, with grain sizes from as small as 0.1 mm. in the Type A rocks, up to 3.0 mm. in the vuggy areas of Type B. Certain minerals, however, are restricted to only one type of rock which presents problems in attempts to postulate a complete series. Olivine was only found in the fine-grained rocks whereas pyroxferroite only occurs in the coarser rocks. The three major minerals, clinopyroxene, plagioclase and ilmenite are present and abundant in all the igneous rocks. Other important

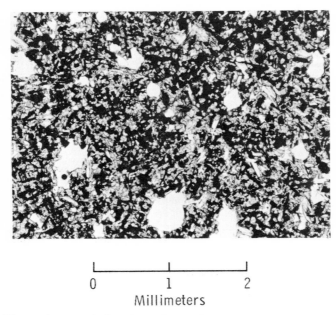

0   1   2
Millimeters

Fig. 2-9. Photomicrograph in plane light of fine-grained basalt. Rock 10057 (Type A) illustrating granular texture (nearly equidimensional mineral grains). White areas are vesicles. (Lunar Receiving Laboratory photograph.)

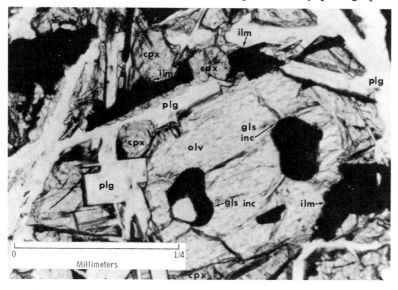

Fig. 2-10. Photomicrograph in plane light of olivine basalt, rock 10020 (Type A) illustrating ophitic texture (elongate feldspar crystals embedded in pyroxene and olivine). This rock also has glass inclusions (gls inc) in the olivine (olv). cpx = clinopyroxene; ilm = ilmenite (black); plg = plagioclase. (NASA photograph S-70-26823.)

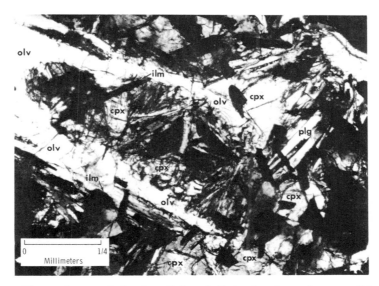

Fig. 2-11. Photomicrograph in plane light of olivine basalt, rock 10022 (Type A) illustrating subophitic texture (distinction between elongate feldspar, and pyroxene or olivine, not as pronounced as ophitic). Abbreviations the same as Fig. 2-10. (NASA photograph S-70-26810.)

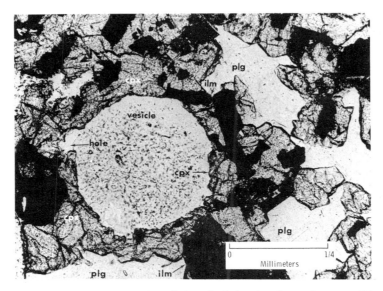

Fig. 2-12. Photomicrograph in plane light of olivine basalt, rock 10017 (Type A) illustrating poikioblastic texture in which the clinopyroxene (cpx) is included within the plagioclase (plg) particularly on the right-hand side of the figure. In this particular rock the vesicle is lined primarily with clinopyroxene. ilm = ilmenite (black). (NASA photograph S-70-26813.)

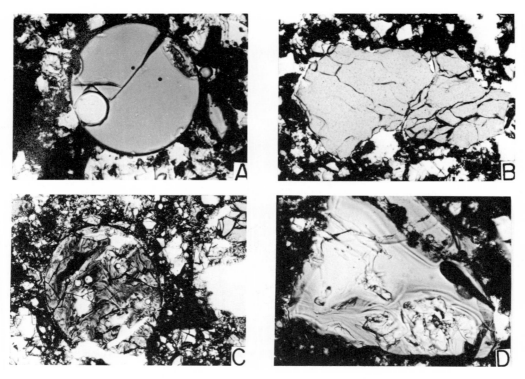

Fig. 2-13. Photomicrographs of glass particles in microbreccias. (A), homogeneous, vesicular spherule. (B), angular colorless glass, short diameter 0.1 mm. (C), inhomogeneous vesicular spherule, 0.08 mm. diameter. (D), brown melt glass with partially melted inclusions, short diameter 0.14 mm. After Quaide and Bunch (NASA Ames Research Center, California).

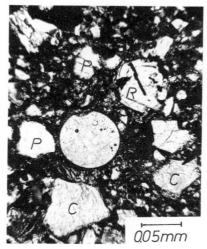

Fig. 2-14. Breccia with fragments of clinopyroxene (C), plagioclase (P), ilmenite (black), basaltic rock (R), and a yellow-brown glass sphere embedded in a fine-grained matrix. Plane light. After von Engelhardt (University of Tübingen, Germany).

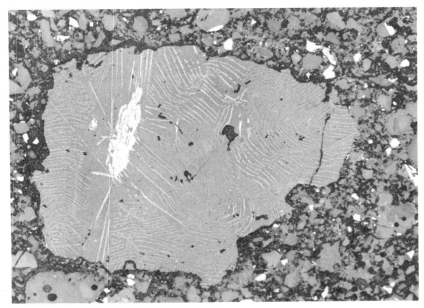

Fig. 2-15. Inclusion in microbreccia (rock 10068) consisting of large ilmenite grain containing titanian chromite, microcrystalline material and glass. Width of field 150 microns; reflected light. After Keil (University of New Mexico).

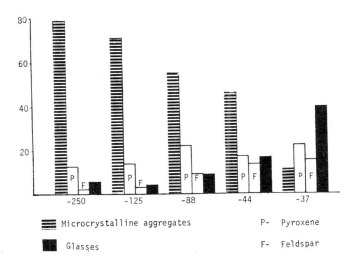

Fig. 2-16. Distribution of minerals and glass in various sieve fractions of the fines (Type D). Note the increase in the percentage of glass with decreasing grain size (from 250 microns to 37 microns). After McKay (NASA Manned Space-craft Center, Houston).

observations are: (1) no hydrous minerals are present; (2) the crystalline rocks and minerals are extremely fresh (unaltered) in comparison with terrestrial rocks; and (3) the rocks are extremely old (approximately 3.7 billion years).

BRECCIAS (TYPE C)

The Type C rocks are the most abundant rock type returned by the Apollo 11 astronauts. Approximately 50% of the rocks are breccias; however for reasons not entirely clear, only 2 out of 45 rocks collected by the Apollo 12 mission are breccias, although this may be related to the fact that the Apollo 12 regolith is less mature and not as thick as that at Tranquillity Base. Breccias are mixtures of all other rock types including some Type C, glass spherules, meteorite fragments, mineral fragments and anything else found in the lunar soils (Fig. 2-8; Plate 3 in frontispiece). They vary in color from gray to dark gray, with some small areas of white, and light gray and brownish-gray reflecting the miscellaneous rock types and minerals. Most breccias are fine-grained; fragments are smaller than 1 cm. in diameter (usually smaller than 0.5 cm.). Most of the fragments are angular, often with abundant microfractures and exhibiting varying degrees of vitrification. No predominance for fragments of either Type A, B or D is found within the breccias. However, a wider range in mineralogy and shock metamorphic features was observed in the breccias (Type C) in comparison with the other rock types (A and B), reflecting a complex origin. Some fragments of single crystals larger than 3 mm. were observed in the breccias which suggests that somewhere on the moon larger crystals than those found in the Apollo 11 rocks are to be expected. Glass fragments are common constituents of some breccias (Fig. 2-13); several different types of glass have been observed, even within single particles. Some breccias are poorly consolidated (soft, friable) whereas others are well-indurated (hard).

In Figs. 2-13 to 2-15 (as well as Fig. 2-8 and Plate 3), the various textures, mineralogical inclusions, and so forth, are presented for breccias which illustrate their complex nature. A mechanism to account for the lithification of such an agglomeration is necessary. Most of those who studied the lunar rocks believe that the breccias were formed by shock metamorphism (see below) from the impact of a large meteorite, and with a resultant induration of the various materials in the soils. There can be no doubt that the breccias are composed primarily of particles which are similar in morphology, composition, and in about the same proportions to those in the soils. However, because of some of the sintering characteristics of the fragments, McKay (NASA Manned Spacecraft Center, Houston) has presented evidence that the breccias are not lithified by shock, but rather are sintered deposits from a hot turbulent lunar base surge generated by a large meteorite. The composition, shock features and origin of the breccias are very complex and, therefore, future studies may modify the present theories.

FINES (TYPE D); ALSO CALLED SOILS

Soils have been arbitrarily defined as any fragment less than 1 cm. (some are as small as 30 microns) in diameter (Plates 4 and 5 color frontispiece). Those fragments from 1 mm. to 1 cm., are largely microcrystalline aggregates of rock (Type A and B) and glass-welded breccias, along with minor amounts of crystal fragments, large glass spherules and some meteoritic metal (Fig. 2-16). The fragments less than 1 mm. in diameter are chiefly glass, plagioclase, clinopyroxene, ilmenite, olivine, breccia and rock fragments. The next smaller fraction (less than 120 microns) consists of larger amounts of angular single mineral grains, and glass with various forms: spherules, dumbbells, rods, and ellipsoids (Plate 6 in color frontispiece). The smallest fraction is mainly glass. All soils are classed by NASA as samples 10085 and 10086 (Table 2-1); 12,486 gm. (about 27.5 lb.) were collected. The term lunar "dust" is only rarely used by scientists. In Table 2-2 the components found in the lunar soils are listed but it must be remembered that the relative abundance varies greatly with grain size (Fig. 2-16).

Glass is an extremely important component of the soils; in some of the finest size fractions it constitutes about one half of the material. Three types of glass were observed: (1) botryoidal, vesicular fragments, dark gray in color; (2) angular fragments, pale or colorless with shades of brown, yellow or orange, with refractive index ranging from 1.5 – 1.6 and (3) spheroidal, ellipsoidal and related shapes, varying in color from red to brown to green and yellow with refractive index ranging from 1.6 – 1.8 (the darker colored glass has a higher refractive index).

Cratering on the glass spherules in the soils is one of the more spectacular observations on the Apollo 11 samples. The cratering is caused by hyper-velocity impacts of micrometeorites (See Plate 7, top, of the frontispiece; Figs. 2-17 to 2-19). The resulting microcraters are usually lined with glass and have raised rims. No evidence of the micrometeorites which formed the craters has ever been found as the micrometeorites undoubtedly vaporized upon impact. According to Frondel (Harvard University), the sequence of events in the formation of the craters initially involves the penetration of a hyper-velocity particle into the glass, with maximum release of its energy near the end of its path, forming a gas cavity. Immediately thereafter, the associated stresses spalled-off the overlying glass surface with accompanying

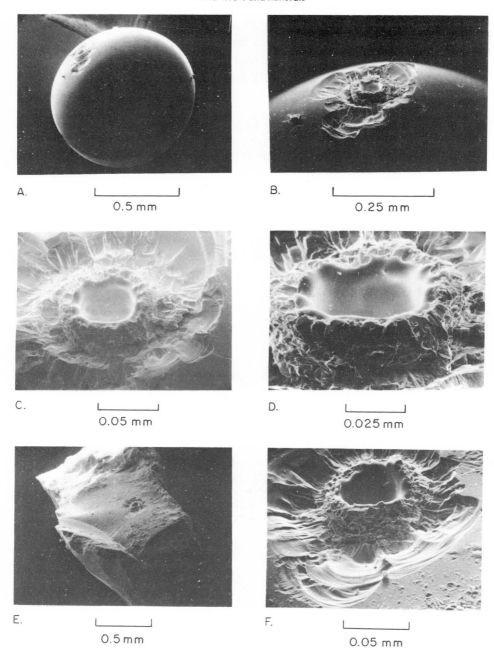

Fig. 2-17. Examples of microcratering in glass spheres and angular fragments from soils by means of scanning electron microscope. (A) microcrater on dark brown glass sphere. (B) same crater showing characteristic raised rim and spalled-off outer region. (C) close-up of crater. (D) close-up of raised rim. (E) microcrater on angular glass fragment. (F) close-up of crater in (E). After Frondel (Harvard University).

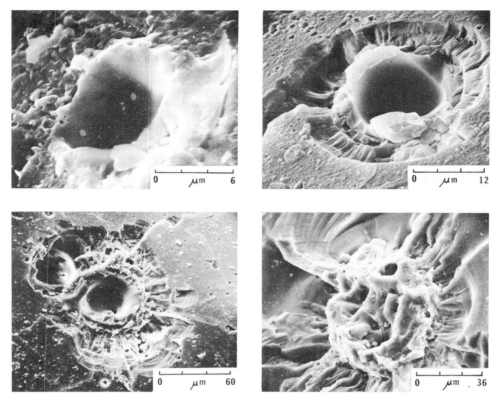

Fig. 2-18. Impact-produced, glass-lined, microcraters on glass spheres from soils (scanning electron microscope illustrations). *Upper left:* flared lip. *Upper right:* radiating fractures surround microcrater; also numerous small craters especially in upper left-hand corner of figure. *Lower left:* rim surrounded by radiating fractures and conchoidal fractures. *Lower right:* hummocky, glass associated with crater. After Carter (University of Texas at Dallas).

extrusion of molten glass to form the inner rim. Craters are also found in iron-nickel of meteorite origin, as is illustrated in Fig. 2-19. It should be emphasized that craters are not found in most spheres; however, some spheres may have many (up to 20 have been reported). Further, microcraters have never been found in any lunar rock. Since the micrometeorites are uniformly distributed on all surfaces of some spheres and metal particles, the impacting event must have occurred when these objects were in free flight related to a major cratering event. It is believed that the glass spheres and metal fragments, and the impacting particles were all generated during and immediately after the meteorite impact. In other words, it appears that the phenomenon was a rare event and was certainly of very limited duration (a few seconds).

Owing to their importance, further detailed discussions of the lunar glasses are presented at the end of this chapter.

Table 2-2. Materials found in soil sample 10085 (Type D); size range 1 – 5 mm. After Wood (Smithsonian Astrophysical Observatory, Massachusetts).

Material	%
breccia (fragments of Type C)	52.4
crystalline basalt (fragments of Type A and B rocks)	37.4
anorthositic material	3.5
glasses	5.8
others (meteorite fragments, etc.)	0.9
	100.0%

ANORTHOSITES IN THE SOILS

For centuries scientists have been predicting, speculating and calculating various properties of the moon. In the past decade the guesswork has been reduced to a somewhat more factual basis because of analyses by moon-orbiting satellites and, more recently, by instrument packages landed in various places on the moon's surface. On the basis of these many speculations, calculations and analyses, it is surprising that anything truly unexpected, except in detail, would be found in the Apollo 11 rocks. Yet there was one truly unanticipated and unpredicted find — anorthosite in the lunar fines. Anorthosite is a relatively rare type of terrestrial rock, being found almost exclusively in outcrop areas of pre-Cambrian rocks such as in the Adirondacks, Labrador and Quebec. It is composed chiefly (more than 90%) of plagioclase (usually andesine or labradorite) plus some accessory pyroxene and olivine; in other words, it is distinctly different from the lunar crystalline rocks which are composed chiefly of plagioclase, clinopyroxene and ilmenite.

The most extensive study of the anorthosite found in the Apollo 11 samples was made by a group of four scientists from the Smithsonian Astrophysical Observatory (Cambridge, Mass.): Drs. J.A. Wood, J.S. Dickey, U.B. Marvin and B.N. Powell. These scientists were studying the lunar fines (Type D) and recognized a small amount of light-colored (see colored frontispiece, Plate 4; Fig. 2-20), low density material, with distinctive chemistry and textures which, upon further analysis, turned out to be anorthosite. A thin-section of anorthosite is illustrated in the colored frontispiece (Plate 5, bottom) and from this one can see the mineralogy and texture which differentiate anorthosite fragments from the usual dark, high titanium lunar rocks. Chemically, anorthosites are Ti-poor and rich in Ca and Al.

It should be noted that of the 5% of the fines being referred to as anorthosites, there are actually three sub-varieties: true anorthosites (plagioclase > 90%), gabbroic anorthosites (77 – 90% plagioclase) and anorthositic gabbros (< 77% plagioclase). Gabbroic anorthosite is the most common. Besides plagioclase, the additional minerals are olivine and pigeonite, along

Fig. 2-19. Microcraters on nickel-iron pellet 3.5 × 3.2 × 2.3 mm., weighing 88 mg. From lunar fines (sample 10085; Type D). Specimen also exhibits furrowing and partial coating of silicate glass. After Mason (Smithsonian Institution).

with minor accessory troilite, titaniferous chromite, kamacite, taenite and spinel so far being reported. Some anorthositic material is found in the breccias and some has been vitrified to glass as would be expected for material blown at least 50 km. (see below). The lunar anorthosites are similar to terrestrial types except for a finer grain size, and the presence of anorthite plagioclase (as opposed to andesine or labradorite).

Because of the fact that the anorthosite fragments are found only in the soils, and are quite small (typically 20 – 100 microns), and because of their distinctive composition and texture, Dr. Wood and associates have postulated that they have been derived from a different area, specifically the lunar highlands. Portions of the highly cratered highlands lie only about 50 km. from Tranquillity Base and it is from here that it is believed the anorthosites have been blown. Until samples are returned from the lunar highlands, the origin of the lunar anorthosites remains one of the most intriguing unanswered questions to emerge from the Apollo 11 studies. The fact that

(unmanned) Surveyor VII chemical analyses of highland material are similar
to those of the anorthosites from Tranquillity Base (Table 2-3) adds
credence to the postulation of Dr. Wood and his colleagues.

Table 2-3. Comparison of composition of Apollo 11 anorthosite and anorthositic glass
with Surveyor VII analyses of ejecta from highlands crater Tycho (in weight %).
After Wood (Smithsonian Astrophysical Observatory).

Element	Average of 6 anorthosites	Average of 10 anorthositic glasses	Tycho ejecta
C	—	—	< 2
O	61.2	61.0	58 ± 5
Na	0.3	0.4	< 3
Mg	2.1	3.9	4 ± 3
Al	12.9	10.6	9 ± 3
Si	16.0	16.6	18 ± 4
"Ca"	6.3	5.5	6 ± 2
"Fe"	1.2	2.1	2 ± 1

Notes:

1. "Ca" = all elements in the range mass numbers 30 – 47 including P, S, K and Ca.
2. "Fe" = all elements in the range mass numbers 47 – 65, including Ti, Cr, Mn, Fe and Ni.
3. Oxygen is calculated.

SHOCK (IMPACT) METAMORPHISM

There are two direct lines of evidence for the recognition of meteorites
in the lunar environment: (1) the presence of minerals of meteoritic origin,
and (2) the detection of chemical elements (or isotopes) which are derived
from meteorites. Both of these are discussed elsewhere, but a third indirect
indication of the presence and importance of meteorites can be found in
shock (also called impact) metamorphic effects observed in the lunar breccias
or soils; none are observed in the lunar crystalline rocks. Shock metamorphic
effects are detectable in the lunar minerals when they have been subjected
to pressures above the dynamic elastic limit. There is no question but that
many shock features are found in certain lunar rocks, and their detection
convincingly adds yet another piece of evidence to a meteorite impact origin
for the lunar craters. For several years preliminary to the lunar studies, a
significant amount of fundamental work had been in progress on known
terrestrial meteorite craters and associated rocks, as well as experimental
laboratory studies, so that the approximately six groups of scientists studying
this phenomenon in the lunar rocks had developed significant expertise in
recognizing shock effects.

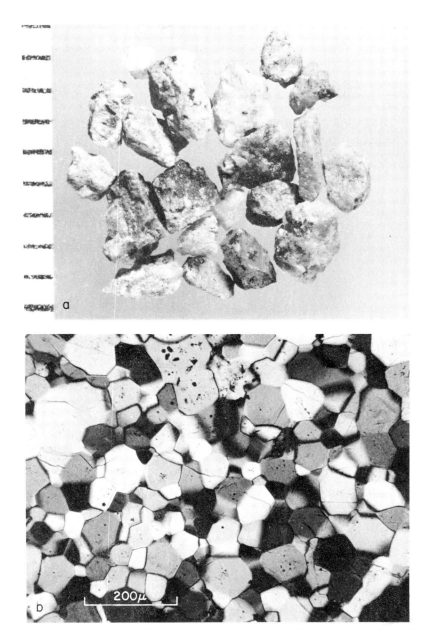

Fig. 2-20. (a) Fragments of lunar anorthositic rocks believed to have been blown in from the lunar highlands; note characteristic light color. (b) Thin section of anorthosite composed of polygonal crystals of anorthite; crossed nicols. After Wood (Smithsonian Astrophysical Observatory).

There are many different features in the lunar rocks and minerals which have been caused by shock waves resulting from meteorite impacts. They can be identified by various means, the most important being microscopic studies, and X-ray diffraction (crystallographic) studies. Some of the shock

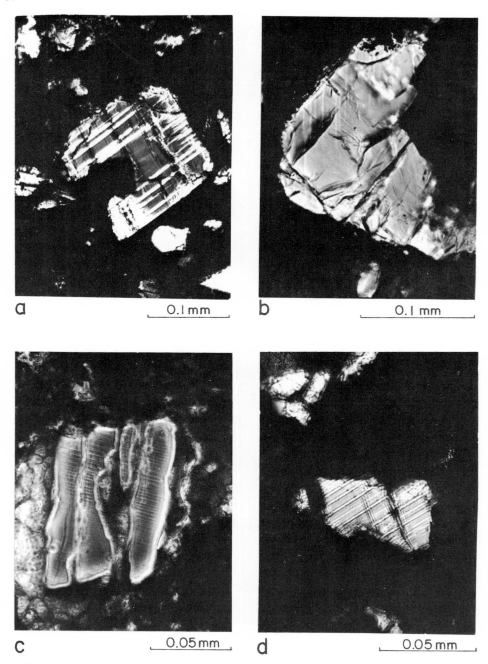

Fig. 2-21. Photomicrographs of structures due to shock deformation in clino-pyroxenes. (a) Twin lamellae (NE trending white bands); from breccia 10023. (b) Shock lamellae (N-S white features); from fines 10084. (c) Shock lamellae linear features); from breccia 10061. (d) Shock lamellae, from breccia 10023. After Carter (Yale University).

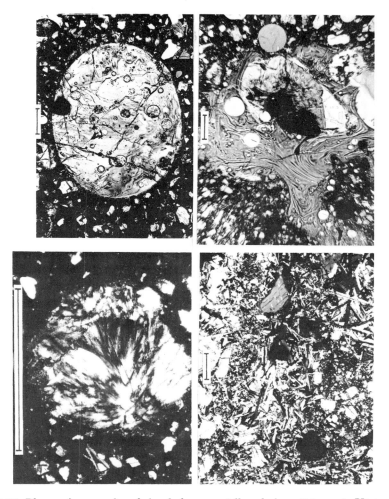

Fig. 2-22. Photomicrographs of shock features (all scale bars 0.1 mm.). *Upper left:* ellipsoidal particle of glass in breccia (rock 10065) showing flow structures as well as vesicles (clear) and nickel-iron spherules (black). Plane light. *Upper right:* glass coating a shocked rock fragment in breccia (rock 10065); the glass is vesicular and shows pronounced flow structure. Plane light. *Lower left:* devitrified plagioclase spherule containing radiating feldspar grains; from breccia (rock 10065). Crossed nicols. *Lower right:* fragment of recrystallized plagioclase-rich glass from fines (10085). Crossed Nicols. After Chao (U.S. Geological Survey).

features are based on textural abnormalities or microstructures such as fracturing, granulation, planar features and multiple twinning; others are based on the recognition of fused glass (scoria, glass spheres and other melting effects); and others are based on very subtle crystallographic variations

Table 2-4. Classification of shock metamorphic effects found in Apollo 11 rocks. Estimated pressure and temperatures based on laboratory experiments. Modified after Chao (U.S. Geological Survey).

Degree of Shock	Description	Pressure	Temperature
weak	no intragranular deformation in plagioclase; sparse mechanical twins in ilmenite and pyroxene; microfractures in all minerals.	150 kilobar	—
moderate	mechanical twins, deformation and shock lamellae in plagioclase; abundant mechanical twins in ilmenite and pyroxene; abundant microfractures.	250 kilobar	?
strong	partial or complete vitrification of plagioclase; intense fracturing and mechanical twinning in pyroxene and ilmenite; etc.	500 kilobar	?
very strong	flowage in feldspar glass	?	700°C.
intense	melting of entire rock by shock-induced heating; etc.	?	1200°C.

found only by X-ray diffraction methods. A few examples of textural features which have resulted from shock effects are illustrated in Figs. 2-21 and 2-22; glass spheres and scoria are illustrated in the colored frontispiece (Plate 6).

Shock features have not been observed in the lunar crystalline rocks (Types A and B), but only in the breccias (Type C) and fines (Type D). Actually, there is every reason to believe the lunar breccias (Type C) owe their existence to the effect of meteorite impacts. The argument is based on the fact that during and immediately after impact, high pressures (250 kilobars or more) and high temperatures (as high as 1200°C.) may be generated. The result is the momentary formation of hot, molten liquid of varying compositions (depending on the material being fused) in the lunar soils which, upon solidification, will "fuse" together fragments of lunar rocks and minerals, glass spheres, and anything else available in the soils. The reason for the lack of shock effects in the crystalline rocks is not readily apparent but because of scarcity of shock effects in these larger rocks, N.L. Carter (Yale University) suggests that small (micrometeorites?) rather than large particles must have been the primary mechanical disintegrating and shock-causing agents once the mare was formed. This would be consistent with the observation of the greatly varying composition of the abundant glass spheres; if large meteorites were responsible for the shock effects, an average composition, similar to the bulk composition of the lunar rocks, would be expected.

Chao (U.S. Geological Survey) has proposed a classification for the shock effects observed in the Apollo 11 rocks and, based on laboratory shock studies, has been able to estimate the pressures developed for several stages (Table 2-4). Further, from selected shock metamorphic textures developed, two temperature estimates (700°C. and 1200°C.) have been made. The pressure scale of Chao establishes the pressure at the "moderate-strong" shock effect boundary as 250 kilobars. Von Engelhardt (University of Tübingen, Germany) suggests that some shock impact pressures corresponding to Chao's "very strong" category range from 600 kilobar to the megabar (1000 kilobar) region. Regardless of the exact pressures and temperatures eventually assigned to the shock effects, there is now no doubt of the importance of shock metamorphism resulting from meteorite impacts as an important process in the evolution of the lunar surface; this applies not only for the formation of the major lunar craters, but also in erosional processes on the regolith, and in the formation of the breccias by shock lithification.

REGOLITH AND SOIL MECHANICS

The lunar surface at Tranquillity Base is composed of a layer of loose, unconsolidated rock fragments and soil technically known as regolith ("mantle rock"). These range in size from the finest soil particles (dust) to blocks as much as 2 meters across. The regolith is porous and, at the surface at least, is very weakly coherent. It grades down into more densely packed material of similar composition. The thickness of the regolith at Tranquillity Base is estimated to be about 3 – 6 meters, after which bedrock is encountered. The 3 – 6 meter estimate is made from study of the craters in the immediate vicinity. In Fig. 1-4, for example, the floor of the crater (about 5 meters deep) can be seen to be strewn with large blocks which are believed to be broken bedrock. All of the smaller craters in the area are within the regolith. Although most of the regolith in the Apollo 11 area is believed to have been derived from local sources, there is undoubtedly some contribution (about 5%) from the highlands (the anorthosites) as well as a small meteoritic component. Because of these additional components, the chemical composition of the regolith is significantly different from the local igneous rocks. Further, the different ages determined for the soil and lunar rocks may also be explained by the contamination of the regolith with small amounts of material formed elsewhere.

A fundamental question is, how did the regolith form? On Earth, the main agents of weathering and erosion are water, wind and ice which break up and carry away rocks, but these are not found on the moon. The unanimous opinion of those who have studied the problem is that the regolith has been formed by the breakdown (comminution) of the local igneous rocks

Fig. 2-23. Undisturbed lunar surface after having been stepped on by astronaut. Bulged and cracked region in front and side of footprint indicates to soil mechanics experts that the lunar soil is cohesive and that shearing deformations have taken place within soil mass. After Costes (NASA Marshall Space Flight Center, Alabama).

(Types A and B) by meteorite impacts, and directly related events (e.g., abrasion resulting from turnover and transport of material during the formation of the rays of a crater, and in the debris-laden explosion cloud). The process has taken about 3.5 billion years, and has involved a multitude of meteorite impacts with varying magnitudes ranging from small-particle bombardment, which is gradually eroding (rounding) exposed rock surfaces (Fig. 2-2), to large crater-forming meteorites. This hypothesis is consistent with the thickness of the regolith, the proportion of shocked debris and amounts of meteoritic material. From this discussion it is clear that the formation of the regolith is complex and extremely slow. Studies by Shoemaker (California Institute of Technology) have shown that the regolith has been turned over to an average depth of 4.1 meters by cratering just once since the mare surface formed billions of years ago. This, coupled with other studies which show the erosion rate to be in the order of 1 – 2 mm. per million years, guarantees that the footprints of the astronauts will be available for study for a very long time — at least a million years!

One of the best known Apollo 11 photographs is that of the astronaut footprint in the lunar soil (Figs. 2-23, 2-24). In addition to its aesthetic appeal, this photograph has great scientific value because it enables those

Fig. 2-24. Astronaut footprints at top edge of soft-rimmed crater penetrate deeper (10–15 cm.) than they do a short distance away. After Costes (NASA Marshall Space Flight Center, Alabama).

experienced in soil mechanics to make deductions about cohesion, deformation and other features of the lunar soil. There was, at one time, a great controversy as to whether lunar modules or astronauts would "sink in" the lunar surface and, although this question was answered by means of unmanned landing craft, many unknown physical aspects of the lunar soil still exist.

The most detailed study of the physical and mechanical behavior of the Apollo 11 lunar soil was made by Costes (NASA, Marshall Space Flight Center, Alabama) who found the soil to be cohesive, but with very little frictional resistance which is believed to be the result of the presence of the glass spherules. The lunar soil at the Apollo 11 site has been described as a brownish, medium-gray, slightly cohesive, granular soil largely composed of bulky grains which range in size from silt to fine sand. Bootprint depths will range from as little as 1 cm. in some areas, to a maximum of 3 – 5 cm. in the softer areas, particularly on the rims of small and relatively young craters. Pre-Apollo 11 calculations predicted that the lunar module footpads should penetrate to a depth of 10 – 12 cm. (5 inches) in a normal landing; they actually penetrated a maximum of about 7.5 cm. This attests to the fact that the lunar surface is relatively soft for the first few inches but beyond that, considerable penetration resistance is encountered. An attempt by the astronauts to drive two core tubes (Fig. 2-25) into the soil was of limited success as they only were able to drive these 10 and 13.5 cm. (4 and 5.4 inches) respectively, which confirms the considerable penetration resistance relatively near the surface. An Apollo 12 core tube was driven about 28 inches and the core revealed some stratification (layering). Notwithstanding the obvious differences in composition, particle size and shape, from a soil mechanics or

Fig. 2-25. Core tube being collected by astronaut Aldrin. Solar wind experiment is in background. (NASA photograph AS-11-40-5964.)

engineering point of view, the lunar soil does not differ significantly in its behavior from what would be expected on Earth of granular, slightly cohesive terrestrial soil with the same particle size distribution and packing characteristics. The one major difference which might be singled out is the intraparticle adhesion which is demonstrated, for example, by the vertical walls produced by the indentations of the footprints (Fig. 2-23).

LUNAR GLASSES

As indicated above, the glasses found in the lunar soils (Type D) and breccias (Type C) are among the more spectacular of the materials returned by the Apollo 11 astronauts (Plates 6 and 7 (top) of the frontispiece; Figs. 2-17 to 2-19). In addition they are of great scientific interest in that they have enabled scientists to learn much about lunar processes, as well as the origin of tektites which have been the subject of scientific debate for decades.

In the following pages the lunar glasses are discussed in a detailed manner in order that their true significance will become more apparent.

Forms

The glassy spheres (Plate 6 in frontispiece) are among the most interesting material returned by the Apollo 11 mission. The spheres are commonly about 100 microns in diameter, but range widely in size. Ellipsoidal shapes are common, as are dumbbells, teardrops, and rods. These are the typical rotational shapes assumed by splashed liquids. Some of the spheroidal forms are flattened, indicating that they were plastic when they landed. In addition to the regular forms, there is a great abundance of angular fragments. Many of these are broken pieces of the more regular forms. Others occur as irregular masses coating rocks or as linings in pits clearly produced by impact of small particles (Plate 6, bottom). The outer surfaces of the spherules occasionally have small craters. In most cases they have resulted from collisions with microparticles (Plate 7 in frontispiece; Figs. 2-17 to 2-19).

Fe/Ni spherules in glasses

Tiny spherules of iron-nickel are present in many of the glasses. They are usually less than 30 microns in diameter and are usually present in the less homogeneous glasses. Commonly these spherules contain about 10% Ni as well as troilite and schreibersite, which are common minerals of iron meteorites.

Albee and Chodos (California Institute of Technology) point out that the glass also contains some nickel-free iron and troilite derived from the lunar rocks, which have formed immiscible droplets in the glass melt. The chief evidence for an external meteoritic origin for the nickel-rich iron spheres is their nickel content. Nickel is very depleted in the Apollo 11 rocks, rarely reaching 20 ppm. These nickel-iron spheres resemble those found in terrestrial glasses which have been formed at meteorite craters (e.g., at Henbury, Australia) by the fusion of country rock by the impacting iron-nickel meteorite. The presence of these globules indicates that most of the glasses bear a genetic relationship to meteorite impact.

Color

A wide range in color is shown by these glasses from colorless through pale yellows, greens, browns, orange to red and black (Plate 6). The colors show a clear relation to refractive index and to composition. Table 2-5, adapted from Frondel (Harvard University), shows the interrelationship of color, refractive index and density.

Chemical Composition

The chemical composition of a representative set of glasses, both fragments and spherules, is given in Table 2-6, adapted from Keil (University of New Mexico). There are no major differences in composition between the angular fragments and the spheroidal forms. The color of the glasses (color frontispiece, Plate 6) is clearly reflected in the chemistry. The lighter colored glasses are similar in composition to the feldspathic or anorthositic fragments, whereas the more numerous red to yellow glasses resemble the bulk analyses of the rocks and the fine material.

Individual spherules are commonly homogeneous, or only slightly heterogeneous. Some of the glasses resemble the Apollo 11 basalts; others resemble the composition of the breccias, some the Apollo 12 rocks, while the lighter colored glasses are similar in composition to the anorthosite fragments and to the Surveyor VII analysis of the ejecta from Tycho in the lunar uplands (Table 2-3). Much of the variation in composition reflects the varying mineralogy of the rock types. Thus glasses with the composition of pure plagioclase and pyroxene are found. Wood (Smithsonian Astrophysical Observatory) and other workers note that there is a tendency for the glass composition to cluster around two main types, the Apollo 11 basalt and the feldspathic or anorthositic compositions.

The variable composition found in the glasses can be due to several causes:

1. Melting of whole rocks and bulk samples of fine material, giving the range in composition found for the rocks.

2. Melting of individual mineral phases by impact of small particles.

3. Selective vaporization or melting. The overall evidence seems to indicate that this process was not effective in altering the composition to any marked degree although some scientists have thought that slight loss of silicon and sodium had occurred.

Skinner and Winchell (Yale University) concluded that the major glass-forming phases were pyroxene and plagioclase and that individual mineral phases were being melted by small particle impact. They noted one inhomogeneous glass sphere which was apparently formed by fusion at the boundary of a feldspar and a pyroxene grain.

Table 2-5. Relationship between color and other properties of lunar glasses. After Frondel (Harvard University).

Color	Refractive Index	% FeO	Density
colorless, transparent light yellow, green to	1.50 – 1.60	0 – 1.6	< 2.7
light green, transparent	1.59 – 1.65	4 – 10	2.7 – 2.8
dark green, transparent	1.65	7 – 16	2.8 – 2.9
yellow-brown, transparent light to dark brown and	1.65	8 – 14	2.7 – 2.8
red-brown, transparent	1.65 – 1.75	9 – 16	2.8 – 3.0
dark brown to opaque	1.75	15 – 25	3.0 – 3.25

Origin of the glasses

The regular forms displayed by the glasses are characteristic of those assumed by splashed liquids and there is general agreement that the glasses are produced by melting, during impact of the surface rock debris, by high velocity meteoritic particles containing nickel-iron.

Two other possibilities have been suggested. The first is that they represent a residual glassy phase formed during the last stages of crystallization of the igneous rocks. Such phases do exist as a glassy residuum, but the composition of this material, described in Chapter 6, does not resemble that of these glass spherules and fragments. Indeed, the composition of these glasses in the fine material does not resemble any that could be produced by any reasonable fractionation process.

The other suggestion, advanced by Gold (Cornell University), is that the glassy crusts observed were created by solar flash melting. This has not received much support from the detailed investigations. Fredriksson (Smithsonian Institution) notes that fragments of the glassy crusts are present throughout the breccias, indicating a prolonged period of glass formation. Shock effects are observed under the crusts, and the glasses contain unmelted crystals at the surface of the crusts.

Resemblance of spherules to chondrules

Fredriksson (Smithsonian Institution) draws attention to some similarities in form between the spherules and chondrules observed in chondritic meteorites. He also emphasizes the general textural similarities between the lunar breccias and the chondrites. This may be considered as supporting evidence for an origin of chondrules and chondritic textures by impact. The meteorites are, of course, different in composition from the lunar breccias but may have originated under analogous conditions on a planetary or asteroidal surface early in the history of the solar systems. There is ample evidence from the Apollo studies that the chondritic meteorites are not derived from the moon.

Microfossils

A final comment on the glasses is the observation by Cloud (University of California) that "the abundant spheroids and ovoids are similar in shape to some algal and bacterial unicells, and the smaller ones are comparable in size. Indeed, if such particles were coated with carbon, they would make impressive pseudomicrofossils. . . . This is *not* to propose that there are or were solid glass Protozoa on the moon, but to add one more warning about a too-ready interpretation of exotic objects as of vital origin on the basis of gross morphology alone. . . . This warning deserves emphasis. Elsewhere on the lunar or martian surface may be lifelike artifacts that will be harder to discriminate from the real thing." (*Proceedings of the Apollo 11 Lunar Science Conference*, vol. 2, pp. 1794-1797)

TEKTITES

One of the achievements of the Apollo missions has been to solve the outstanding scientific question of a terrestrial versus lunar origin for tektites. Tektites are small glassy objects which have been melted and splashed during the impact of a large meteorite, asteroid or comet. These impact events have been on a large scale, for the tektites have been sprayed over immense distances. In the youngest and best preserved example, the Australian strewn field, tektites occur across the entire southern half of the continent. The numerous occurrences in Southeast Asia are probably related to the same event and the recent discovery of microtektites in deep-sea cores (curiously within the zone marking the 700,000 year reversal of the Earth's magnetic field; Bruhnes-Matuyama reversal), has extended the strewn field to dimensions of about 4% of the Earth's surface. No normal observed geological processes (e.g., volcanic action) are capable of explaining this distribution, although many theories have been suggested. Neither do these small objects come from deep space for they record no evidence of any exposure to cosmic radiation outside the Earth's atmosphere. These considerations have restricted their origin to the Earth or the moon, from where they could be transported within a few days. If they were formed from material excavated beneath the lunar surface by impact, they would lack the evidence of exposure to cosmic radiation which is apparent in the lunar regolith. Because no obvious terrestrial crater has been recognized as a source for the Australasian group of tektites, lunar origins have been popular. However, a large cometary impact analogous to the Tunguska, Siberia event of 1908 might produce them without leaving a recognizable crater. Certainly many features suggest a terrestrial origin, in particular, the chemistry which resembles that of upper crustal sedimentary rocks.

Several facts revealed by the Apollo 11 and 12 studies weigh heavily against a lunar origin for tektites:

1. The chemistry of the maria material is totally dissimilar to the composition of tektites, and tektites could not be derived from such material by selective melting, vapor fractionation or other processes which have been considered to act during impact events. The available evidence from studies of terrestrial impact glasses formed at meteorite craters, and the lunar glasses, indicates that only very minor changes occur during fusion of country rock. The chemistry of the uplands so far established by Surveyor VII (and from the possible upland material in the lunar soil material) is totally dissimilar to that of tektites.

Table 2-6. Electron microprobe analysis of glass fragments and spherules in microbreccias and fines (weight %). After Keil (University of New Mexico).

	Fragments (9) * (Clear)	Fragments (8) * (Green)	Fragments (12) * (Orange to Brown)	Fragments (8) * (Red to Black)
SiO_2	44.7	43.0	43.0	37.7
Al_2O_3	26.8	25.2	11.7	5.5
Cr_2O_3	0.20	0.17	0.35	0.64
TiO_2	0.30	0.54	7.8	10.8
FeO	5.5	5.9	18.5	24.6
MgO	6.5	8.2	8.1	12.9
MnO	0.06	0.09	0.25	0.28
CaO	15.0	16.0	10.8	7.5
Na_2O	0.13	0.27	0.37	0.29
K_2O	0.02	0.08	0.12	0.06
ZrO_2	0.02	0.02	0.08	0.06
P_2O_5	0.02	0.10	0.12	0.06
Total	99.19	100.15	100.79	100.19
	Spherules (15) * (Clear)	Spherules (10) * (Green)	Spherules (20) * (Orange to Brown)	Spherules (22) * (Red to Black)
SiO_2	45.5	44.2	40.1	37.2
Al_2O_3	27.0	21.0	14.8	5.2
Cr_2O_3	0.12	0.17	0.32	0.61
TiO_2	0.45	1.81	7.6	10.7
FeO	3.8	7.9	15.3	24.7
MgO	6.9	8.6	8.4	13.1
MnO	0.8	0.15	0.22	0.30
CaO	15.0	14.7	12.9	7.7
Na_2O	0.24	0.41	0.14	0.27
K_2O	0.02	0.39	0.05	0.04
ZrO_2	0.02	0.04	0.07	0.06
P_2O_5	0.04	0.14	0.04	0.05
Total	99.17	99.51	99.94	99.93

* Number of grains analyzed.

2. The ages of the lavas filling the lunar maria as given by the Rb-Sr method are much older than that of the parent material of tektites studied by the same method. The ages for the Apollo 11 rocks (3.7 billion years) and the Apollo 12 sample (3.3 billion years) compare with ages for the *parent* material of the Australasian tektites strewn field of 100 – 300 million years. There is, accordingly, a difference of at least 3 billion years between the lunar rocks and the parent material of tektites. The case for deriving tektites from the still older uplands (e.g., Tycho, as commonly suggested) is even more difficult.

3. The lead isotopic evidence was considered by many of the Apollo 11 workers to be among the most significant data telling against a lunar origin for the tektites. In the section on lead isotopes, the highly radiogenic nature of the lunar lead is shown to be a consequence of a low initial lead content and a high Th/Pb and U/Pb ratio. Lead, a volatile element, has apparently been depleted in the moon, before or during accretion, and most of the lunar lead has been derived from the radioactive decay of U^{238} and Th^{232}, giving high ratios of the daughter products Pb^{208}, Pb^{207} and Pb^{206} to the stable lead isotope Pb^{204}. Terrestrial lead contains a much higher proportion of Pb^{204} and has not been depleted in primordial lead to the same extent as the moon. The Pb isotopic composition of tektites is identical to that of modern terrestrial lead found in ocean sediments or in the Earth's crust. It has clearly had an identical history to lead in the crust of the Earth. (Some loss of lead and uranium relatively and thorium has occurred recently in tektites, either during the impact event, or equally likely in leaching during surface weathering of the parent material.) The tektite lead isotope ratios are thus widely different from the lunar lead isotope ratios and reflect a different isotopic history.

4. Numerous glassy spherules, exhibiting all the forms characteristic of splashed silicate melts (e.g., spheres, dumbbells, teardrops) were found in the lunar fine material. Might these resemble tektites? The consensus among workers is that they do not. There is a superficial resemblance in external form, since both are formed by impact melting processes. However, all workers on the lunar glass specimens agree that they do not resemble tektites in chemistry, refractive index, or internal structure.

5. The oxygen isotope data (O^{18}/O^{16} ratios) are likewise unfavorable to a lunar origin for tektites. The δO^{18} values in tektites are typically in the range + 9.0 to 11.5 per mil (see Chapter 7 section on oxygen isotope ratios for explanation of this ratio). The Apollo 11 rocks and minerals show much lower values for this ratio ranging from about 4 for ilmenites to 7 for cristobalite, with total rock values of about 6. H.P. Taylor and S. Epstein (California Institute of Technology) conclude that "suitable tektite parent materials are rare or nonexistent on the lunar surface."

6. Many workers commented on the glassy potassium-rich mesostasis in the lunar basalts. The composition of this phase was typically granitic, similar to late stage granophyres formed by differentiation from terrestrial basalts. This material does not resemble the composition of tektites, being heavily depleted in magnesium and enriched in potassium, in particular. Similar comments apply to the late immiscible globules of silicate of "granitic" composition observed by Roedder (U.S. Geological Survey) and Weiblen (University of Minnesota). The tektite chemistry is quite distinct from that of granitic material.

3

THE MINERALS

Detailed studies by approximately 50 groups of scientists concerned with the mineralogy and petrography of the lunar rocks and soils have identified 28 minerals of lunar origin and four minerals from meteorites. Seven of the 28 lunar mineral identifications are provisional but considering the qualifications of the scientists, most of these identifications are probably correct. Two new minerals, pyroxferroite and armalcolite, were discovered as well as three new mineral varieties among the chromites and ulvöspinel. Several minerals which are extremely rare on Earth, for example native iron and troilite, are common accessories in the lunar rocks. There are at least six minerals in the lunar rocks and soils which have been recognized, but not named, some of which may be new minerals; all are present in very small amounts. In addition to fragments of Type A and B rocks, the lunar soils and breccias have mineral representatives of the anorthosites (which were probably projected in from the lunar highlands by some meteoritic impact in the highlands), and also of meteorite fragments mostly of the iron meteorite types. As a result, the widest variety of minerals are found in the soils and breccias. Various types of natural glasses, which are considered as minerals by some scientists, are not included in our discussion of minerals. The minerals which have been identified are listed in Table 3-1 along with their chemical compositions, an estimate of their abundance, and other comments considered appropriate.

All the silicate minerals in the lunar rocks are remarkably free of hydrothermal alteration and weathering so common in terrestrial igneous rocks, and, as a result, are unusually transparent and clear (except for some affected by shock). All iron present in the lunar minerals (except native iron) is ferrous (Fe^{+2}) because of the highly reducing environment; the oxygen pressure of the lunar rock system has been estimated to be at least five times lower than that of the terrestrial equivalents.

Attempts have been made to quantitatively determine the amount of each mineral in the various rock types, and although these are undoubtedly correct for the rock specimen studied, attempts to project these values to the entire Apollo 11 mare area are not justified considering the very small frac-

Table 3-1. The Minerals found in Apollo 11 samples.

Mineral	Generalized Composition	Relative Abundance	Rock Occurrence	Remarks
pyroxene; augite	$(Ca, Mg, Fe, Al, Ti)_2 Si_2O_6$	very abundant	all types	composition very variable
pyroxene; pigeonite	$(Mg, Fe, Ca, Al, Ti)_2 Si_2O_6$	abundant	all types	composition very variable
pyroxene; hypersthene	$(Mg, Fe)_2Si_2O_6$	rare	soils	probably of meteoritic origin
* pyroxferroite	$Ca_{0.15}Fe_{0.85}SiO_3$	moderate	Type B	new lunar mineral
plagioclase	$CaAl_2Si_2O_8 - NaAlSi_3O_8$	very abundant	all types	anorthite-bytownite
potassium feldspar	$KAlSi_3O_8$	rare	in residuum	occasionally with Ba
ilmenite	$FeTiO_3$	high (10 – 20%)	all types	most abundant opaque
olivine	$(Mg, Fe)_2SiO_4$	high (up to 7%)	Types A, C, D	more abundant in Apollo 12
fayalite	Fe_2SiO_4	rare	in residuum	——
* chromite (Ti and Al)	$FeCr_2O_4$	moderate	all types	new lunar mineral varieties
* ulvöspinel (chromian)	Fe_2TiO_4	moderate	all types	new lunar mineral variety
spinel	$MgAl_2O_4$	rare	soils	from lunar highlands (?)
* armalcolite	$(Mg_{0.5}Fe_{0.5})Ti_2O_5$	low (rare?)	Types A, C, D	new lunar mineral
troilite	FeS	up to 1.3%	all types	only definite lunar sulfide
iron	Fe	low (0.03%)	all types	low Ni content
rutile	TiO_2	rare	Type A	exsolution in ilmenite
cristobalite	SiO_2	high	late stage (residuum)	reaches 6% in Type B
tridymite	SiO_2	low	in residuum	
quartz	SiO_2	rare	in residuum	least common form of SiO_2
apatite	$Ca_5(PO_4)_3(F,Cl)$	up to 0.15%	in residuum	high rare-earth content
whitlockite	$Ca_3(PO_4)_2$	rare	soils, Type A	tentative identification
copper	Cu	rare	soils, Type A	high in Zn
tin	Sn	rare	in soils	——
zircon	$ZrSiO_4$	rare	in residuum	tentative identification
baddeleyite	ZrO_2	rare	in residuum	tentative identification

Table 3-1 *(Continued)*

Mineral	Generalized Composition	Relative Abundance	Rock Occurrence	Remarks
mica	complex silicate	rare	soils, Type A	needs further substantiation
amphibole	complex silicate	rare	Type B	needs further substantiation
aragonite	$CaCO_3$	rare	Type B	possibly of meteoritic origin
pentlandite	$(Fe, Ni)_9S_8$	rare	Type A	tentative identification
** iron-nickel	(Fe, Ni)	low	soils, Type C	chiefly of meteoritic origin
** cohenite	$(Fe, Ni)_3C$	rare	in soils	only in meteorite fragments
** schreibersite	$(Fe, Ni, Co)_3P$	rare	in soils	only in meteorite fragments
unidentified minerals		rare	all types	at least 6 recognized

* New lunar minerals or new varieties not known on Earth.
** From meteorites; iron-nickel may also be indigenous to some lunar rocks.

tion of the moon's surface these represent. Variations in mineral content for Apollo 12 rocks with similar chemical composition to those of Apollo 11 are, in some instances, great. For example, olivine may constitute as much as 55% of some Apollo 12 rocks, but will rarely reach 7% in similar Apollo 11 rocks. With these limitations in mind, approximate mineral percentages for Type A and B rocks are presented in Table 3-2, which shows that less than 10 of the 28 lunar minerals account for 94 – 98% of the volume of the lunar rocks; in fact almost 90% of the minerals from the Tranquillity Base rocks can be accounted for by pyroxene, plagioclase and ilmenite. Hence many reported mineral species are, at this stage at least, little more than curiosities.

The remainder of this chapter will be devoted to descriptions of each observed mineral. In many cases the lunar minerals will show both differences and similarities to terrestrial equivalents. Where this occurs, we have chosen to stress the similarities, describing the lunar minerals in terms of reference (chemical, structural, textural) to their nearest terrestrial equivalent. Aside from the two new minerals and three new varieties, which are primarily a reflection of the chemical composition of the lunar rocks, another unusual aspect of lunar mineralogy may be summarized as one of relative abundance. For example, basalts on Earth rarely, if ever, have 10% ilmenite, a reflection again of unusual chemical composition (high TiO_2). Similarly, on Earth occurrences of troilite and native iron are extremely rare owing to the fact that the required reducing conditions are normally not achievable in our oxidizing environments.

Table 3-2. Approximate percentage of minerals in Type A and B Apollo 11 rocks
(in volume %).

Mineral	Type A (basalt) Range	(average)	Type B (gabbro) Range	(average)
pyroxenes	50 – 59	(53)	45 – 51	(46)
plagioclase	20 – 29	(27)	29 – 37	(31)
ilmenite	10 – 18	(13)	10 – 14	(11)
chromite-ulvöspinel	1 – 2	(1)	0 – 0.1	(0.05)
troilite	.05 – 1.3	(1)	0.1 – 0.5	(0.3)
iron	.01 – 0.1	(0.04)	.01 – .05	(0.03)
olivine	trace – 7	(3)	0	0
cristobalite	trace – 1	(trace)	4 – 6	(5)
pyroxferroite	0	0	0.5 – 2	(1)
others	1 – 7	(2)	4 –8	(6)
		100%		100%

Much attention has been given to the search for evidence of meteorites and meteoritic minerals, especially in the lunar soil. There is no question but that most of the lunar craters were formed by meteorite impacts, although extreme views as to the meteorite versus volcanic origins for the lunar craters can be found in various pre-Apollo studies. Much of the meteoritic material is found in the finest fractions of the lunar soil and some is in the breccias, but because the greatest percentage of any meteorite is vaporized on impact with the lunar surface, surviving meteoritic material is rare. Agrell (University of Cambridge, England) has estimated that meteoritic material constitutes less than one or 2% of the soils based on his mineralogical studies; Anders (University of Chicago) calculates about 2% (specifically 1.88%) based on trace element distributions in the soils. In the latter case, Anders suggests that most of the meteoritic material striking the moon is very fragile carbonaceous chondrites, essentially none of which would be expected to survive.

Those fragments of meteoritic materials which are found in the lunar fines are related only to the iron meteorites rather than the stony meteorites, except possibly for hypersthene and aragonite. Iron meteorites are more durable and a small amount would be expected to survive almost any impact. Study of the well-known Canyon Diablo meteorite crater, Arizona, shows that an iron meteorite of many millions of tons would be required to form a crater of its dimension (maximum diameter of 1,295 meters) yet only about 30 tons have been recovered; the recovered portion was probably from the back-side of the meteorite which was not vaporized. It is not surprising therefore that (a) meteorite material in the moon's soils is rare, and (b) what is found is from the more tenacious iron meteorites.

The minerals on the lunar surface so far determined to come exclusively from meteorites are only (1) iron-nickel (kamacite and taenite), (2) cohenite and (3) schreibersite. There is, additionally, some evidence for modified or melted material probably of meteoritic origin associated with the lunar glasses. Troilite of meteoritic origin is probably present in the soils but at present is not easily distinguished from the relatively abundant troilite in the igneous lunar rocks. However, Goldstein (Lehigh University) made a careful study of the lunar metal particles containing iron-troilite intergrowths and concluded that components of both meteoritic and lunar origin are present. The two types can be differentiated on the basis of the significant Ni and P contents of the meteorite material. The cobalt contents and structures of both meteorite and lunar troilite are similar.

AUGITE-PIGEONITE (THE PYROXENES)

Members of the pyroxene group of minerals are the most abundant of all minerals in the Apollo 11 rocks and soils from Tranquillity Base, generally ranging in size from 0.1 – 2 mm. Detailed studies have shown that many varieties of pyroxenes are found in the various rocks: augite, subcalcic augite, ferroaugite, titanaugite and pigeonite. For this discussion it is only necessary to consider the two major varieties, pigeonite and augite, as understanding of the others will automatically follow. In many of the lunar studies the term pigeonite is used synonymously with 'low calcium pyroxene,' augite with 'high calcium pyroxene,' and 'pyroxene' for both. For the present it suffices to know that the pyroxenes are a closely related group of minerals with physical and chemical properties which are similar, although significant variations are possible. Terrestrial pyroxenes are known to crystallize in both the orthorhombic (called "orthopyroxene") or monoclinic (called "clinopyroxene") crystal systems. All lunar pyroxenes so far found (augite, pigeonite, etc.) are clinopyroxenes, except for a few grains of hypersthene (orthopyroxene) which have been reported in the soils, but these are likely of meteoritic origin and are not discussed further.

The chemical properties of the various lunar pyroxenes will vary appreciably but are still within the general chemical requirements of the group. The generalized formula for any pyroxene is XYZ_2O_6, and for lunar pyroxenes X = Ca; Y = Mg, Fe, Ti, Al, Mn and Cr; Z = Si and Al. In the coarse-grained rocks, the pyroxenes are usually cinnamon-brown, lustrous grains and can be seen with the naked eye.

In its simplest form, the chemical composition of the clinopyroxenes can be considered in relationship to the triangle illustrated in Fig. 3-1, in which the corners are $MgSiO_3$, enstatite (abbreviated "En"); $FeSiO_3$, ferrosilite

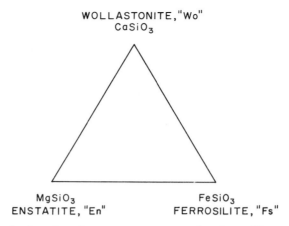

Fig. 3-1. Triangle showing the components enstatite, ferrosilite and wollastonite which are present in the pyroxenes.

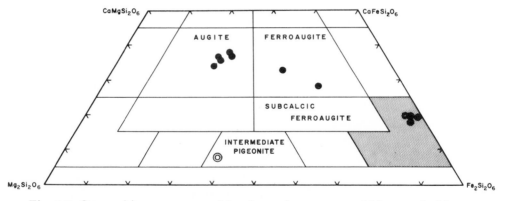

Fig. 3-2. Compositions, represented by dots, of pyroxenes within a typical lunar rock (rock 10047; Type B), illustrating the variability which has been found. The composition of the new mineral pyroxferroite falls in the shaded area at the lower right; terrestrial minerals are not known to fall in this compositional region. After Mason (Smithsonian Institution).

(abbreviated "Fs"); and $CaSiO_3$, wollastonite (abbreviated "Wo"). In actual practice, only a section of the triangle (a trapezohedron) is required to plot known analyses (Figs. 3-2, 3-3) as the $CaSiO_3$ ("Wo") component is less than 50%. The additional corners now introduced represent $CaMgSi_2O_6$ (diopside) and $CaFeSi_2O_6$ (hedenbergite). Whereas terrestrial mineral representatives of the corners of the triangle (En, Fs, and Wo) crystallize as orthopyroxenes or triclinic pyroxenoids, the lunar minerals so far found have compositions which fall within the triangle or trapezohedron and are all clinopyroxenes.

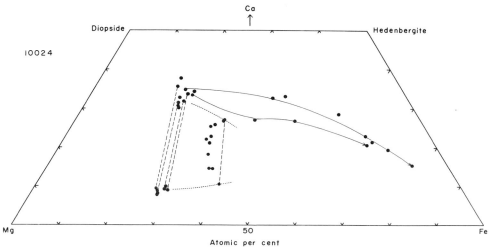

Fig. 3-3. Plot of the variations in the compositions within pyroxene crystals for rock 10024 (Type B). Solid lines indicate ranges of continuous chemical zoning within a single crystal; note the change from augite to ferroaugite to pyroxferroite. Dashed lines illustrate change of composition from pigeonite (lower dots) to augite (upper dots); these minerals are in contact with each other. Dotted lines indicate a possible solvus between augite and pigeonite. After Kushiro and Nakamura (University of Tokyo, Japan).

The most striking characteristic of the lunar pyroxenes is their chemical variability (Table 3-3; Figs. 3-2 and 3-3). Two generalized types have been recognized: (1) a high-Ca group with the wollastonite component from $20 - 40\%$ (Wo_{20-40}) and (2) a low-Ca group with the wollastonite component from $10 - 14\%$ (Wo_{10-14}). In the high calcium group are the varieties augite, ferroaugite and subcalcic augite, whereas in the low calcium group pigeonite is the only mineral (Fig. 3-2). Variations in composition (zoning) from pigeonite to the high calcium types have been observed within most pyroxene grains by means of electron probe studies which are capable of analyzing areas as small as 1 micron (Figs. 3-3 and 3-4). In general, cores of pyroxene crystals are likely to be pigeonite with a gradual chemical transition to edges of augite. In some cases, the pyroxene grains are rimmed with the new lunar mineral pyroxferroite (described below). In many grains there is no optical or color evidence for the change pigeonite-augite-pyroxferroite, and only by careful chemical measurements by the electron probe have they been observed. The compositional changes essentially involve a decrease in Ca, Mg and Cr, followed in the last stage by a dramatic increase in Fe. This is another way of explaining the most characteristic chemical feature of lunar pyroxenes: low calcium cores and high iron rims. In Table 3-6 and Fig. 3-9 of the pyroxferroite section below, the changes from pigeonite to augite to pyroxferroite found in a zoned crystal are presented. As mentioned

Fig. 3-4. Photomicrograph showing basal sections of well developed prisms of pyroxene crystals. Note the strong compositional zoning. Plane light. Rock 10069 (Type A). After Dence (Geological Survey of Canada).

Table 3-3. Chemical analysis of lunar pyroxenes (in weight %).

	1	2	3	4	5
SiO$_2$	49.0	49.96	50.78	49.09	43.3
Al$_2$O$_3$	3.9	2.83	1.92	3.49	7.9
TiO$_2$	1.20	3.29	2.03	3.30	7.0
FeO	17.0	15.90	10.59	8.71	18.4
MgO	22.5	13.93	16.35	13.80	8.1
MnO	0.20	0.29	0.28	0.22	–
Cr$_2$O$_3$	0.50	–	–	–	–
CaO	5.0	14.19	16.47	20.10	13.5
Na$_2$O	< 0.03	–	–	–	–
K$_2$O	–	–	–	–	–
Total	99.20	100.39	98.42	98.71	98.5
Wo (CaSiO$_3$)	10	31	34	44	34
En (MgSiO$_3$)	63	42	48	41	29
Fs (FeSiO$_3$)	27	27	18	15	37

Notes:

1. Pigeonite from rock 10067 (Type C). Analysis by Keil (University of New Mexico).
2. Subcalcic augite from rock 10045 (Type AB). Analysis by Agrell (University of Cambridge, England).
3. Augite, pale-colored crystal from lunar fines. Analysis by Agrell.
4. Augite, darker-colored crystal from lunar fines. Analysis by Agrell.
5. Titanaugite from lunar fines. Analysis by Frondel (Harvard University).

above, recognition of these chemical variations by optical means (e.g., color, changes in index of refraction) is very difficult, if not impossible in some cases. In other cases, zoning in pyroxenes is readily recognized (Fig. 3-4). Titanaugite (7.0% TiO_2), on the other hand, which is reported only from the soils, can be identified optically because of its very dark purplish color. Detailed studies by various authors have shown variations and complications from the simplified trends described above.

Petrographic (microscopic) studies have failed to reveal some of the more interesting heterogeneities in chemistry and structure of many pyroxene grains because of the inherent inability of these techniques to resolve changes in crystal structure and composition across areas of less than 1 micron. X-ray diffraction and high voltage electron microscopy studies, both of which have resolving power into the angstrom (Å.) range, or many times greater than optical microscopic methods, have revealed a fascinating degree of phase and chemical heterogeneity in the lunar pyroxenes.

These two significantly different techniques have enabled mineralogists to observe that lunar pyroxene crystals are generally heterogeneous. Crystals may appear to be augite, but under great magnification will be found to be composed of intergrowths of augite and pigeonite in varying proportions. What is actually present are exsolution lamellae (thin plates) of either phase (usually pigeonite in augite), many about 60 Å. in thickness, although thicker ones are found (generally less than 1000 Å.). These lamellae have been described by Ross (U.S. Geological Survey) by X-ray diffraction methods, and more spectacularly by Radcliffe (Case Western Reserve University), and others, with the relatively new technique of high voltage electron microscopy (Figs. 3-5 and 3-6). Considering the very small size of the pigeonite exsolution lamellae, it is not surprising that only rarely are these seen by conventional petrographic methods. Where pigeonite lamellae have been thick enough for electron probe work, studies have shown the pigeonite to contain more Fe than the augite host, as would be expected. Other studies have shown that there is chemical substitution involving Ca for Fe and Ti for Al, as well as other elements, as would be predictable from the variation in the composition of pigeonite and augite. Within each individual augite sector, minor variations of the Ca and Fe contents, corresponding with the general pyroxene crystallization chemical sequence described above (Fig. 3-3), are also found.

The explanation for the pigeonite-augite lamellae displayed by the lunar pyroxenes may be attributed to the rapid crystallization of these minerals from a melt continually changing composition. It is believed that initially a single clinopyroxene began to crystallize and it had the composition between augite and pigeonite. On cooling, by complex methods not yet fully understood, the pigeonite component which has a slightly different

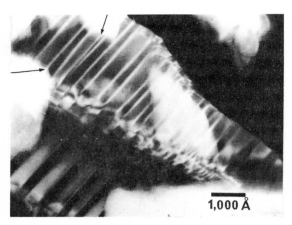

Fig. 3-5. Transmission (high voltage) electron microscope photograph showing narrow lamellae (thin bands) approximately 60 Å. in thickness (arrows); the bands are pigeonite in augite. In the lower left of photograph the bands are about 400 Å. in thickness. After Ross (U.S. Geological Survey).

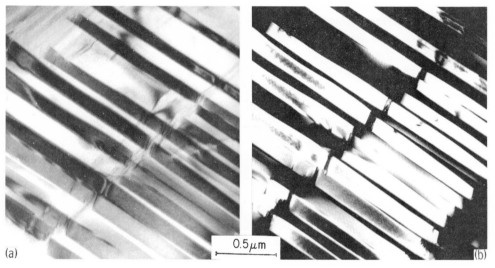

Fig. 3-6. High-voltage electron microscope photographs illustrating exsolution lamellae of pigeonite in augite. Different types of contrast are shown in (a) and (b). After Radcliffe (Case Western Reserve University).

crystal structure (but is still a clinopyroxene) was not able to remain within the augite, and exsolution resulted. Finally, it should be observed that Radcliffe reports fine-scale exsolution lamellae are also found in terrestrial pyroxenes, but their exact nature and causes are not known. Radcliffe studied lunar ilmenite and plagioclase by this same method, and found some microstructures (e.g., slip dislocations, twins, evidence of deformation), but no exsolution phenomenon.

PYROXFERROITE

Pyroxferroite has received special attention for two reasons: (1) it is the first new mineral to be observed, described and named from the moon, and (2) its bright yellow color undoubtedly qualifies it for the most attractive of the lunar minerals (see color frontispiece, Plate 7). Aside from these points, pyroxferroite is a very interesting and important mineral in the study of lunar rocks, specifically the Type B microgabbros or gabbros, the only rocks in which it occurs.

The composition of pyroxferroite is simple, being ideally defined as $FeSiO_3$. Lunar pyroxferroite, however, contains approximately 6% CaO resulting in the formula $Ca_{0.15}Fe_{0.85}SiO_3$ (with minor Mn, Mg, Ti and Al, as well). Pyroxferroite is the iron analogue of pyroxmangite, $MnSiO_3$, a relatively rare mineral which is known on Earth from certain manganese deposits and metamorphic rocks. About 20 examples of terrestrial minerals which fall within the series from pyroxmangite toward the pyroxferroite end-member have been described but none of these minerals approach the ideal pyroxferroite closer than 28% FeO, in comparison with the approximately 47% FeO for the Tranquillity Base material (See Table 3-4).

In order to understand the significance of pyroxferroite, and its relationship to other silicates, it is necessary to digress to a brief discussion of the

Table 3-4. Chemical analysis of selected minerals in the pyroxferroite-pyroxmangite series (the Siebenerketten pyroxenoids) (in weight %).

	1	2	3	4	5
SiO_2	45.0	44.7 – 46.4	45.5 – 47.0	45.74	47.14
TiO_2	0.5	0.3 – 0.5	0.2 – 0.5	–	–
Al_2O_3	0.2	0.5 – 1.2	0.2 – 0.4	–	2.38
FeO	47.2	45.0 – 46.4	46.0 – 47.9	0.39	28.34
Fe_2O_3	–	–	–	Trace	–
MnO	1.0	0.6 – 1.3	0.1 – 0.5	52.42	20.63
MgO	0.9	0.6 – 0.9	0.4 – 1.0	0.68	–
CaO	6.0	5.7 – 6.3	5.4 – 6.1	0.46	1.88
Total	100.8	100.2	100.1	99.69	100.70

Notes:

1. Pyroxferroite from Tranquillity Base (rock 10047). Analysis by Frondel (Harvard University).
2. Pyroxferroite from Tranquillity Base (rock 10044). Analysis by Smith (University of Chicago).
3. Pyroxferroite from Tranquillity Base (rock 10047). Analysis by Dence (Geological Survey of Canada).
4. Pyroxmangite ($MnSiO_3$) from Ajiro Mine, Japan. Analysis by Lee (1955).
5. Manganoan pyroxferroite from Iva, South Carolina. Analysis by Ford and Bradley (1913). The total of 100.70% includes 0.33% H_2O.

pyroxenoids. The pyroxenoids are a group of minerals related to the much more abundant pyroxenes (of which augite is an example), but there are important differences based on the internal atomic arrangement of the respective families. Although both pyroxenes and pyroxenoids are structurally based on chains of linked SiO_4 tetrahedra of composition $(SiO_3)_n$, many different arrangements are possible (Fig. 3-7). The more abundant pyroxenes are either orthorhombic or monoclinic, but the pyroxenoids are triclinic. In Table 3-5 data on several pyroxenoids are presented which illustrate the differences among these chain silicate (SiO_3) minerals. The SiO_3 chains of linked (SiO_4) tetrahedra differ in their nature and arrangement, as for example the pyroxenes (augite) whose chains are parallel to the c-axis and have a repeat every second SiO_4 tetrahedron, Si_2O_6. In the triclinic pyroxenoid wollastonite, on the other hand, the chains are parallel to the b-axis and the repeat is every third SiO_4 tetrahedron, Si_3O_9, (hence the technical name — Dreierketten, German equivalent for "three chain"); in rhodonite the repeat distance of the silicate chains is every fifth tetrahedron, Si_5O_{15} (Fünferketten); and in pyroxmangite it is the seventh tetrahedron, Si_7O_{21} (Siebenerketten). It is believed that the repeat lengths of the pyroxenoid chains are controlled, at least in part, by the average octahedral cation size of the substituting elements (i.e., Ca, Fe, Mn, Mg). From Table 3-5 we see that rhodonite and pyroxmangite have the same composition, but because of their different structures (called polymorphs), they can be distinguished with certainty only by X-ray diffraction methods and certain optical properties, such as indices of refraction. The pyroxenes and pyroxenoids are often related texturally by oriented intergrowths which can be explained by their close similarity in structure.

From the chemical composition of several selected examples of pyroxmangite-pyroxferroite minerals presented in Table 3-4, the following important points are observed: (1) Mn and Fe are the dominant octahedrally coordinated cations; (2) calcium reaches a maximum of about 6% and tends to increase with iron; (3) essentially all the iron is in the ferrous state, indicating extreme reducing conditions; and (4) the lunar pyroxferroite has a variable composition, but the variation is over a very narrow range, with very little Mn or Mg. The composition taking the minor elements into account can be written as:

$(Fe_{0.85} Ca_{0.14} Mg_{0.03} Mn_{0.02}) (Si_{0.97} Ti_{0.01} Al_{0.01}) O_3$.

Other properties of lunar pyroxferroite include:

color: yellow
refractive indices: $\alpha = 1.753$ $\beta = 1.755$ $\gamma = 1.766$
$2 V_z = 35° - 41°$ optical sign $= +$
cleavage: good in one direction, possibly (010), and poor (001)
specific gravity: 3.68 - 3.76

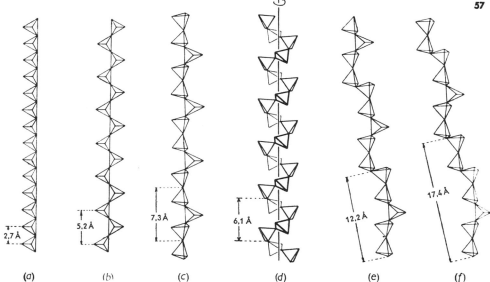

Fig. 3-7. Schematic representation of the structural relationship between pyroxenes and pyroxenoids. Repeat distance for SiO₄ tetrahedra are (a) every
tetrahedron; (b) every second tetrahedra as in augite; (c) every third tetrahedra
as in wollastonite; (d) every fourth tetrahedra; (e) every fifth tetrahedra as in
rhodonite; and (f) every seventh tetrahedra as in pyroxferroite, the new lunar
mineral. After F. Liebau (1959) and reprinted with permission of *Acta Crystallo-
graphica*.

Pyroxferroite occurs only as a late stage accessory mineral (up to 2%)
in the Type B rocks, often in intimate growth relationships with pyroxene
(augite) as is illustrated in Fig. 3-8. Some bright yellow pyroxferroite crystals will also be found lining the vugs in these rocks; it is from this occurrence that a few single crystals and crystal fragments have been isolated
(color frontispiece, Plate 7). Occurrences in the late-stage mesostasis (residuum), associated with fayalite, silica minerals and potassium-rich intergrowths have been reported by Brown (University of Cambridge, England).

Fe-Ca silicates approximating the composition of lunar pyroxferroite have
been known since 1933 when they were synthesized by the famous petrolo-
gist, N.L. Bowen. Bowen's pyroxenoids, however, were probably of the

Table 3-5. Data on selected pyroxenoids. (All are terrestrial except pyroxferroite which
is from the moon.)

Mineral	Color	Composition	Repeat Distance	Technical Name
wollastonite	white	CaSiO₃	3 tetrahedra	Dreierketten
bustamite	pink-red	(Mn, Ca) SiO₃ with significant Fe	3 tetrahedra	Dreierketten
rhodonite	rose-red	MnSiO₃ with significant Fe and Ca	5 tetrahedra	Fünferketten
pyroxmangite	pink	MnSiO₃	7 tetrahedra	Siebenerketten
pyroxferroite	yellow	FeSiO₃	7 tetrahedra	Siebenerketten

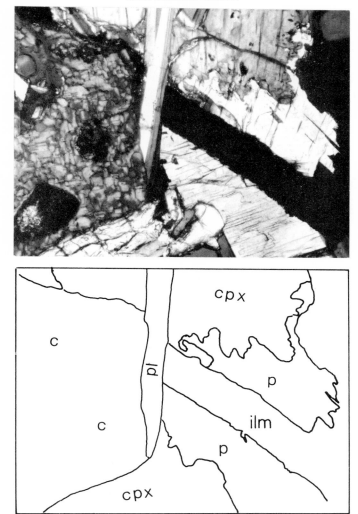

Fig. 3-8. *Upper:* Photomicrograph (using crossed polars) of thin section from rock 10047 (Type B).

Lower: Key to above photomicrograph in which p = pyroxferroite; ilm = ilmenite; cpx = clinopyroxene; pl = plagioclase; c = cristobalite. Note the interfingering of pyroxferroite with clinopyroxene, demonstrating intimate growth relation. Also, the numerous lines across the pyroxferroite indicates good cleavage. The cristobalite exhibits "tile" structure, which is the result of structural inversion from high temperature cubic structure to low temperature tetragonal structure. After Trail (Geological Survey of Canada).

wollastonite type (Dreierketten). Material essentially identical chemically and structurally to lunar pyroxferroite was synthesized by D.H. Lindsley at the Geophysical Laboratory, Washington, D.C., in 1967, certainly without any realization of the importance of his work to lunar mineralogy. One interesting point observed then, and reconfirmed more recently, is that the pyroxferroite is not stable below approximately 10 kilobars and 1190°C. From these synthetic studies it has been shown that at lower pressures, pyroxferroite decomposes to a combination of Ca-enriched pyroxenoid (such as wollastonite) or clinopyroxene, fayalitic (high Fe) olivine, and a SiO₂ phase; at lower temperatures, it transforms into a clinopyroxene. From the petrographic studies of the minerals associated with lunar pyroxferroite (such as cristobalite) and its occurrence in vugs, a low pressure origin for pyroxferroite, along with high temperature conditions, is suggested (Fig. 3-8). From other evidence, we also know lunar pyroxferroite crystallized from an iron-rich residual liquid which was cooling rapidly. It is because of this rapid cooling that pyroxferroite crystallized and still persists in its undecomposed metastable state after 3 billion years. Only in a few cases has the association of (Ca-enriched) pyroxene, fayalite, and a silica mineral been found which could represent the breakdown of metastable pyroxferroite when cooling could have been sufficiently slow to permit the transformation.

The close relationship between the pyroxenes and pyroxenoids mineral families is mentioned above. This relationship is remarkably illustrated in some lunar rocks, in which zoned pyroxenes show gradations from a core of pigeonite, to a middle portion consisting of subcalcic ferroaugite, and from here the pyroxenes will grade into rims of pyroxferroite; a gradual change from monoclinic to triclinic symmetry is also required (Table 3-6). The chemical variations associated with these changes have been discussed

Table 3-6. Analysis of zoned crystal from rock 10058 grading from pyroxene to pyroxferroite (in weight %). Analysis by Agrell (University of Cambridge, England).

	3	4	5	6	7	8	9
SiO₂	50.36	49.76	48.31	46.92	46.31	45.92	45.86
TiO₂	1.67	1.30	0.66	0.74	0.63	0.63	0.59
Al₂O₃	1.97	1.49	0.81	0.76	0.64	0.88	0.74
Cr₂O₃	0.31	0.24	0.14	0.12	0.10	0.09	0.10
FeO	17.31	22.97	36.11	42.48	42.45	42.45	44.19
MnO	0.32	0.43	0.65	0.65	0.64	0.62	0.64
MgO	14.17	11.69	5.90	2.41	1.63	1.59	1.38
CaO	13.85	12.07	8.97	6.69	6.37	6.48	6.21
Total	99.68	99.95	101.55	100.77	98.77	98.66	99.71

Notes:

1. Analyses 3 to 9 correspond with points on Fig. 3-9 and illustrate a continuously zoned crystal. Note decrease in Ca and Mg (and to a lesser extent Ti, Al and Cr) and a corresponding increase in Fe (and Mn) from core (Anal. 3) to rim (Anal. 9).
2. Points 3, 4 and 5 correspond with pyroxene; points 6, 7, 8 and 9 are pyroxferroite areas.

in the pyroxene section, but it is important to restate that this gradation correlates with a decrease in Ca and Mg (and to a lesser extent Ti, Al and Cr) and an increase in Fe (and Mn) in the crystallizing phases from the pigeonite core to pyroxferroite rims. Its outside position in the zoned crystals also indicates that pyroxferroite is a late-crystallizing mineral phase, which is further borne out by its association in the final residuum with apatite, tridymite, cristobalite, more sodic plagioclase and some small patches of potash feldspar, as well as its occasional occurrence as well-developed late-forming crystals in the vugs.

Fig. 3-9 beautifully illustrates such a zoned pyroxene grading into a zoned pyroxferroite. The mineralogical changes can be followed by detailed optical measurements, but for our purposes the corresponding chemical changes can be observed from the data in Table 3-6, where the numbered points indicated on the crystal (Fig. 3-9) correspond with those in Table 3-6. The reason for the crystallization of the pyroxferroite in this relationship has not been definitely established and will probably be the subject of exhaustive study, but its presence does give some ground for speculation. On the basis of the apparent lack of a compositional break between the pyroxene and pyroxferroite, it is believed that at its high temperatures the original lunar magma (high in Ca and Mg) crystallized pyroxenes. Later when Ca and Mg were depleted, and the residual magma was enriched in Fe, a triclinic mineral (pyroxferroite) was the metastable structural form which crystallized from the magma.

Terrestrially, the pyroxenoids wollastonite and rhodonite are well-known, pyroxmangite is rare, and pyroxferroite is unknown. The closest terrestrial approach to lunar pyroxferroite is the rare mineral from Iva, South Carolina (Table 3-4, Anal. 5), which is actually a manganoan pyroxferroite with a Fe/Mn ratio of 55/45 on an atomic basis.

The name "pyroxferroite," especially for the first new mineral found in lunar rocks, may seem unappealing to many scientists as well as laymen; it is hardly glamorous and certainly not euphonious. Yet mineralogical nomenclature must adhere to strict rules to prevent a multitude of unnecessary, incorrect or otherwise undesirable mineral names. The name pyroxferroite is scientifically appropriate because it indicates a relationship to the pyroxenes (or pyroxenoids) and, more importantly, it is consistent with the nomenclature of the previously well-defined terrestrial mineral pyroxmangite — its manganese analogue (Table 3-5). Thus it is possible to refer to all minerals with similar chemical, structural and optical properties as belonging to the pyroxmangite (Mn-rich)-pyroxferroite (Fe-rich) series. As with all proposed new minerals, the name pyroxferroite was approved by the Nomenclature Committee of the International Mineralogical Association, thereby establishing its status officially.

Fig. 3-9. *Upper:* Photomicrograph of strongly zoned pyroxene-pyroxferroite crystal, showing optical gradations (variation in birefringence) from clear core (pyroxene) to darker rim (pyroxferroite). Analysis obtained at points 3, 4, 5 and 6 are presented in Table 3-6. Width of field 3.5 mm. Crossed polars. Rock 10058 (Type B).

Lower: Englargement of the lower left corner of the crystal shown above, in the area of pyroxferroite crystallization. Analyses obtained at points 6, 7, 8 and 9 are presented in Table 3-6. Pyroxferroite is in contact with residuum composed of cristobalite, tridymite, (twinned crystal, upper right), sodic plagioclase, alkali (potassium) feldspar and opaques. Width of field 1.5 mm. Crossed polars. After Agrell (University of Cambridge, England).

PLAGIOCLASE (AND POTASSIUM FELDSPAR)

The most abundant group of minerals on Earth are the feldspars and for this reason they are the basis of classification for terrestrial igneous rocks. The feldspars are generally divided into two subgroups: (1) the plagioclases and (2) the potassium feldspars. Both types of feldspars also have been found on the moon but the abundance of the plagioclases far exceeds that of the potassium feldspars; this is to be expected because of the basaltic nature of the lunar rocks. In terrestrial basalts, plagioclase and pyroxenes combined constitute most of the mineral assemblage, and the same is true for the lunar maria rocks.

The mineralogical classification of the plagioclases (both on the Earth and on the moon) is based upon the fact that a continuous solid solution series exists between a sodium end-member (albite, $NaAlSi_3O_8$) to a calcium end-member (anorthite, $CaAl_2Si_2O_8$). The plagioclase series can be considered as a solid solution series in which sodium and calcium end-members are mutually interchangeable within the plagioclase crystal structure. Because of the great abundance of plagioclases in nature, and their importance in igneous rock classification, six convenient arbitrarily defined species have been named for the plagioclases. The variation can be expressed as the percent of the anorthite member, which is commonly abbreviated as "An."

$NaAlSi_3O_8$	albite	An_0-An_{10}
	oligoclase	An_{10}-An_{30}
	andesine	An_{30}-An_{50}
	labradorite	An_{50}-An_{70}
	bytownite	An_{70}-An_{90}
$CaAl_2Si_2O_8$	anorthite	An_{90}-An_{100}

Thus "An_{72}" means that on a chemical basis the plagioclase contains 72% anorthite ($CaAl_2Si_2O_8$) and the remaining 28% is albite ($NaAlSi_3O_8$); the mineral name in this case would be bytownite.

In the lunar rocks, plagioclases show a range of composition (Table 3-7) and for all practical purposes the range of compositions falls within An_{70} – An_{92} (bytownite-anorthite), although some mineralogists have reported pure anorthite (An_{100}) and others have reported An contents in the labradorite range. Several independent statistical studies of the many plagioclases analyses from the Type B (or AB) rocks (gabbros) show that the average composition is in the range An_{88-92} (Table 3-7, Anal. 3 and 4). This even takes into account the fact that some zoning, on a minor scale in comparison with the pyroxenes, does take place in the plagioclase crystals and a range of from perhaps An_{84-94} would not be unusual. The Type A rocks (basalts), on the other hand, have been shown to have a lower An content — in other words, they have more of the sodium component (albite). Plagioclases from Type A rocks commonly range from An_{71-77}, as is illustrated in Table 3-7 (Anal. 1 and 2). If the observations on the varying chemistry of the plagioclases from the Type A and B rocks stand the test of time and are found to be significant, they could be the basis for the postulation that the basalts and gabbros were formed from chemically dis-

Table 3-7. Chemical analysis of feldspar (plagioclase and potassium feldspar) from Tranquillity Base (in weight %).

	1	2	3	4	5	6
SiO_2	53.3	51.2	44.8	46.3	64.6	61.2
TiO_2	0.08	0.11	–	0.05	–	–
Al_2O_3	29.3	30.0	34.5	34.0	19.9	19.1
FeO	1.0	0.5	0.63	0.99	0.6	–
MnO	–	–	–	0.03	–	–
MgO	0.2	0.3	–	0.3	–	–
CaO	14.5	15.6	18.5	17.1	0.72	0.9
Na_2O	2.0	2.1	0.94	1.05	0.33	0.0
K_2O	0.34	0.23	0.05	0.09	13.1	13.9
BaO	–	–	–	0.01	–	3.2
Total	100.7	100.00	99.42	99.90	99.25	98.3
"An" content	71	77	91	90	–	–

Notes:

1. Small plagioclase crystal (with An_{71}) next to residual glass. Rock 10022 (Type A). Total includes 0.02% P_2O_5. Analysis by Smith (University of Chicago).
2. Interior of large plagioclase (with An_{77}) from same rock as above. Total also includes 0.02% P_2O_5. Analysis by Smith.
3. Plagioclase (An_{91}); average of 20 grains from medium-grained igneous rock 10045 (Type B). Analysis by Keil (University of New Mexico).
4. Plagioclase (An_{90}); from fine-grained gabbro from sample 10050 (Type AB). Total includes 0.01% Cr_2O_3 and 0.01% SrO. Analysis by Frondel (Harvard University).
5. Potassium feldspar of late stage differentiate. Rock 10045 (Type AB). Analysis by Keil.
6. Potassium-barium feldspar associated with cristobalite and other late stage minerals. Rock 10020 (Type A). Analysis by Dence (Geological Survey of Canada).

tinct magmas. Indirect preliminary evidence for this suggestion has been obtained from several crystallographic studies on the lunar plagioclases by Stewart (U.S. Geological Survey) and Gay (University of Cambridge, England) who find differences in the structural state of the plagioclases from the different rock types, which could be a reflection of not only the above mentioned compositional differences, but also thermal history.

From Table 3-7, in addition to the variation of An content, one other item of chemical interest with respect to the minor elements is worthy of mention. Iron is present in the feldspar structure up to about 1% FeO; iron in the structure of terrestrial plagioclase is rare and often attributed to impurities. Other elements present in minor amounts, such as TiO_2 and MgO, appear to be within a normal range based on terrestrial equivalents in basalts and gabbros.

Plagioclase is the second most abundant mineral in all types of lunar rocks. In comparison with its occurrence in terrestrial rocks, lunar plagioclase is remarkably unaltered and relatively free of inclusions, although inclusions of small grains of pyroxene and ilmenite are not unusual. Grain size varies from 0.1 – 2mm. depending primarily on rock type, and a wide variety of forms, such as tabular, lathlike or acicular and hourglass (Figs. 2-5 through 2-12), are found. Weill (University of Oregon) reports an

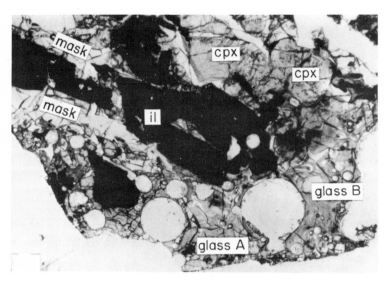

Fig. 3-10. Photomicrograph of maskelynite (mask), a glass of plagioclase composition caused by shock effects, seen in microbreccia with ilmenite (il) and clinopyroxene (cpx). Note maskelynite retains external form of original plagioclase. Clinopyroxene has developed fine mosaic structure. Glasses of two different compositions (glass A and B) have developed reflecting different parental material. Plane light. After Quaide and Bunch (NASA Ames Research Center, California).

unusual hollow form which he concludes is the result of rapid cooling and suggests that perhaps this form may be found in quick-cooled plagioclases from terrestrial lavas. Large-sized plagioclase crystals will always show the characteristic albite twinning, but other less common types of twinning are also observed. In the fines, and in some vugs, some well-developed anorthite crystals have been isolated and crystal faces identified. The crystals are flattened on the pinacoid (010).

Meteorite impacts have had great shock and metamorphic effects on lunar rocks and minerals (Fig. 2-22). The results of these impacts are particularly evident on the plagioclases which are converted to glass (vitrification). The name maskelynite has been applied to such shock-vitrified material (Fig. 3-10). Maskelynite is relatively abundant in the breccias (Type C) and the fines (Type D). Chemical analyses of maskelynite are very similar to some of the plagioclases in Table 3-7, indicating that little chemical (as opposed to physical) change has taken place in the process of maskelynite formation. The close chemical similarity also confirms the (bytownite) plagioclase origin for maskelynite.

Potassium feldspars, in some cases with considerable barium, have been found in small amounts in the lunar rocks (Table 3-7, Anal. 5 and 6). These potassium feldspars are probably distinctly different from the plagioclases in structure, but because of their small size and limited abundance they have not been isolated for the necessary crystallographic investigations (Fig. 3-9). No name has been used in discussions of these feldspars other than their chemical designation, potassium (or K) feldspar or potassium-barium feldspar. Sanidine is the potassium feldspar usually found in potassium-rich terrestrial volcanics such as rhyolite and trachyte, but the lunar rocks are significantly different in bulk composition from rhyolite or trachyte. Regardless of the name eventually associated with the lunar potassium feldspars, the important point to be kept in mind is their occurrence — which is in the very late residual (mesostasis) stages associated with such minerals as cristobalite, tridymite, apatite and zircon and other as yet incompletely defined minerals.

ILMENITE

Ilmenite is the third most abundant lunar mineral (ranging from $10 - 18$ weight % in most rocks) and is one of the most conspicuous features of the Apollo 11 rocks, with crystals occasionally reaching several millimeters in size. It occurs in all types of lunar rocks, shows a large crystallization range (from an early to a late stage), and exhibits several distinctive forms which may be correlated with time of crystallization. Ilmenite is unquestionably the most important opaque lunar mineral, and in large part accounts for the dark black appearance of many specimens.

Chemically, lunar ilmenite is almost pure $FeTiO_3$, as is illustrated by the several analyses of Table 3-8. Most investigators have found that ilmenite crystals are generally uniform in composition. However, a few studies have noted an excess of Ti (for example, Table 3-8, Anal. 6), and a deficiency of Fe in comparison with the theoretical composition (Table 3-8, Anal. 1). This has lead to the tantalizing possibility that excess titanium may exist in the rare, reduced trivalent state (Ti^{+3}), whereas titanium usually is tetravalent (Ti^{+4}); this hypothesis remains to be proved. Other aspects of the chemistry of the lunar ilmenites which warrant mention are the relatively high chromium and magnesium contents. Variations in the abundance of some of the elements, such as magnesium, can be correlated with time of crystallization — early formed ilmenite is usually higher in Mg than that which crystallized later, a situation analogous to what occurs

Table 3-8. Chemical analysis of ilmenites from Tranquillity Base rocks illustrating relatively uniform composition (in weight %).

	1	2	3	4	5	6
SiO$_2$		0.14	–	–	0.09	0.09
TiO$_2$	52.66	53.95	52.6	52.0	52.22	55.05
Al$_2$O$_3$		–	0.0	0.14	< 0.03	< 0.03
Cr$_2$O$_3$		0.66	0.51	0.46	0.53	0.53
FeO	47.34	43.80	45.3	45.4	44.38	44.84
MnO		0.40	0.37	0.95	0.15	0.15
MgO		0.97	0.83	1.46	1.39	1.14
CaO		0.08	–	0.23	0.21	0.21
ZrO$_2$		–	~ 0.3	0.03	0.24	0.24
Total	100.00	100.00	100.0	100.71	99.21	102.25

Notes:

1. Theoretical ilmenite, FeTiO$_3$.
2. Ilmenite from rock 10017 (Type A). Average of 9 analyses. Analyses by Agrell (University of Cambridge, England).
3. Ilmenite from rock 10050 (Type B). Analysis by Frondel (Harvard University).
4. Ilmenite from rock 10068 (Type C). Average of 57 grains. Total of 100.71% includes 0.04% V$_2$O$_3$. Analysis by Keil (University of New Mexico).
5. Imenite from rock 10057 (Type B). Illustrates normal TiO$_2$ abundance. Analysis by Lovering and Ware (Australian National University).
6. Ilmenite from the same rock as above (5) except this ilmenite has high TiO$_2$ content which may represent presence of Ti^{+3}; see text.

in the pyroxenes and pyroxferroite which is discussed in greater detail above. Weill (University of Oregon) has noted that Mg in ilmenite may vary from 0.1 – 4.7%, and that there is a distinct hiatus between the platy, more commonly occurring ilmenites with 0.1 – 1.6% Mg, and the rare variety with 3.6 – 4.7% Mg. The high-magnesium ilmenites occur as small tabular grains totally enclosed in pyroxene. The explanation for the high-Mg ilmenites is not known. Another unexpected observation is the high zirconium content (ZrO$_2$~0.3%) of several ilmenites (Table 3-8, Anal, 3, 4, 5, 6) which lead the observers to suggest that ilmenite is apparently one of the main host minerals for zirconium in the lunar rocks.

Many textures have been observed and described for ilmenite. These include blocky, tabular, platy, skeletal, herringbone, equant, anhedral, euhedral and circular. A selection of textures is presented in Figs. 3-11 and 3-12. There are numerous suggestions that in some rocks the morphology of ilmenite crystals can be related to time of crystallization and chemistry. For example, the above-mentioned high-magnesium ilmenites, observed by Weill (University of Oregon) as inclusions within pyroxene, are tabular and believed to form early; the more abundant platy variety is believed to have

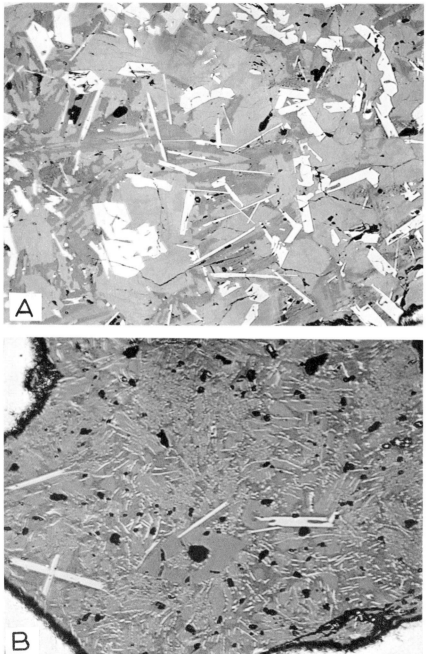

Fig. 3-11. Photomicrograph showing ilmenite textures as seen in reflected light. (A) ilmenite (white) showing both platy and tabular textures. Pyroxene is light gray and plagioclase darker gray. Rock 10022 (Type A). (B) phenocrysts of ilmenite (white) in a groundmass containing abundant skeletal ilmenite. Magnification 70X. After Cameron (University of Wisconsin).

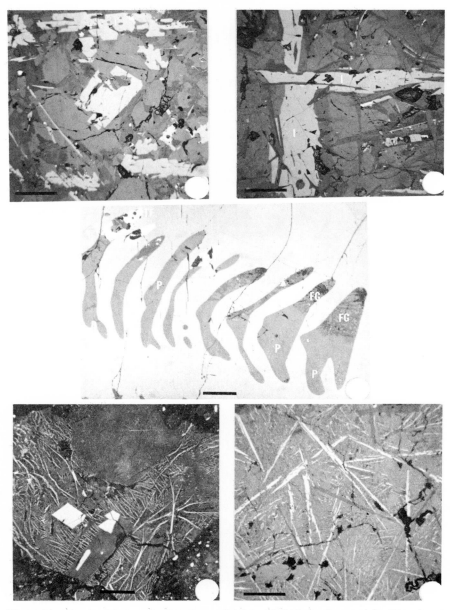

Fig. 3-12. Photomicrograph showing selection of ilmenite textures as seen in reflected light. *Upper left:* blocky ilmenite (I) in rock 10071 (Type AB). *Upper
right:* cross-cutting grains of ilmenite (I) in rock 10020 (Type A). *Center:*
herringbone structure in ilmenite (I). Trapped inclusions are pyroxene (P),
feldspar glass (FG) and troilite-iron (TF). Rock 10047 (Type B): scale bar =
50 microns. *Lower left:* blocky, skeletal and dendritic textures of ilmenite
(white). Rock 10073 (Type C): *Lower right:* radiating, subskeletal laths of
ilmenite (white) in glass matrix. Rock 10061 (Type C). Scale bar = 50 microns.
After Haggerty (Geophysical Laboratory).

formed later. Under any condition, there is almost unanimous agreement that ilmenite crystallized over most of the solidification range of the crystalline lunar rocks.

Some very distinctive textures involving ilmenite have been described by Haggerty (Geophysical Laboratory, Washington, D.C.). These include (a) exsolution of various minerals from ilmenite, and (b) ilmenite overgrowths on several minerals, the most spectacular being armalcolite (color frontispiece, Plate 8, top). The exsolution consists chiefly of secondary rutile and spinel (Plate 8). The overgrowth texture of ilmenite on armalcolite is believed to result from the incomplete reaction of early formed armalcolite with lunar melt (armalcolite + melt → ilmenite). Nevertheless, the many textures and exsolution phenomenon are complex and not fully understood. It should be kept in mind, however, that most lunar ilmenite is homogenous, and the ilmenites representing the two features (exsolution and overgrowth) just mentioned are relatively rare and quantitatively minor.

In terrestrial rocks ilmenite is a common accessory mineral and is often found as disseminations or segregations in basic igneous rocks such as gabbros and anorthosites. Important localities are in Wyoming, Quebec, Norway, and other places; but only rarely is ilmenite ever found in as great abundance as it is in the lunar rocks because terrestrial rocks rarely contain as much of the essential TiO_2 as do the Apollo 11 rocks. In recognition of their high ilmenite content, the lunar rocks are sometimes referred to as ilmenite basalts or ilmenite gabbros.

OLIVINE

Olivine is the fourth most abundant lunar mineral occasionally constituting as much as 7% of the Apollo 11 rocks. It is found in the breccias, fines, and, most importantly, in the fine-grained basalts (Type A) which are, therefore, sometimes referred to as olivine basalts (Figs. 2-10 and 2-11). Olivine was not found in the coarse-grained (Type B) crystalline rocks. In the Apollo 12 samples, on the other hand, olivine was observed in almost all crystalline rocks where it sometimes reaches as much as 55% of the total, in sharp contrast to the approximately 7% maximum in the Apollo 11 rocks. Most of this discussion will be concerned with the better documented Apollo 11 occurrences.

Chemically, both terrestrial and lunar olivines are explained as a continuous solid solution of two end-members: (1) Mg_2SiO_4, forsterite (abbreviated "Fo"), and (2) Fe_2SiO_4, fayalite (abbreviated "Fa"). The pure end-members are rarely found in nature, and most olivines contain varying proportions of each end-member. The resulting generalized formula of olivine is $(Mg,Fe)_2 SiO_4$, which expresses the mutual substitution of "Fo" and "Fa". Lunar olivines generally contain between 60 – 75% of the forsterite molecule (Fo), but some analyses show additional variation of a few percent on either side of this range (Table 3-9).

There are at least three groups of investigators who quite surprisingly report the identification of essentially pure fayalite (Table 3-9, Anal. 4). This high-iron variety of olivine, which represents another lunar mineral, is rare and occurs only as small grains associated with cristobalite, K-rich areas and other minerals of the residuum (Fig. 3-13). Quantitatively, fayalite is very minor in comparison with the more important forsteritic (high Mg) olivines, and will not be discussed further.

In Table 3-9 (Anal. 1, 2 and 3) the analyses of the forsteritic olivines are presented. In general, these are very similar to terrestrial olivines from basalts except for (1) the chromium content which is higher by a factor of two in comparison with terrestrial olivine, and (2) the nickel content which is significantly lower than would be expected.

Table 3-9. Analysis of lunar olivines (in weight %).

	1	2	3	4
SiO_2	37.5	37.53	37.3	29.2
TiO_2	0.09	0.16	0.09	0.06
Al_2O_3	0.05	–	0.17	–
Cr_2O_3	0.21	0.27	< 0.02	0.03
FeO	25.5	25.46	29.2	68.5
MnO	0.30	0.67	0.41	1.01
MgO	36.5	36.08	31.9	–
CaO	0.33	0.32	0.12	0.40
NiO	< 0.01	0.03	–	–
Total	100.5	100.12	99.19	99.20
"Fo"	72	72	66	0

Notes:

1. Olivine from rock 10020 (Type A). Analysis by Haggerty (Geophysical Laboratory).
2. Olivine from rock 10085 (lunar soil). Analysis by Agrell (University of Cambridge, England).
3. Olivine from anorthositic basalt fragment in breccia. From rock 10059 (Type C). Analysis by Keil (University of New Mexico).
4. Olivine, variety fayalite, from late-stage mesostasis (residuum) phase in rock 10058 (Type B). Note high iron and absence of magnesium. Analysis by Brown (University of Durham, England).

Physically, lunar olivines appear completely fresh, exhibiting none of the alteration effects so common in terrestrial olivine. They are transparent and vary in color through various shades of yellow, green and orange, and crystals exhibit only slight zoning. Olivine crystals occur as a phenocryst constituent in the Type A (fine-grained) igneous rocks where they will, on occasion, attain dimensions of up to about 2 mm., although 0.5 mm. is more typical. In the same rock, however, they may be as small as 0.02 – 0.04 mm. Texturally, olivine crystals are frequently enclosed in augite. On the other hand, olivine may contain inclusions of devitrified glass and early forming minerals, such as ilmenite or plagioclase. Most olivine (except the rare faya-lite) began to crystallize at an early stage, but crystallization also ceased at a comparably early stage, certainly before the bulk of the augite crystallized.

Fig. 3-13. Photomicrograph of olivine, variety fayalite (Fe_2SiO_4) in residuum (mesostasis) of rock 10058 (Type B). There are 3 fayalite crystals; two are above, and one is below the horizontal feldspar lath. Magnification about 60X. After Brown (University of Durham, England).

CHROMITE-ULVÖSPINEL-SPINEL

One of the most important terrestrial mineral groups is the spinel group which contains at least twelve common, as well as rare, members. The group includes such well-known and abundant minerals as magnetite and chromite, but takes its name from spinel which was the first member of the group whose internal structure was determined in detail. Spinel structures are also known from synthetic laboratory materials, as well as from the slags from steel and metallurgical processes. All spinels have the same internal position for atoms (crystal structure) but exhibit a wide variation in color owing to the numerous possible substitutions of one element for another in the equivalent atomic positions. When the exact nature of the spinel-group mineral is not known, it is perfectly acceptable to refer to it by the general name "spinel," or "spinel-group mineral."

Chemically, the spinel group is described as a "double oxide" of the type AB_2O_4 in which the A is one or more divalent metals (such as Fe^{+2}, Mg, Zn or Mn) and the B is one or more trivalent metals (such as Al, Fe^{+3}, Cr or Ti^{+4}) Thus:

Spinel	A^{+2}	B^{+3}_2	O_4
1. spinel	Mg	Al_2	O_4
2. hercynite	Fe	Al_2	O_4
3. franklinite	Zn	Fe_2	O_4
4. chromite	Fe	Cr_2	O_4
5. ulvöspinel	Fe_2	Ti	O_4

Ideal end members such as are illustrated above are not commonly found because extensive solid solution (element substitution) is possible and likely in terrestrial spinels, as well as lunar spinels, as will be illustrated below.

Study of the lunar rocks has shown that several spinel-group minerals are present and, similar to their terrestrial equivalents, extensive solid solution is also found (frontispiece, Plate 8; Fig. 3-14). Not surprisingly, in view of the high Fe content and reducing environment of the lunar rocks, all have ferrous iron (Fe^{+2}). The three lunar spinel group end-members are:

chromite: $FeCr_2O_4$
ulvöspinel: Fe_2TiO_4
hercynite: $FeAl_2O_4$

The two most important end-members in the lunar spinels are chromite and ulvöspinel; no examples of minerals with the hercynite (aluminum) end-member predominant have been reported so far. The observed extensive solid solutions give rise to such variations as titanian chromite, aluminian chromite and chromian ulvöspinel. Examples of typical analyses are presented in Table 3-10. It is also evident from the selected analyses that small amounts of other elements (V, Mn, Mg and Ca) are also present in the lunar spinel structures. For all practical purposes, it may be said that spinel itself ($MgAl_2O_4$) is not represented in the lunar maria rocks, except as represented by the small Mg component in the chromite and ulvöspinel. One exception to this statement is the secondary spinel exsolution lamellae, associated with rutile, in ilmenite surrounding armalcolite (frontispiece, Plate 8). In addition, some true spinel has been reported in the anorthosite fragments (Table 3-10, Anal. 4) of primary origin, probably originating from the lunar highlands (but this is not of mare origin). The anorthosite fragments are discussed separately above.

From analyses 2a and 2b, Table 3-10, which represent the core and rim of a single zoned grain, it is apparent that great variability is possible in the chemistry of the lunar spinel group minerals. It may also be concluded that there is a progressive fractionation trend in the substitution of Cr and Al (in **core**)

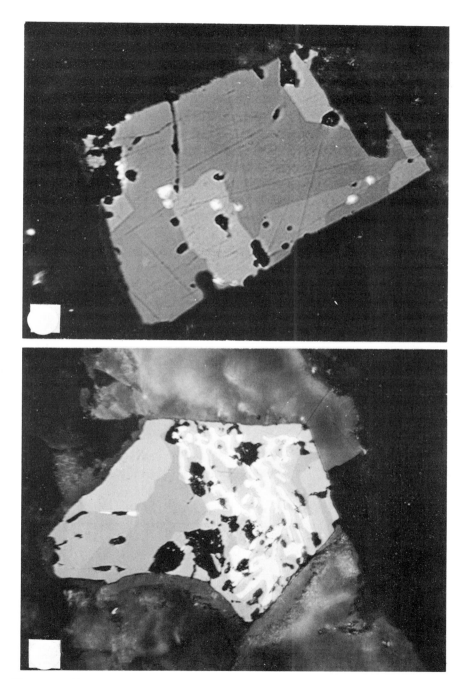

Fig. 3-14. Photomicrograph of ulvöspinel (dark gray) in complex intergrowth relations with ilmenite (lighter gray) and native iron (white). The three minerals (ulvöspinel, ilmenite and native iron) are found in both upper and lower photomicrographs; reflected light, magnification 700X. After Cameron (University of Wisconsin).

Table 3-10. Analysis of chromites, ulvöspinels and spinel from Apollo 11 rocks (in weight %).

	1	2a	2b	3	4
TiO$_2$	21.9	9.1	23.2	32.7	–
Al$_2$O$_3$	7.05	15.0	4.6	1.88	68.0
Cr$_2$O$_3$	22.1	32.1	16.3	3.5	2.16
V$_2$O$_3$	–	0.57	0.59	–	–
FeO	44.4	38.1	51.9	62.2	3.33
MnO	0.17	0.33	0.39	0.22	–
MgO	3.7	2.1	1.3	0.04	25.9
CaO	–	0.11	0.15	0.03	–
Total	99.32	97.41	98.43	100.57	99.39

Notes:

1. Titanian chromite. Rock 10020 (Type A). Analysis by Dence (Geological Survey of Canada).
2a. Aluminian chromite. Core of grain from rock 10084 (Type D). Analysis by Cameron (University of Wisconsin).
2b. Chromian ulvöspinel. Rim of same grain as 2a illustrating extreme chemical zonation. Analysis by Cameron.
3. Ulvöspinel; close to theoretical Fe$_2$TiO$_4$; from loose fines (Type D). Analysis by Keil (University of New Mexico).
4. Spinel; close to theoretical MgAl$_2$O$_4$. From anorthositic fragment in microbreccia rock 10019 (Type C). Analysis by Keil.

to Fe and Ti (in rim). Variations have been observed between different grains in the same rock, and certainly between grains from different rocks.

The various varieties of lunar chromite and ulvöspinel are found as opaque phases, generally tan in color when seen under high magnification oil immersion methods (see frontispiece, Plate 8), in all types of lunar rocks. The mineral grains are usually well-formed and range from 100 – 200 microns in their largest dimensions. They are often found within ilmenite grains; they are also found in association with olivine and pyroxene, but in these occurrences they are not mantled. The spinel group opaques constitute about 10% (by volume) of the Fe-Ti oxides within one sample (10020; Type A) and this may be considered representative of their maria abundance, at least for the present.

Chromite is a well-known mineral on Earth and, although occurrences of ulvöspinel are rare, they are being recognized more frequently generally as exsolution blebs in magnetite, and other ores. However, in these ulvöspinel occurrences some ferric (Fe^{+3}) iron is usually present. Further, chromite and other spinels will rarely have more than about 2% TiO$_2$, but as much as 12.8% TiO$_2$ has been reported in one unusual chromite from Bushveld, South Africa. Because the end-members — chromite, ulvöspinel and hercynite — have been previously reported on Earth, new names are not justified for the lunar phases. But because they do differ so markedly in comparison with their terrestrial equivalents (high Ti and Al; no ferric iron), the lunar examples are considered as new varieties of the long established minerals chromite and ulvöspinel. Further experimental work on these phases to establish the extent of the substitutions possible between chromite-ulvöspinel-hercynite, and the structural positions of the substituting elements will no doubt be made.

ARMALCOLITE

Armalcolite is the second new mineral to be identified in the lunar rocks (the first being pyroxferroite). It is likely that with time armalcolite will become the most famous, although not necessarily the most important, lunar mineral because it is named after the three astronauts who were instrumental in collecting the Apollo 11 lunar rocks and returning them to Earth: *Arm*strong, *Al*drin and *Col*lins. It has so far been found in the Type A crystalline rocks, in the breccias and in the soils; no occurrence has yet been reported in Type B rocks. Estimates of its abundance have not been made, but it is certainly uncommon, if not rare.

Armalcolite is an opaque mineral, is gray in reflected light and is always (except in one rare case) bordered or rimmed by ilmenite; this type of occurrence for ilmenite is minor, as is mentioned in the discussion of ilmenite. Armalcolite occupies extremely small, generally rectangular areas (longest dimension is 100 – 300 microns) within the ilmenite grains and because of this intimate association and small size, armalcolite is seen only under high power magnification in polished thin sections, where it is always observed to be homogenous (frontispiece, Plate 8; Fig. 3-15). All chemical analyses have been accomplished by the electron probe.

Chemically armalcolite is defined as $(Mg_{0.5}Fe_{0.5})$ Ti_2O_5; however, the name is not intended for this composition only. Rather the name armalcolite is used for a range of compositions approximating the above formula. From a compositional point of view, armalcolite can be considered as intermediate, both chemically and structurally, between two end-members, $FeTi_2O_5$ and $MgTi_2O_5$ (Fig. 3-16). Neither end-member is known to occur naturally, but both have been synthesized; it is important to remember that the Fe is ferrous iron (Fe^{+2}). Variations in the abundance of all elements in the lunar armalcolite have been observed, such as TiO_2 ranging from 70.9 – 75.6% (Table 3-11). The Fe/Mg ratio of the lunar mineral varies from 1.83 to 0.57, or roughly 65% of the $FeTi_2O_5$ component, to 64% of the $MgTi_2O_5$ component. This corresponds closely with the middle third of the series $MgTi_2O_5$ – $FeTi_2O_5$ as illustrated in Fig. 3-16; if at a later date either of these end-members are found on the Earth, moon, or in meteorites, names will be assigned

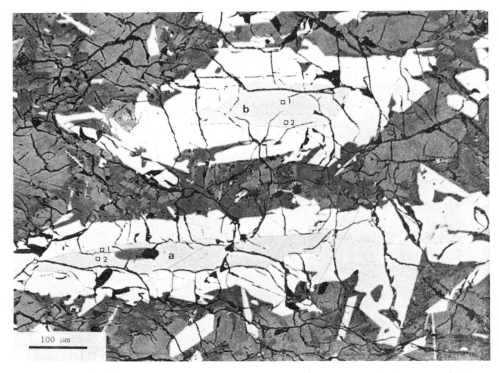

Fig. 3-15. Photomicrograph of armalcolite (medium gray; labelled a and b) grains in characteristic occurrence rimmed by ilmenite (light gray). Points 1 and 2 are where chemical analyses by means of the electron probe have been carried out. Dark gray colored minerals are chiefly pyroxene and feldspar. Oil immersion, reflected light. Rock 10022 (Type A). After Anderson (University of Chicago).

but until that time formulas must be used when referring to them. In addition to the major constituents in armalcolite, minor amounts of Al, Cr and Mn have been detected, along with traces of Ca, V, Co, Ni, Cu and Zn (not reported in Table 3-11).

All studies have shown armalcolite to be homogeneous and free of exsolution or alteration minerals, even though the bordering ilmenite may have several exsolution minerals included (frontispiece, Plate 8). Variations in the composition of individual armalcolites from different rocks have been observed, but any one armalcolite crystal is generally uniform in composition and unzoned.

The end-members $FeTi_2O_5$ and $MgTi_2O_5$, as well as armalcolite compositions, have been synthesized by heating the chemically pure components in sealed silica tubes for 2 hours, at 1300°C. and then quenching. The $FeTi_2O_5$ end-member breaks down to $FeTiO_3$ (ilmenite) + TiO_2 (rutile) when cooled below 1140°C. From several synthetic experiments involving armalcolite and

Table 3-11. Analysis of armalcolite from Tranquillity Base illustrating range of compositions observed (in weight %).

	1	2	3	4	5	6
TiO_2	70.9	73.4	71.63	75.6	72.0	71.9
Al_2O_3	1.8	1.62	2.18	1.87	1.48	0.97
Cr_2O_3	1.3	2.15	1.38	1.81	1.92	1.26
FeO	16.9	15.3	18.01	11.9	14.7	11.32
MnO	0.02	0.08	0.05	–	0.07	0.01
MgO	8.6	7.70	5.52	8.12	8.7	11.06
Total	99.52	100.25	98.77	99.30	99.28	96.52

Notes:

1. Sample 10022 (Type A). Analysis by Smith (University of Chicago).
2. Sample 10071 (Type AB). Small amounts of Ca, V, Co, Ni, Cu and Zn also detected. Analysis by Haggerty (Geophysical Laboratory).
3. Sample in soil fragment (Type D). Analysis by Cameron (University of Wisconsin).
4. Sample 10059 (Type C). Analysis by Ramdohr and El Goresy (University of Heidelberg, Germany).
5. Sample 10068 (Type C). Small amounts of Ca and V also detected. Analysis by Keil (University of New Mexico).
6. Sample 10084 (Type D). Analysis by James (U.S. Geological Survey).

ilmenite, it has been found that armalcolite forms above 1130°C. whereas ilmenite forms at 1100°C. In other words, armalcolite crystallized as a primary, early-forming mineral before ilmenite, when the lunar rocks were cooling. This confirms the petrographic evidence which shows armalcolite forms cores of well-developed crystals which are mantled by ilmenite. Several textural studies of the lunar minerals have shown the crystallization sequence to be armalcolite-pyroxene-ilmenite.

The implication of all these textural and synthetic studies may be summarized by saying that (a) armalcolite was one of the early minerals to form on cooling of the molten lunar melts (lavas); (b) when the temperature of the lava fell to approximately 1130°C., armalcolite tended to disappear by reaction with the remaining melt and to form ilmenite (armalcolite + melt → ilmenite); (c) the small amount of armalcolite observed today represents material which did not have time to completely react with melt to form ilmenite before the lava completely solidified.

TROILITE

The only sulfide mineral positively identified in the lunar rocks is troilite, FeS. It is the second most abundant opaque (after ilmenite) in the lunar rocks ranging from 0.3 – 1.3% on a volume basis according to Cameron

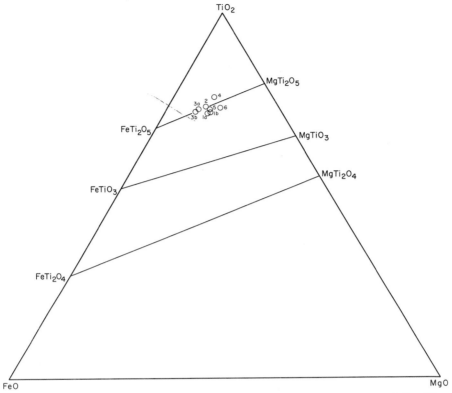

Fig. 3-16. Armalcolite analyses plotted on the join $FeTi_2O_5$ and $MgTi_2O_5$. The points 1–6 represent plotted armalcolite analyses. Note restricted range of composition for armalcolite in the system TiO_2-MgO-FeO. After Anderson (University of Chicago).

(University of Wisconsin), but Simpson and Bowie (Institute of Geological Sciences, London) found considerably less (0.03 – 0.2%). Chemically it is pure Fe and S with only very minor amounts of other elements such as Cr, Ti, Co and Ni. Selected analyses are listed in Table 3-12.

Troilite in the lunar samples is found in several types of occurrences such as in thin stringers or ovoid droplets in ilmenite, or as interstitial blebs up to 0.3 mm. in size which are usually finely polycrystalline and always in association with native iron (Figs. 3-14 and 3-17 to 3-19). On rare occasions troilite has been observed on the walls of cavities or vugs, where it forms bright yellow areas; possibly this occurrence is the result of vapor phase movement into the vesicle, and is clearly late in the crystallization sequence. From this last occurrence Evans (U.S. Geological Survey) isolated two excellent crystals (Fig. 3-20) for single crystal X-ray diffraction and crystallographic studies. He found the troilite to have a hexagonal habit consistent with the high-temperature NiAs-type structure, and with the unit cell measurements (a = 5.962 ± 0.002 Å. and c = 11.750 ± 0.003 Å.) in close agreement for previously determined stoichiometric FeS. This is the only detailed crystallographic analysis so far completed for any lunar mineral.

Troilite has not been observed in the Apollo 11 lunar rocks without included iron (except as the rare euhedral crystals lining vugs); however, preliminary studies show this relationship may not be as constant in the Apollo 12 rocks. Quantitative measurements of selected intergrowths of troilite and iron by Skinner (Yale University) show that iron averaged 8.5% by volume (range 3.3 − 14.6%) and, in agreement, other studies show the troilite to iron ratio is generally about 10:1 although one study shows a 35:1 ratio. The troilite and iron intergrowths crystallized late, after ilmenite and pyroxene, as evidenced by textural relations (Fig. 3-21). The constant association of troilite and iron in a reasonably consistent ratio suggests they were derived from an initially homogeneous sulfide liquid that separated immiscibly from the silicate magma and, as indicated above, the textural evidence shows this to have occurred after the start of crystallization of ilmenite and pyroxene. From knowledge of the phase relations in the system Fe-S, Skinner has been able to show that separation of the immiscible sulfide liquid had to take place at 1140° C., or above. Thus Skinner concluded that most crystallization of the Apollo 11 igneous rocks must have taken place above 1140°C., as the troilite-iron was among the last minerals to crystallize.

Table 3-12. Lunar troilite and native iron analysis (in weight %).

	1	2	3	4	5
Fe	65.3	61.50	62.9	63.53	99.1
S	34.1	37.72	35.2	36.47	–
Ni	–	–	–	–	0.13
Ti	0.1	–	–	–	–
Cu	–	0.31	–	–	–
Co	–	–	–	–	0.17
Cr	0.1	–	0.03	–	–
Mn	–	–	0.43	–	–
P	–	–	–	–	–
Total	99.6	99.53	98.56	100.0	99.40

Notes:

1. Troilite. Rock 10020 (Type A). Analysis by Dence (Geological Survey of Canada). Authors note slight excess of Fe over stoichiometric proportions may be due to inclusion of native iron.
2. Troilite. Rock 10045 (Type AB). Analysis by Simpson and Bowie (Institute of Geological Sciences, England).
3. Troilite. Rock 10067 (Type C); average of 10 grains. Analysis by Keil (University of New Mexico).
4. Troilite, FeS, theoretical.
5. Native iron. Average of 25 grains from breccias (Type C). Analysis by Keil (University of New Mexico).

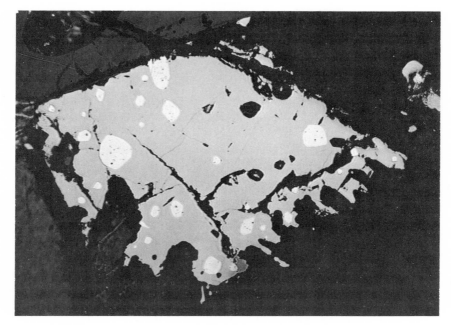

Fig. 3-17. Photomicrograph of troilite (gray) containing crystals of native iron (white). Note distinct crystal outline of some iron crystals. Rock 10058 (Type B). Reflected light. Magnification 330X. After Cameron (University of Wisconsin).

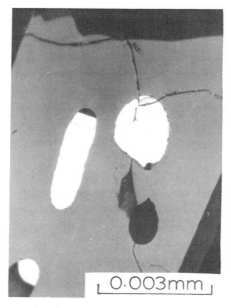

Fig. 3-18. Photomicrograph of native iron (white) and troilite (light gray) droplets in ilmenite (dark gray); silicates (black). Rock 10072 (Type A). Reflected light. After Simpson and Bowie (Institute of Geological Sciences, London).

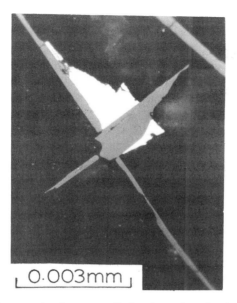

Fig. 3-19. Photomicrograph of two small droplets of native iron (white) in troilite (light gray) associated with slender blades of ilmenite (dark gray) in silicates (black). Reflected light. Rock 10072 (Type A). After Simpson and Bowie (Institute of Geological Sciences, London).

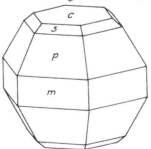

Fig. 3-20. Troilite crystal habit. Forms (indexed on high-temperature unit cell) are: $c\{0001\}$; $m\{10\bar{1}0\}$; $p\{10\bar{1}1\}$; $s\{10\bar{1}2\}$. From rock 10050 (Type AB). After Evans (U.S. Geological Survey).

Troilite of meteoritic origin would be expected in the lunar soils and breccias inasmuch as troilite is a common phase in iron meteorites. Mason (Smithsonian Institution) has described such an occurrence, in the form of a conclusive description of iron (taenite)-troilite spheroids. These do not appear to be abundant in the soils and without the association of high-Ni taenite or other diagnostic features would not be distinguished from the lunar igneous troilite.

On Earth, troilite is a very rare mineral and, as in the lunar rocks, strong reducing conditions are necessary. However, troilite is common as an accessory in most classes of meteorites.

IRON

Native iron (with low Ni) is found in the opaque phase of all igneous rocks and can be considered a common, but not necessarily abundant, lunar mineral. In this type of occurrence, it is *always* associated with troilite, FeS, in Apollo 11 rocks (but native iron is commonly *not* associated with troilite in the Apollo 12 rocks). The troilite to iron ratio is variable, but usually about 10:1. On a volume basis, one study showed native iron constitutes less than 0.03% of the rocks. In the coarse rocks (Type B), the troilite and iron form aggregates up to 300 microns but in the finer grained rocks the aggregates become so small as to be unresolvable (less than 1 micron). The aggregates appear late in the crystallization sequence, occupying space remaining after the crystallization of the more abundant silicates and oxides (Fig. 3-21); they may represent droplets of immiscible sulfide-rich liquids which separated from the parent magma, but several other explanations are possible.

The native iron in the lunar igneous rocks is usually in the range of 1-30 microns in diameter. It has various shapes ranging from nearly spherical, to areas with distinct crystal outlines, to elongate vein-fillings within other opaque phases (Figs. 3-14; 3-17 to 3-19; 3-21).

Many chemical analyses have been made for Ni, Co and other minor elements, all of which are present only in minor amounts (Table 3-12, Anal. 5):

$$Ni = 0 - 0.9\% \qquad\qquad Ti = 0 - 0.3\% \qquad\qquad Mn = 0 - 0.2\%$$
$$Co = 0 - 1.2\% \qquad\qquad Cr = 0 - 0.2\%$$

Structurally, the iron from the igneous rocks is kamacite (low Ni) with the α-structure.

Terrestrial occurrences of native iron (kamacite; low nickel) are known from several localities, the most striking being the iron-bearing basalts of Disko Island, Greenland. There are several similarities between the lunar iron and the iron in the Disko Island basalts: iron in both cases (1) is kamacite, (2) is associated with sulfides, and (3) is in interstitial positions. The similarity is explainable on the basis of the reducing environment (low oxygen fugacities) of both the lunar and Disko Island basalts; both have high FeO contents. Other terrestrial occurrences of native iron usually are in volcanic rocks that cut coal seams or other reducing (e.g., carbonaceous) rocks.

There is one exception to the above statements that only low-nickel kamacite is indigenous to lunar rocks, and the high-nickel iron (taenite; γ-Fe) is of meteoritic origin. In the (non-meteoritic) anorthosites from the Apollo 11 and 12 soils, some taenite (28.6% Ni) associated with kamacite (6.2% Ni) and troilite (0.1% Ni) has been found by Wood (Smithsonian Astrophy-

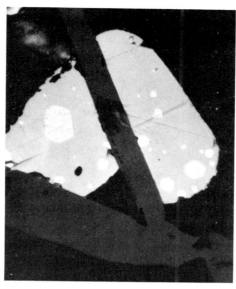

Fig. 3-21. Photomicrograph of intergrowth of troilite (light gray) and iron (white) crystals between branching arms of a skeletal ilmenite crystal (dark gray). This relationship shows that the troilite-iron crystallized after ilmenite. Rock 10072 (Type A). Width of field 0.01 mm. After Skinner (Yale University).

sical Observatory). He notes the consistent presence of nickel-bearing minerals associated with terrestrial anorthosites. Further discussion on this point should await return of samples from the lunar highlands on some future Apollo flight.

RUTILE

Rutile, TiO_2, is a rare constituent in the Tranquillity Base rocks, whereas on Earth it is a common accessory (but not necessarily abundant) in many igneous and metamorphic rocks; it would not necessarily be expected in basaltic rocks. For all practical purposes, most of the rutile so far observed is as exsolution lamellae within the uncommon variety of ilmenite which rims or surrounds armalcolite in the Type A rocks (frontispiece, Plate 8; Fig. 3-22). It has been stressed above that most ilmenite is homogeneous; therefore the exsolution rutile (usually associated with a spinel-group mineral of similar exsolution origin) in this uncommon type of ilmenite is expected to be rare. The rutile lamellae are extremely fine, usually less than 10 microns in thickness, and visible only in reflected light under high magnification. Rutile, associated spinel-group mineral, and native iron exhibit several textural and intergrowth relationships within this host ilmenite. From a study of these relationships, there can be no doubt but that the exact nature of the

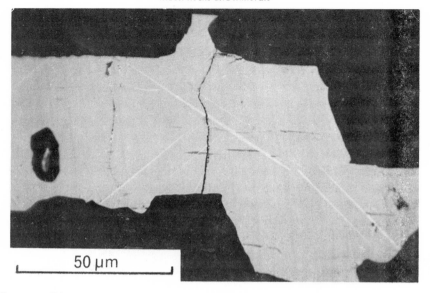

Fig. 3-22. Photomicrograph of rutile (diagonal white thin lamellae), and chromium-rich spinel mineral (short, dark, horizontal lamellae in center), which may be chromite, in host ilmenite. Both rutile and spinel-mineral are of exsolution origin. Rock 10017 (Type A). Reflected light. After Dence (Geological Survey of Canada).

exsolution and the sequence of crystallization are complex. No such identical textures are found in terrestrial rocks, but similar ones have been observed in selected meteorites.

The origin of the rutile lamellae is difficult to explain, but it is worthwhile recalling that experimental studies have shown that $FeTi_2O_5$, one of the end-members of the armalcolite (see above), breaks down to $FeTiO_3$ (ilmenite)+TiO_2(rutile) when cooled below 1140°C. However, it has also been suggested that the rutile may be formed by the reduction of ilmenite, possibly by:

$$2FeTiO_3 \rightarrow 2TiO_2 + 2Fe + O_2$$
$$\text{(ilmenite) (rutile) (iron)}$$

In some rocks native iron is associated with the exsolution rutile, complying with this reaction, but in other rocks native iron is absent. Therefore, it is possible that several mechanisms can account for exsolution rutile lamellae.

Another type of occurrence for rutile has also been reported, which indicates a primary origin, as opposed to secondary exsolution origin. Primary rutile inclusions, characterized by complex twinning and roughly hexagonal form, occur randomly oriented in some ilmenite from Type B rocks. The relative abundances of the primary and secondary occurrences is not known at present.

A word of caution must be expressed here in that the identification of the white lamellae in ilmenite as rutile is based on chemical and optical properties. Because of their extremely small size, the needles have not been isolated for confirmatory identification by such methods as X-ray diffraction. The composition (TiO_2) has been unquestionably verified by several scientists by the electron probe method. One analysis suggests that small amounts of Al, Cr, Fe, Mn, Mg and Ca may be in the rutile structure — a situation not uncommon in terrestrial rutiles.

CRISTOBALITE, TRIDYMITE AND QUARTZ

Three polymorphs of SiO_2 have been found in the lunar rocks and fines in small amounts. On occasion they occur together in pairs, for example tridymite-cristobalite and quartz-cristobalite. In some cases the pairs are associated in fine-grained intergrowths, but coarse intergrowths of euhedral cristobalite and tridymite have also been observed. Cristobalite is the most abundant and important of the three polymorphs sometimes reaching 6% of selected rocks (generally Type B; Fig. 2-7). Quartz is rare.

The silica minerals occur primarily in interstitial aggregates and have crystallized late (Figs. 3-8 and 3-9). Cristobalite will also be commonly found as euhedral or subhedral crystals often projecting into the cavities of rocks. The cristobalite will range from as small as 10 microns to coarse mosaic patches. The coarse-grained cristobalite of Type B rocks is characterized by curved fractures and complex twinning which is optical evidence that it has inverted from its high temperature polymorph to its low temperature polymorph, which is also metastable (Fig. 3-23). The low temperature form of tridymite has been reported as needle-like grains, often in association with late stage apatite, potassium feldspars, incompletely defined rare-earth and zirconium mineral phases, and other silica minerals, but it also occurs in coarser patches in vugs (Fig. 3-24). Low-tridymite has been found in the soils as anhedral grains and crystal fragments.

Several studies have stressed that the silica minerals crystallized with the fine-grained residual phases. The silica minerals, therefore, are primary igneous phases which have crystallized from a saturated residual liquid differentiated from the initial ultrabasic melt. The important point to be kept in mind is that these silica rich areas are of limited extent and are late differentiates of the basalts, and *not* indicators of large areas of granitic (acidic) rocks on the moon. Further study of the lunar highlands is needed to confirm this feeling, which is currently prevalent among most lunar geologists, that granitic rocks are not abundant.

Fig. 3-23. Photomicrograph of cristobalite showing mosaic (tile) structure resulting from inversion from high to lower temperature form. Rock 10058 (Type B).
Magnification about 200X. After Brown (University of Durham, Englai d).

Fig. 3-24. Photomicrograph of large crystal of SiO_2 (probably tridymite), below
center, enclosed in mosaic of cristobalite. Rock 10058 (Type B). Magnification
about 100X. After Brown (University of Durham, England).

Analyses of cristobalite and tridymite are presented in Table 3-13. Noteworthy is the small amount (2 – 3%) of Si^{+4} replaced by Al^{+3} and other
elements (e.g., Ti, Fe). These elements are also characteristic of terrestrial
cristobalite and tridymite. The introduction of alkali (Na^+, K^+) or alkaline
earth (Ca^{+2}, Mg^{+2}) ions balances the charge deficiency.

The occurrence of more than one polymorph of SiO_2 in terrestrial lavas is rather common, as rapid cooling delays, or alkalis prevent, the inversion to the more stable quartz polymorph. Tridymite or cristobalite are rarely found in igneous rocks of deep-seated origin. The presence of tridymite in particular permits the placing of upper limits of pressures the rocks have been subjected to, and this is not more than 3 kilobars. Cristobalite and tridymite are characteristically found in crevices and cavities in terrestrial volcanic rocks similar to their occurrence in lunar rocks.

Table 3-13. Chemical composition of silica minerals (in weight %).

	1	2	3	4
SiO_2	97.6	98.0	96.2	98.0
TiO_2	0.2	0.27	0.37	0.22
Al_2O_3	1.1	0.92	1.72	0.63
FeO	0.3	0.05	0.11	0.55
MgO	0.0	–	< 0.02	–
CaO	0.3	0.16	0.50	0.33
K_2O	0.0	–	0.03	0.17
Na_2O	0.0	0.15	0.09	–
Total	99.5	99.55	99.02	99.90

Notes:

1. Cristobalite from rock 10020 (Type A). Analysis by Dence (Geological Survey of Canada).
2. Cristobalite from late-stage mesostasis phase. Rock 10058 (Type B). Analysis by Brown (University of Durham, England).
3. Tridymite from rock 10045 (Type AB). Analysis by Keil (University of New Mexico).
4. Tridymite (?) from late-stage mesostasis. Rock 10058 (Type B). Analysis by Brown (University of Durham, England).

APATITE

Two varieties of apatite have been identified in the Apollo 11 rocks: 1. fluorapatite $Ca_5F(PO_4)_3$ with up to 2.6% of rare earth (RE) oxides (plus 1.2% Y_2O_3), by Fuchs (Argonne National Laboratory, Illinois). 2. chlor-fluorapatite $Ca_5(Cl,F)(PO_4)_3$ from the soils by Albee and Chodos (California Institute of Technology) and from Type A rocks by Adler (NASA Goddard Space Flight Center, Maryland). This variety also contains some rare-earth elements, but less than the fluorapatite variety.

Although the apatite is found only in very small amounts (about 0.15%) as an accessory mineral in the lunar rocks, it is apparently widespread in certain associations such as within the interstitial high-K phase (glass and fine-grained crystalline material), and particularly as inclusions in pyroxferroite where it may occupy up to 5% of the pyroxferroite volume (Fig. 3-25). In all cases the crystals are exceedingly small (25 – 100 microns) which makes identification difficult. One noteworthy aspect of the apatites is their rare-earth content, which represents a concentration of over 100 times that found in the bulk lunar rocks. Also, the occurrence of the halogens (fluorine and chlorine) is further evidence for the presence of volatiles in lunar rocks (see discussion below of mica). Hydroxyl (OH) is apparently not present in these apatites.

Fig. 3-25. Photomicrograph of fluorapatite crystals (dark gray; in center) within pyroxferroite grain (medium gray). Light colored grain is ilmenite; mottled dark area (left) is mounting media. Rock 10044 (Type B). Reflected light. Scale bar is 25 microns. After Fuchs (Argonne National Laboratory, Illinois).

Chemical analyses of lunar apatites are shown in Table 3-14. In addition, the analyses of several terrestrial apatites are also included for comparison. The rare-earth elements substitute for Ca in the apatite structure, while SiO_4 groups substitute for PO_4 (Si^{+4} for P^{+5}) to compensate for the trivalent rare-earth elements substituting for calcium (RE^{+3} for Ca^{+2}).

It is interesting to note that fluorapatite has never been discovered in meteorites (only chlorapatite), but on Earth fluorapatite is a common mineral found in many geological associations. The lunar fluorapatites show strikingly different chemical characteristics and associations from their terrestrial counterparts. For example, the apatite in terrestrial basalts or mafic

Table 3-14. Chemical analysis of lunar apatites and terrestrial apatites (in weight %).

	1	2	3	4
P_2O_5	38.7	38.6	41.30	35.75
CaO	52.1	50.9	55.16	56.47
FeO	1.5	0.58	0.14	–
SiO_2	2.3	1.12	–	0.01
F	3.3	3.12	3.67	–
Cl	.03	1.10	0.09	–
CO_2	--	–	0.50	3.36
H_2O	–	–	0.01	4.44
Y_2O_3	1.2	0.07	–	–
RE_2O_3	2.54	< 1.0	--	–
Total	100.7	97.0	102.14	100.69

Notes:

1. Rock 10044 (Type B). Analysis by Fuchs (Argonne National Laboratory, Illinois).
2. Rock 10085 (Type D). Analysis by Albee and Chodos (California Institute of Technology). Total includes 0.21% Na_2O , 0.30% MgO , and 0.23% Al_2O_3.
3. Fluorapatite, Ontario. Total includes 0.12% MnO , 0.63% Fe_2O_3 , 0.24% Al_2O_3 and 0.28% insolubles.
4. Carbonate-apatite. St. Paul's Rocks, Atlantic Ocean. Total includes 0.30% MgO and 0.36% SO_3.

RE_2O_3 = sum of oxides Ce, La, Pr, Nd, Sm and Gd.

igneous rocks would likely be fluorapatite but would not have high rare-earth contents as do the lunar examples; high contents of RE elements are primarily restricted to apatites of alkaline igneous rocks or pegmatites, based on present knowledge. The Si and Fe contents of the lunar fluorapatites are somewhat higher than terrestrial apatites.

The lunar phosphate minerals (apatite and whitlockite) are also associated with high concentrations of K, Ba, U and Th, as well as with pyroxferroite and the K-rich interstitial phase. But a still unanswered question is whether or not all (or at least a large part) of the rare-earth elements in the lunar rocks are found in the apatite and related whitlockite. The preliminary calculations of both the Illinois and California scientists clearly suggest that a significant amount of the RE elements are present in other minerals, some of which could well be opaque.

WHITLOCKITE

A mineral tentatively called whitlockite, $Ca_3(PO_4)_2$, by Albee and Chodos (California Institute of Technology) has been found in one "exotic" fragment from the lunar soils and also in one Type A rock (10064). It has been named solely on the basis of its chemistry; neither X-ray data nor optical properties have been reported.

The lunar soil whitlockite is characterized by a high rare-earth content (nearly 10% rare earth oxides), and a chemical composition corresponding to $Ca_3(PO_4)_2$ with some Na^{+1} and rare earths (RE^{+3}) substituting for Ca^{+2}; Si^{+4} substitutes for P^{+5}. Whitlockite in the Type A rock, on the other hand, contains little or no rare-earth elements. This latter variety is chemically more in accord with terrestrial and meteoritic whitlockites which have very low rare-earth element contents.

Whitlockite is somewhat more abundant than chlor-fluorapatite in the same "exotic" soil sample. Physically it is similar to apatite, as it is found as minute elongate grains ranging fom 5 – 20 microns. Whitlockite co-exists with apatite in the "exotic" soil sample and in this association at least, the rare-earth elements are highly concentrated in the whitlockite (about 10% as RE_2O_3) in comparison with the apatite ($<1\%RE_2O_3$).

COPPER (INCLUDING BRASS)

Native copper (Cu) has been observed in small amounts in the lunar rocks by Simpson and Bowie (Institute of Geological Sciences, England) in association with troilite. An alloy of copper and zinc was detected by Gay (University of Cambridge, England) from several golden-colored metallic fragments which they extracted from both soils and Type A rock, and they refer to this material as brass. X-ray diffraction confirmed the structure, and chemical analysis showed Cu (variable 55 – 70%) and zinc (variable in the range 30 – 45%) with minor amounts of tin (0.3 – 0.5%). Contamination appears to have been ruled out. Small amounts of native copper have also been tentatively identified in Apollo 12 samples.

Native copper on Earth is well-known from several important localities (such as in the basalts of northern Michigan) and in many cases it is commonly associated with basic extrusive rocks, not dissimilar to the Tranquillity Base basaltic rocks. Normally, native copper will have small amounts of silver, arsenic, iron, bismuth or antimony, but never significant amounts of zinc or tin, so in this respect the lunar Cu-Zn alloy has no terrestrial equivalent.

TIN

The rare occurrence of tin has been reported only by Gay (University of Cambridge, England) in the Tranquillity Base soils. It is embedded in native iron containing about 1% nickel, hence the iron is of lunar origin (meteorite iron contains significantly more Ni). Structurally the tin is the β-Sn variety. Native tin is known on Earth as a mineral, but it is extremely rare. Owing to its occurrence in placers, for example in Ceylon, its original source is unknown, but native tin appears to be associated in some localities with volcanic rocks, as is the lunar tin.

ZIRCON

Zircon, $ZrSiO_4$, has been mentioned as occurring in lunar rocks by several scientists. Weill (University of Oregon) suggests its occurrence in the residual phases of crystallization of the lunar igneous rocks but the mineral has not been definitely identified owing to its very small size. Fleischer (General Electric Co., Schenectady) suggests that zircon may be the source of uranium in the sample they studied by the fission track method but again the identification is not confirmed. At this time, the presence of zircon in the lunar rocks must be considered tentative.

BADDELEYITE

Baddeleyite, monoclinic ZrO_2, has been observed as a late crystallizing mineral in the groundmass of a Type B rock by Agrell (University of Cambridge, England). It is associated with ilmenite either in composite grains, or small adjacent tabular crystals. The possibility of micron-sized grains of baddeleyite (a reddish phase) as the source of high (40 ppm.) uranium concentrations in some specimens is suggested by Lovering and Kleeman (Australian National University). Dence (Geological Survey of Canada) also mentions baddeleyite as one of three late stage minerals associated with two other incompletely described zirconium minerals. X-ray diffraction or other diagnostic studies have not been completed on any of the above phases, and the identification must be regarded as tentative. Baddeleyite is a rare mineral in terrestrial rocks, occurrences being reported in gravels or placers (Ceylon), as an accessory in basic igneous rocks and associated contact zones (Brazil), and in vugs of the volcanics of Mt. Somma, Italy.

MICA

Micas are members of the phyllosilicate ("layered silicate") family, and contain water in the form of hydroxyl groups (OH). Identification of minerals in this family has been reported independently by Gay (University of Cambridge, England) in the soils by X-ray diffraction and chemical methods, and by Drever (Scripps Institution of Oceanography, California) in the soils and a Type A rock by electron microscopy and diffraction. In both instances, the authors state their identifications are provisional owing to the small amount of material, and the possibility of contamination from many sources (such as airborne dust). From electron diffraction studies, Drever sees evidence for both dioctahedral mica (muscovite is an example), and trioctahedral mica (such as biotite). From a chemical analysis, Gay interprets the micaceous component in the lunar soil as biotite.

Although the amount of micaceous minerals is admittedly minute, the significance is great, should its presence be confirmed. The reason for this is that there is very little, if any, unequivocal evidence for water-containing minerals on the moon — the lunar rocks have been referred to as "dry." Presence of water (or other volatiles), even in very small amounts (micas have about 4% water in their structure), can be of great significance in any lunar origin theory. The fact that small amounts of apatite (containing F and Cl), hornblende (hydroxyl-containing) and aragonite*(carbonate-containing) have been reported by various scientists in the Apollo 11 samples supports the belief that some volatiles are (or have been) present on the moon; and the moon's interior may contain more of these elements than previously believed. Adding some strength to this belief is the observation that gas eruptions at the crater Alphonsus have been reported by a Russian scientist (Kozyrev) in a paper written in 1962.

AMPHIBOLE

A rare occurrence of an amphibole mineral has been reported by Gay (University of Cambridge, England) from a vug in rock 10058 (Type B). Single-crystal X-ray diffraction studies show that the dark green mineral is a clinoamphibole but chemical analyses show it to be unusual in comparison with terrestrial amphiboles owing to its very low alumina content (0.75%) and high sodium content (Na_2O = 8.69%). Technically, an amphibole with these chemical characteristics would be classed as a magnesio-arfvedsonite-richterite. Of more importance than the name, however, is the fact that this mineral contains fluorine and hydroxyl, whose significance has been discussed above in conjunction with mica. Although Gay is the only one to definitely identify an amphibole, Frondel (Harvard University) mentions the possibility of an amphibole in another rock.

ARAGONITE

A rare, and unexpected, occurrence of a small pink lath-like fragment of crystallites of aragonite (orthorhombic $CaCO_3$) has been reported by Gay (University of Cambridge, England) from rock 10058 (Type B). The

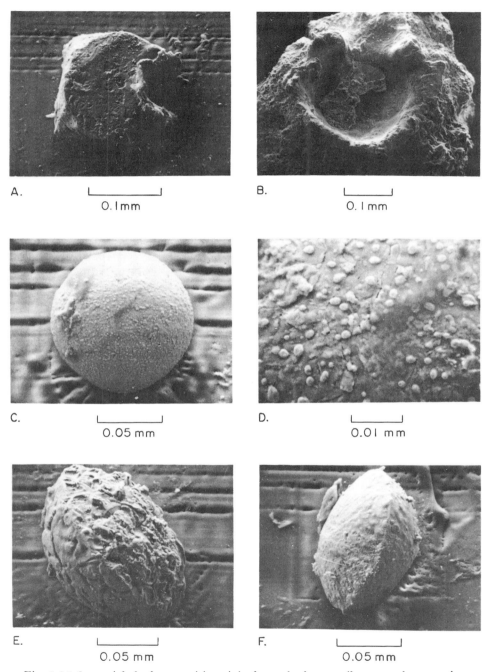

A. 0.1mm

B. 0.1mm

C. 0.05 mm

D. 0.01 mm

E. 0.05 mm

F. 0.05mm

Fig. 3-26. Iron-nickel of meteoritic origin from the lunar soils as seen by scanning electron microscope. (A) iron-nickel crystal with impact crater on right side. (B) irregular fragment of iron-nickel with two impact craters. (C) spherule of iron-nickel. (D) blebs on surface of sphere. (E) and (F) discoidal body of iron-nickel. After Frondel (Harvard University).

identification is still considered tentative but if confirmed is of importance because (1) it is the only occurrence of inorganically combined carbon, and (2) yields another, admittedly small, example of a volatile component (namely CO_2) in the lunar rocks. The possibility exists that the aragonite may well have been recovered from the lunar rock, but may actually have been formed elsewhere in the solar system, specifically in a carbonaceous chondrite type of meteorite. Such meteorites occasionally contain aragonite as well as other carbonates; and small amounts of carbonaceous chondrites and other types of meteorites have been added to the lunar surface over geologic time.

PENTLANDITE

Pentlandite, $(Fe,Ni)_9S_8$, has been tentatively suggested by Simpson and Bowie (Institute of Geological Sciences, London) as the name for an unidentified "flamelike exsolution" opaque mineral within troilite, and associated with native iron, in rock 10072 (Type A).

IRON-NICKEL

Iron of meteoritic origin, with from 3 – 30% Ni, has been recorded from the lunar soils, disseminated throughout the microbreccias, and in glass fragments by several investigators; at least two scientists recognized the two known varieties, kamacite (α-Fe) and taenite (γ-Fe). Frondel (Harvard University) has described several different morphologies, some of which are illustrated in Fig. 3-26. He reports that iron-nickel constitutes from 0.05 – 0.1% of the fines less than 1 mm. in diameter. Agrell (University of Cambridge, England) described a fragment about 2.5 mm. in diameter which was composed of kamacite crystals, the largest of which was about 0.5 mm. across. The kamacite contains 92.5% Fe, 6.5% Ni, and 0.5% Co and is typical of meteorite material, including the development of the characteristic Neumann lines. Mason (Smithsonian Institution) illustrated a dendritic intergrowth of taenite and kamacite (Fig. 3-27). Several groups have noted that the Ni content of the iron-nickel ranges from 3 – 14%, with 6 – 7% as the most common range, in good agreement with other studies. Iron-nickel of meteoritic origin in the lunar soils is normally easily distinguishable from iron originating in the lunar igneous rocks on the basis of Ni content (<1.0% Ni for lunar igneous). On the other hand, Wood (Smithsonian Astrophysical Observatory) reports both kamacite and taenite from the lunar anorthosite (highland material) both of which have high Ni contents but these are of relatively limited abundance in the Apollo 11 and 12 rocks.

Iron-nickel (24 – 77% Ni) has been found on Earth only very rarely such as in some placer deposits in a number of localities. At localities in Oregon, the mineral occurs in large masses (some exceeding 100 lb.), and the Ni content reaches 67% (in this case the mineral name is awaruite). Terrestrial iron-nickel with high Ni has been regarded as a magmatic segregation from peridotites, as in Oregon, but it has also been found veining

Fig. 3-27. Photomicrograph of polished section of iron-nickel pellet of meteoritic origin, showing dendritic pattern of taenite (white) and troilite (gray). Length of section is 2.5 mm. After Mason (Smithsonian Institution).

serpentinized rocks; the former association is a high temperature origin, whereas the latter is low temperature. The important point, however, is that both environments must be reducing, even if only on a local scale. For a further discussion of the low-nickel iron of the lunar igneous rocks, see Iron above.

COHENITE

Cohenite, $(Fe,Ni)_3C$, has been reported by Frondel (Harvard University) intimately associated with schreibersite in a metallic iron-nickel fragment in the fines. It is rare in the lunar fine material, and is believed to come from an iron meteorite as this mineral has been reported in several types of meteorites (octahedrites and enstatite chondrites). Cohenite has also been found on Earth in some terrestrial irons (e.g., Greenland) but is extremely rare.

SCHREIBERSITE

Schreibersite, $(Fe,Ni,Co)_3P$, is another mineral similar to cohenite in that it is commonly found in iron meteorites. Frondel (Harvard University) has identified schreibersite intergrown with cohenite in one lunar sample. This mineral does not occur naturally on Earth.

UNIDENTIFIED MINERALS

There is no question but that future studies will report additional minerals in lunar samples, in all probability even in the intensively studied Apollo 11 rocks on which most of this discussion has been based. There is already a strong indication that additional mineral phases have been recognized, but that identification has not been successful. For example, one scientist (Frondel, Harvard University) mentions "hairlike inclusions of a greenish birefringent mineral with inclined extinction, possibly an amphibole," and also "a yellow-brown birefringent mineral, with a peculiar grid-like structure . . . which contains Fe and probably Cl." Another (Cameron, University of Wisconsin) gives preliminary description of an unnamed, probably new, yttrium-zirconium-iron-titanium-calcium-silicate from two rocks, and notes it is similar to a mineral reported by some investigators in Germany from another specimen. Canadians report an unnamed Fe, Ti, Y, Zr silicate. Several other examples of incompletely described minerals could be cited but in view of the preliminary nature of the data, no useful purpose would be served.

4.

CHEMISTRY OF SAMPLES
BROUGHT BY APOLLO 11 AND 12

INTRODUCTION

The chemical composition of the lunar rocks is unique and is one of the most interesting features to emerge from the study of the rocks brought back by the Apollo 11 and 12 missions. Some previous information was available from the Surveyor soft landing missions and the Russian Luna-10 orbiter. This latter mission, in April 1966, carried a γ-ray spectrometer which indicated that the concentration of the natural γ-ray emitters K, U and Th, did not exceed those in terrestrial basalts. (The upper limits were about 1% K, 1 ppm. U and 3 ppm. Th). Despite some uncertainty, the uplands appeared to be deficient in these elements relative to the maria. These data seemed to cast doubt on the then popular beliefs that substantial amounts of granitic rocks occurred either in the maria or in the uplands, or that material of tektite composition was widespread.

Three Surveyor spacecraft, V, VI and VII, soft landed and carried out chemical analyses of the surface at two maria and one upland site using the α-scattering equipment developed by Turkevich at the University of Chicago. Surveyor V landed in Mare Tranquillitatis 25 km. northwest from the historic site of Tranquillity Base, two years prior to the manned landing. Surveyor VI landed in Sinus Medii, nearly in the center of the visible face of the moon. Data from both Surveyor V and VI indicated a basaltic-like composition, and a high titanium content at the Surveyor V site. (Apollo 12 landed 600 feet from the earlier Surveyor III which did not carry chemical analysis equipment). Surveyor VII landed on the out thrown apron of debris from Tycho. The analysis of soil and a rock indicated a lower iron and higher calcium content (Table 4-1).

The first analysis carried out by the Preliminary Examination Team on July 28, 1969 revealed that the Tranquillity Base material was basaltic, high in titanium, with low concentrations of nickel and other siderophile elements, with low concentration of alkalies, lead and other volatile elements.

Table 4-1. Chemical analysis of soil and rock at Surveyor Landing Sites carried out by unmanned Surveyor Spacecraft prior to Apollo landings (in weight %).

	1	2	3
SiO_2	46.4	49.1	46.1
TiO_2	7.6	3.5	–
Al_2O_3	14.4	14.7	22.3
FeO	12.1	12.4	5.5
MgO	4.4	6.6	7.0
CaO	14.5	12.9	18.3
Na_2O	0.6	0.8	0.7
Total	100.0	100.0	99.9

Notes:

1. Turkevich, A. L., Franzgrote, E. J. and Patterson, J. H. (1969) Chemical composition of the lunar surface in Mare Tranquillitatis, *Science* 165, 277–279.
2. Franzgrote, E. J., Patterson, J. H., Turkevich, A. L., Economou, T. E. and Sowinski, K. P. (1970) Chemical composition of the lunar surface in Sinus Medii, *Science* 167, 376–379.
3. Patterson, J. H., Turkevich, A. L., Franzgrote, E. J., Economou, T. E. and Sowinski, K. P. (1970) Chemical composition of the lunar surface in a terra region near the crater Tycho, *Science* 168, 825–828.

CHEMICAL ABUNDANCE DATA

The chemical composition of the rocks (Type A = high K and Type B = low K), breccias (Type C), and fine material or soil (Type D) are given in Tables 4-3 — 4-10. The sources for each value quoted are listed in the tables. Many data are available. Considering the number of analysts, and methods used, the variation is smaller than would have been predicted on the basis of experience with the analysis of terrestrial international rock standards. An attempt has been made in the tables to provide the best numbers for the various elements. Occasionally, where the spread is small, averages of all data have been used. For many of the trace elements, data of superior quality obtained by experienced analysts using highly precise or accurate methods (e.g., isotope dilution) have been used although the other values may not be very different. This procedure has occasionally led to rather arbitrary use of data of good quality from one laboratory rather than equivalent data from another, or to averaging both or several sets. The choice has usually depended on the number of rocks analyzed, the number of elements reported and is not meant to indicate that the chosen data are the only "true" values, or to imply that the data not used are necessarily inferior. The procedure adopted enables each value in the tables to be identified, checked back against the source and compared with other data if necessary.

PRIMITIVE, PRIMORDIAL

OR

COSMIC ABUNDANCES

In much of the discussion which follows, and in the sections on the origin of the moon, many comparisons are made with "cosmic" element abundances. In current usage, the term "cosmic" refers to the chemical composition of the original disk-shaped cloud of dust and gas (the solar system nebula) from which the solar system condensed about 4.5 billion years ago. The element concentrations in the nebula are the result of a combination of "initial" element abundances (mainly hydrogen and some helium) from a period before 10 billion years ago, and heavier elements formed subsequently by element synthesis processes in stars and supernovae. The heavy elements, derived from a variety of nucleosynthetic processes, are mixed back into the interstellar medium, as stars give off mass, or explode in supernovae events. The net result is a steady increase of the heavy element content of the interstellar dust, with perhaps local enrichment from supernovae explosions, of those elements produced in an intense neutron flux (rapid or r-process); these include gold, uranium and thorium. The sun contains about 2% of elements heavier than helium. Younger stars (Population I) contain up to 5%, and older stars (Population II in the galaxy) may have less than 0.3% of elements heavier than He.

The solar system nebula is considered to have been well mixed both with respect to isotopic and elemental abundances. Its composition, for the nongaseous elements, is usually assumed to be close to that of the Type I carbonaceous chondrite meteorites. The rationale for this is the similarity between the relative abundances in this class of meteorites and the sun as revealed by spectroscopic examination of the photosphere and corona. Recent work has revealed that an outstanding anomaly in this interpretation (the apparent high iron abundance in meteorites relative to the sun) is an analytical artefact of the solar spectral interpretation.

Hence the abundances in the Type I carbonaceous chondrite class of meteorites are now used as a first approximation to the composition of the original solar nebula.

The great interest in the chemistry of the moon arises partly from the extensive differences in concentration (by factors of $50 - 100$) between the element abundances in the lunar rocks and the assumed primitive values. This includes both enrichments of involatile elements (RE, Y, Th, U, Ba, Zr, Hf) and depletion of volatile elements (Pb, Tl, Bi, Ag, Zn, Hg) and siderophile elements (Ni, Au, Ir, Pt, Pd).

MAJOR AND MINOR ELEMENTS

These are usually defined by geochemists as those elements present as principal constituents of the main rock-forming minerals. Their abundance usually exceeds 1% by weight. In the Apollo 11 and 12 rocks, seven elements, O, Si, Al, Fe, Mg, Ca and Ti, are major constituents. K, Na, Mn and Cr are minor constituents within the concentration range of $0.1 - 1.0\%$. Other constituents at levels between $100 - 1000$ ppm. $(0.01 - 0.1\%)$ include Zr, Ba, Sr, Y and total rare-earths, (and Ni in the fines). The other elements are generally present at levels below 100 ppm. (0.01%) and do not contribute significantly to the total.

Although all data are given here as weight percent, parts per million $(10^{-4}$ weight %) or parts per billion $(10^{-7}$ weight %), it should be recalled that alternative representations in terms of atomic percent or volume percent often give a different sequence. In terms of volume, the large cation, potassium, is much more important than its weight percentage would indicate. On this basis, all the cations are reduced to occupying interstices among a packing of oxygen anions, comprising over 90% of the volume.

The four distinct sample types (A, B, C, D) recognized by LSPET (1969) also show distinct compositional differences.

CHEMICAL CLASSIFICATION OF ROCKS

The Apollo 11 rocks were divided by LSPET into two types, A and B, on the basis of texture. Further divisions were Type C (breccias) and Type D (fine material). Type A were fine-grained vuggy rocks of "volcanic" appearance whereas Type B were coarser-grained and had a more plutonic aspect. The major element composition of both types was similar for many of the major constituents. Thus there are only slight differences in the amounts of Si, Fe, Mg, Ca, Na and Ti.

However, it was noted by many investigators that the rocks fell into two chemical groups, which approximated to the textural classification. These groups were distinguished by the abundances of K, Rb, Cs, Ba, Pb, Y, RE, Th, U, Zr, Hf and Li.

Since there is a general overlap with the initial textural classification, the terminology of Type A and Type B rocks has been retained by most authors. Type A are higher in K and the elements noted above (see Table 4-3) as well as higher Cr, Ni, Co and Ti.

Type B has higher Al, Cu and Mn. A number of investigators (Compston, Australian National University; Tera, California Institute of Technology; Gast and Hubbard, Columbia University) suggest that they represent two separate flows, and workers dealing with age dating have had to take this fact into account. These chemical distinctions are a good example of the usefulness of trace elements (potassium may be so regarded in the lunar rocks) to distinguish rocks of rather similar major element chemistry. Most of the Apollo 12 rocks, in contrast, show a continuum in composition, without the clear distinctions in element abundance shown by the Apollo 11 samples. They show a much wider variation in the abundances of elements such as Ni and Cr and this may indicate some near surface fractionation. It is possible that the Apollo 12 rocks come from several related flows rather than from one unit. (See page 127.)

Table 4-2. Chemical composition of lunar basalt, compared with achondritic meteorites and deep sea basalts (in weight %). After Mason and Melson (Smithsonian Institution).

	1	2	3	4
SiO_2	39.79	48.16	48.47	49.21
TiO_2	11.44	0.32	0.37	1.39
Al_2O_3	10.84	15.57	9.46	15.81
FeO	19.35	15.69	17.16	8.18
MgO	7.65	8.41	12.00	8.53
CaO	10.08	11.08	8.08	11.14
Na_2O	0.54	0.45	0.46	2.71
K_2O	0.32	0.09	0.05	.26

Notes:

1. Lunar basalt 10057.
2. Moore County eucrite.
3. Kapoeta howardite.
4. Average composition of deep sea basalts.

The general chemical correlation of high potassium content (and other elements typical of residual phases in lunar rocks) with the finer-grained, more quickly chilled rocks may be of genetic significance, in that elements not already incorporated may be trapped in the residual *mesostasis* by rapid chilling. In the more coarsely crystalline rocks, some of this material escapes into other parts of the cooling unit. It is possible that an acid residuum, similar to the rock 12013, might form in this manner. A subdivision of the rocks into Type A or Type B, based on the chemical classification as far as possible, is given in Table 2-1.

As will be discussed later, the experimental data indicate that material of the composition of the Type A and B rocks cannot be representative of the overall element abundances in the moon since it will invert to more dense mineral phases, forming the rock type eclogite at depth. There is no evidence for more dense phases at depth within the moon.

Table 4-3. Major and minor element content of Apollo 11 rocks expressed as weight %. Oxides (above) and elements (below). Type A rocks (A); Type B rocks (B); Type C breccias (C); Type D fines (D).

	A	ref.	B	ref.	C	ref.	D	ref.
				Oxides				
SiO_2	40.5	h, i	40.5	h, i	41.7	h, i	41.9	h, i
TiO_2	11.8	h, i	10.5	h, i	8.5	h, i	7.5	h, i
Al_2O_3	8.7	h, i	10.4	h, i	12.7	h, i	13.8	h, i
FeO	19.0	h, i	18.5	h, i	15.9	h, i	15.6	h, i
MgO	7.6	h, i	7.0	h, i	7.8	h, i	8.0	h, i
CaO	10.2	j	11.6	j	11.6	j	11.9	h
Na_2O	.50	h	.41	h	.49	h	.44	h
K_2O	.29	j	.096	j	.18	j	.13	j
MnO	.25	ave.	.28	ave.	.25	ave.	.21	ave.
Cr_2O_3	.37	ave.	.25	ave.	.31	ave.	.29	ave.
ZrO_2	.075	h	.049	h	.055	h	.054	h
NiO	–		–		.025	l	.029	b
Total	99.3		99.6		99.5		99.8	
				Elements				
Si	18.9		18.9		19.5		19.6	
Ti	7.1		6.3		5.1		4.5	
Al	4.6		5.5		6.7		7.3	
Fe	14.8		14.4		12.4		12.1	
Mg	4.6		4.2		4.7		4.8	
Ca	7.3		8.3		8.3		8.5	
Na	.37		.31		.36		.33	
K	.24		.08		.15		.11	
Mn	.19		.22		.17		.16	
Cr	.25		.17		.21		.20	
Zr	.056		.036		.041		.040	
Ni	–		–		.020		.023	
O	38.5	r	39.4	r	41.1	r	40.8	

BRECCIAS (TYPE C)

The Apollo 11 sample return was notable for the large number of rocks composed of fragments produced by shock lithification of the fine material during meteorite impact. In contrast, the Apollo 12 material, collected from a thinner regolith, had few breccias. The postulated mode of origin implies that the breccias will be the result of the smaller cratering events, confined mostly within the regolith. Thus the breccias should closely resemble the local fine material, and this is found to be the situation. Only minor differences in composition exist between the soils and the breccias. Once again the principal differences for the rocks are the lower Ti and Fe contents. As is the case for the soils, the interesting differences from the rocks occur in the trace element abundances.

FINE MATERIAL (SOIL) (TYPE D)

For the major elements, the soil composition generally resembles that of the rocks, so there is *prima facie* evidence for a strong local component in the regolith. This is consistent with models of development of the regolith derived from geological studies. The degree of local cratering indicates that the bedrock should dominate, although material from more distant sources also contributes. The observed distribution of rays from craters such as Tycho indicates this. A ray from Tycho, 1500 km. distant passes near to Tranquillity Base. Thus the soil may be predicted to contain components from many parts of the moon. As noted above, the composition indicates that about 90% is derived locally. There is also a local component in the Apollo 12 fines. Among the major constituents, the most striking differences are the lower Ti and Fe contents and the higher Al contents, reflecting some dilution of the local component. Various authors have carried out calculations. Compston (Australian National University) suggests that 7% anorthosite plus the removal of 5% ilmenite (possibly by sorting during the "gardening" process) produces the composition of the average soil. The complexity of the contributions to the soil are illustrated by the Apollo 12 regolith. District stratification was observed and the "light gray" fine material was widespread as a thin veneer at the site. This material may possibly be a ray from Copernicus. It has a composition much richer in potassium and associated elements than the local rocks, and is more closely related to the breccia No. 12013.

Sources of data for chemical abundances listed in Tables 4-3 − 4-10.

(a) Taylor (Australian National University).
(b) Wanke (1970) average fine material (Max Planck Institute, Mainz).
(c) Ganapathy (University of Chicago).
(d) Reed and Jovanovic (Argonne National Laboratory).
(e) Wasson and Baedecker (University of California, Los Angeles).
(f) Haskin (University of Wisconsin).
(g) Lovering and Butterfield (Australian National University).
(h) Wakita, Schmitt and Rey (1970) Averages (Oregon State University).
(i) Compston Averages (Australian National University).
(j) Tera (California Institute of Technology).
(k) Kohman (Carnegie-Mellon University).
(l) Annell and Helz (U.S. Geological Survey).
(m) Tatsumoto (U.S. Geological Survey).
(n) Gast (Columbia University).
(o) Turekian and Kharkar (Yale University).
(p) Morrison (Cornell University).
(q) Moore (Arizona State University).
(r) Ehmann and Morgan (University of Kentucky).
ave = average

COMPARISON
OF
MAJOR ELEMENT ABUNDANCES
WITH TERRESTRIAL ROCKS AND METEORITES

The Apollo 11 and 12 rocks are completely distinct in composition from typical upper crustal rocks on Earth, such as granodiorites and granites. Other materials which are dissimilar include sedimentary rocks, ultrabasic rocks, iron and chondritic meteorites and tektites.

The closest resemblances in element abundances are to the terrestrial basalts and to a rare type of stony meteorite, the basaltic achondrites (eucrites and howardites). Mason and Melson (Smithsonian Institution) among many other workers have made comparisons of the lunar abundance data with terrestrial basalts and achondrites. Interest attaches to these comparisons for several reasons. It has long been suggested that some classes of meteorites were derived from the moon. The Apollo 11 data effectively ruled out the chondrites since the element abundances are widely different. However the basaltic achondrites, although too low in Ti (and differing in some trace elements), show some remarkable similarities in chemistry. One of the Apollo 12 rocks (12038) is particularly close in composition (Fig. 4-16) although Ti is still too high in the Apollo 12 rocks.

In general, the high Ti content of both Apollo 11 and 12 rocks serves to distinguish them from most other terrestrial and meteoritic specimens so far examined. Mason and Melson find that, after subtracting the composition of the mineral ilmenite, the remaining abundances are quite close to the basaltic achondrites.

Among the terrestrial basalts, the low potassium "oceanic tholeiites," which appear to form most of the oceanic crust, are the most primitive lava being extruded from the Earth's interior, and immediately invite comparison with the lunar basaltic rocks. Although there are some similarities, the sodium content of the terrestrial basalts is much higher, and the iron and titanium contents much lower than the lunar lavas. Table 4-2 from Mason and Melson illustrates these comparisons. (See page 130 for detailed comparisons of Apollo 12 rocks.)

The significance of these differences, when taken in conjunction with the more informative trace element data and the experimental work, indicates that both appear to be products of local partial melting deep in the interior. The chemical differences of the resulting lavas indicate that the parent material is different, so that the lunar interior does not have the same composition as the Earth's mantle.

TRACE ELEMENT ABUNDANCES

Data for a total of 57 trace and minor elements and 8 major elements are given in Tables 4-3 – 4-10. These comprise most of the cations which can be determined at the levels encountered, by the present analytical techniques, and include concentration ranges down to the parts per billion levels. Data in the tables are given in weight percent for the major elements and in parts per million (ppm.) and parts per billion (ppb.) for the minor and trace elements. The purpose of using the three different units (although all are simply related) is to provide numbers which are convenient to use (e.g., it is much easier to use and compare a number such as 8.5 ppm. than 0.00085%). The relations of weight %, ppm. and ppb. are as follows:

$$
\begin{aligned}
\text{One million ppm.} &= 100\% \\
100{,}000 \text{ ppm.} &= 10\% \\
10{,}000 \text{ ppm.} &= 1\% \\
1{,}000 \text{ ppm.} &= 0.1\% \\
100 \text{ ppm.} &= 0.01\% \\
10 \text{ ppm.} &= 0.001\% \\
1 \text{ part per million (ppm.)} &= 0.0001\% \ (= 10^{-4}\%) \\
1{,}000 \text{ ppb.} &= 1 \text{ ppm.} \\
100 \text{ ppb.} &= 0.1 \text{ ppm.} \\
10 \text{ ppb.} &= 0.01 \text{ ppm.} \\
1 \text{ part per billion (ppb.)} &= 0.001 \text{ ppm.} \ (= 10^{-7}\%)
\end{aligned}
$$

GEOCHEMICAL CLASSIFICATION OF THE ELEMENTS

The terms *siderophile, chalcophile* and *lithophile* elements are used in many places in the text. They were introduced by the geochemist Goldschmidt to describe the distribution of elements among *metallic, sulfide* and *silicate* phases and much of the classification stems from the observed distribution of elements among metallic, troilite (FeS) and silicate phases in meteorites. The behavior of an element is dependent on local conditions of temperature, pressure, oxidizing or reducing conditions and so on, but the classification remains a useful first approximation to indicate the geochemical behavior of the elements. The term *volatile elements* is used by many authors to indicate those elements volatile at temperatures below 1500°C. *Involatile* or *refractory* elements are those with oxides having boiling points above about 2500°C.

ARRANGEMENT OF DATA

Abundance data are available for most of the chemical elements in the lunar samples. The selection of the individual element data is discussed on page 98. In this section, the trace elements are divided into several groupings in which the elements exhibit similar geochemical behavior. This classification is based on the geochemical distribution of elements in minerals, where the size of the cations is a critical factor in determining element behavior. Thus the normal periodic classification of the elements, while remaining the ultimate base, needs some modification to allow for such effects due to the strict geometric requirements for entry into crystal lattices. The abundance of the major elements, Si, Al, Fe, Mg, Ca, Ti (and Na and K), control the type of mineral lattices which form and which the trace elements can enter or not on the basis of similarity in ionic size, valency, bond type (ionic-covalent-metallic) and, for the transition elements, crystal field effects.

The groupings used are as follows:

1. The large cations (Ionic radii > 1.2Å.).
      monovalent K, Rb, Cs, Tl; divalent Ba, Sr, Eu, Pb.
2. The rare-earths La-Lu (trivalent). Ionic radii $0.85 - 1.14$Å.
3. The large highly charged cations
      Th^{+4}, U^{+4}, Zr^{+4}, Hf^{+4}, W^{+6}, Nb^{+5}.
4. The ferromagnesian elements, which occupy sixfold coordination sites:
      monovalent Li,
      divalent Ni, Co, Cu, Mn (Fe),
      trivalent Cr, V, Sc,
      quadrivalent Ti.
5. The small cations Si, Be, B, P.
6. The chalcophile elements, entering sulfide phases.
7. The Pt group elements (mainly siderophile)
      Pt, Pd, Ru, Re, Os, Au.
8. The anions, O, S, F, Cl, Br, I.

The advantages of this classification are:

a. elements whose geochemical behavior is similar are brought together;

b. tables are arranged in order of decreasing ionic size and this order is preserved within each table except for the ferromagnesian elements where a tabulation based on crystal field site preference energy is used;

c. the large number of elements is broken up into tables of convenient size.

THE LARGE CATIONS (SEE TABLE 4-4.)

These comprise the elements which mainly accompany potassium. In contrast to most terrestrial surface rocks, potassium is so low in the lunar rocks
as to constitute a minor or trace element, and resembles the concentration
levels in low-K oceanic tholeiites or in chondritic meteorites. In the lunar
rocks, potassium and the other large cations are principally contained in the
interstitial material or *mesostasis*, and enter the lattice sites in the main rock-
forming minerals only to a minor degree. Although the total potassium content in the low-K rocks is about 0.08% and about 0.24% in the high-K rocks,
up to 9% K has been found in some of the residual material, (see section on
mineralogy, page 60, for discussion on occurrence of potassium feldspar).
Rb, Cs, Ba (and Li) and possibly other elements (e.g., RE, Th, U, Hf etc.),
as discussed later, are concentrated in the interstitial material.

Some of the potassium will enter plagioclase feldspar. Wasserburg (California Institute of Technology) and Wanless (Geological Survey of Canada)
report levels of about 0.25% potassium in the rocks, which are probably
upper limits. On crystal chemical grounds, it is unreasonable to suppose that
the olivines, ilmenites, or pyroxenes contain appreciable amounts of potassium
and related elements. Rubidium and cesium are systematically depleted relative to potassium when compared to the chondritic abundances. Since Cs and
Rb will preferentially enter a liquid phase during partial melting, this implies
that the source region was even more depleted with respect to these volatile
elements than the lavas. Type A-high K rocks show lower K/Rb ratios than
the Type B-low K rocks. The increased amount of Rb and many other

Table 4-4. Abundances of large cations in Apollo 11 samples. Type A rocks (A);
Type B rocks (B); Type C breccias (C); Type D fines (D).

		A	ref.	B	ref.	C	ref.	D	ref.
Cs+	ppm.	.16	j	.03	j	.13	j	.12	j
Rb+	ppm.	5.6	j	.9	j	3.7	j	2.7	;
Tl+	ppb.	.6	c	.6	c	2.8	c	2.2	c
Ba+2	ppm.	280	j	100	j	200	j	180	b
K+	ppm.	2400	j	800	j	1500	j	1100	j
Pb+2	ppm.	1.7	m	.4	m	1.7	m	1.4	m
Sr+2	ppm.	155	j	170	j	160	j	160	j
Ca+2	%	7.3	j	8.3	j	8.3	j	8.5	h
Na+	%	.34	j	.31	j	.34	j	.33	j
K/Rb		430		890		405		410	
Ba/Rb		50		111		54		67	
Rb/Cs		35		30		28		23	
Ba/Sr		1.8		.59		1.25		1.1	
Rb/Sr		.036		.005		.023		.017	

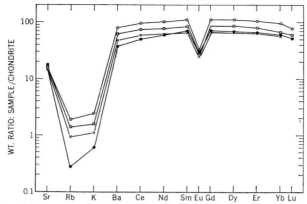

Fig. 4-1. Chondrite normalized Sr, Rb, K, Ba, and rare earth concentrations in crystalline rocks, breccia and soil. After Philpotts and Schnetzler (NASA Goddard Space Flight Center).

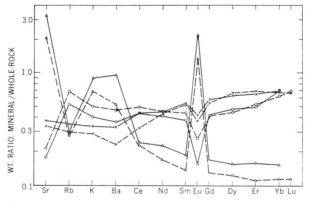

Fig. 4-2. Sr, Rb, K, Ba and rare earth concentrations in plagioclase (Δ), py-roxenes (x), and opaques (o) relative to whole rocks. After Philpotts and Schnetzler (NASA Goddard Space Flight Center).

elements in Type A may indicate derivation from a different source from the Type B rocks. The strontium isotopic data provide some evidence for this with differing initial ratios for the two rock types, according to Wasserburg.

The abundance of barium calls for special comment. It is relatively much more abundant compared to potassium than in the Earth. The cosmic or primitive abundance is about 4 ppm. and at least 50% of all the barium in the Earth is concentrated in the continental crust, which comprises 0.4% of the mass of the Earth. The abundance levels of 200 – 300 ppm. barium in the lunar rocks imply similar concentration in the outer regions of the moon. Thus much of the Ba has been selectively melted and concentrated upwards. The high Ba abundance is thus contributory evidence for partial melting processes in the interior as the source of the Apollo 11 lavas, rather than an origin by impact melting of surface rocks. The fact that the alkalies (e.g., rubidium) do not show comparable surface enrichment indicates that the moon must be depleted in alkalies relative to Ba. Cs and Rb should be concentrated upwards to at least the same degree as barium.

Strontium is also strongly enriched by about 15 times over the chondritic abundances (Fig. 4-1). This element is mainly contained in the plagioclase feldspars where it readily substitutes for calcium (Fig. 4-2). Divalent europium is similar in ionic radius to strontium and, like it, is concentrated in plagioclase feldspar. Strontium is less strongly enriched in the lavas than barium. This is consistent with its geochemical behavior, since it enters calcium sites rather readily. Hence it will occur in the main mineral phases in the interior of the moon and will be less readily partitioned into the liquid phase than barium, which will accompany potassium, probably mainly in interstitial phases.

Sodium may be conveniently considered here. It is rather uniform in the Apollo 11 rocks in contrast to the behavior of the heavier alkalies, K, Rb and Cs. This is a consequence of its entry into plagioclase, which the larger alkalies enter only with difficulty. It is depleted relative to terrestrial basalts by a factor of about five. As Wasserburg (California Institute of Technology) points out, the Na/Ca ratio is constant. Sodium will be partitioned into the liquid phase during partial melting, so that the source rocks will be depleted even more in sodium. This evidence is consistent with loss of volatile elements generally. Suggestions of loss of volatile elements at the surface to account for the alkali loss during lava flow have not received much support. The surface will rapidly freeze over due to very effective radiation cooling (see Chapter 8, page 196, section on viscosity). The strontium isotopic evidence indicates that the depletion of rubidium relative to strontium did not occur at the time of the melting of the lavas (3.7 billion years) but much earlier at about 4.6 billion years. The consensus is that the depletion in the volatile elements occurred early in the history of the moon, most likely during accretion, or before.

THE RARE EARTHS (RE) (SEE TABLE 4-5.)

The rare-earth elements have been extensively studied by geochemists in recent years. The interest arises from the fact that they form a closely related series of 14 elements (and yttrium). They are usually trivalent (except for europium which may be divalent, and cerium, which may be quadrivalent under oxidizing conditions in geological environments). The significant geochemical difference is a regular decrease in ionic radii from La^{+3} (1.14 Å.) to Lu^{+3} (0.85 Å.). The only common cations close in size are Ca^{+2} (1.02 Å.) and Na^+ (0.97 Å.). Substitution of the trivalent rare-

Table 4-5. Abundances of rare earths in Apollo 11 samples. Type A rocks (A); Type B rocks (B); Type C breccias (C); Type D fines (D).

		A	ref.	B	ref.	C	ref.	D	ref.
La	ppm.	27	f, n	11.4	f, n	21	f, n	16.6	f, n
Ce	ppm.	76	f, n	36	f, n	57	f, n	47	f, n
Pr	ppm.	13	h	7	h	–	–	7	h
Nd	ppm.	63	f, n	33	f, n	40	f, n	39	f, n
Sm	ppm.	21	f, n	12	f, n	14	f, n	13	f, n
Eu	ppm.	2.2	f, n	1.9	f, n	1.9	f, n	1.7	f, n
Gd	ppm.	27	f, n	17	f, n	20	f, n	15	f, n
Tb	ppm.	4.6	f, n	2.5	f, n	3.6	f, n	3.1	f, n
Dy	ppm.	32	f, n	20	f, n	24	f, n	20	f, n
Ho	ppm.	6.8	f, n	3.3	f, n	4.7	f, n	4.5	f, n
Er	ppm.	19	f, n	12	f, n	14	f, n	12	f, n
Tm	ppm.	3.0	h	–	–	2.0	h	1.8	h
Yb	ppm.	19	f, n	15	f, n	12	f, n	12	f, n
Lu	ppm.	2.6	f, n	1.5	f, n	1.9	f, n	1.6	f, n
RE (total)	ppm.	316		173		216		194	
Y	ppm.	184	h	104	h	91	h	96	h
RE+Y	ppm.	500		277		307		290	
La/Yb		1.4		.76		1.75		1.38	

earth elements (hereafter abbreviated to RE) for monovalent sodium does not occur but they substitute for Ca^{+2} in a variety of minerals. However, valency difficulties ensure that they concentrate in residual phases and a substantial portion occurs in the interstitial material in the lunar rocks. The individual rare-earths are difficult to separate, but due to the radius difference rather smooth changes in the relative abundance patterns occur. Two regular patterns have been observed. These are in chondritic meteorites and in sedimentary rocks. The first is interpreted as equivalent to the primitive solar nebula abundances, and the second as equivalent to the upper crustal rare-earth abundances, for all sediments give similar patterns.

The terrestrial crustal pattern is enriched in the large rare-earths (La-Sm) relative to the chondrites, and this is the typical pattern observed during fractional crystallization. A convenient way to depict the abundance patterns is to divide the abundances element by element, by the chondritic abundances. Enrichment, depletion or inflections of the abundance patterns are clearly shown by such a procedure. The data so treated are shown in Figs. 4-1, 4-2, 4-3, and 4-4. Ba is often included in the plots since it is often determined by the same investigators.

The first feature is that the rare-earth patterns are more or less parallel to the chondritic abundance patterns although they are enriched by factors of about 40 for the low K-Type B rocks and by about 100 for the high K-Type A rocks. The large RE (La-Sm) do not show relative enrichment, but instead show slight depletion, a pattern reminiscent of the low-K oceanic

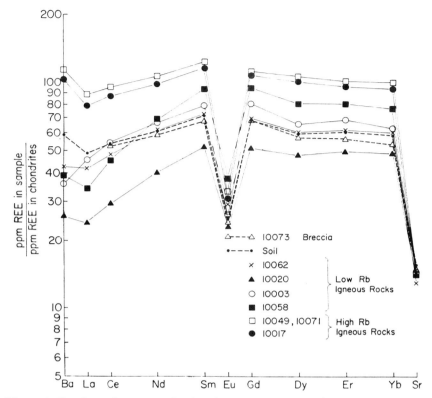

Fig. 4-3. Ba, Sr and rare earth abundances, ratioed to chondritic values. After
Gast and Hubbard (Columbia University).

basalts. The lack of enrichment of the large RE relative to the smaller is
consistent with limited or no fractional crystallization during cooling of the
melt. A significant fraction of the rare-earths is concentrated in the interstitial material. Some of the accessory minerals, such as apatite, contain substantial amounts.

The strong enrichment of the rare-earths relative to the chondritic abundances parallels that of the large cations, especially Ba, and Th, U, Zr and Hf.

EUROPIUM DEPLETION

One major distinction, apart from the relative enrichment, is observed
between the lunar and chondritic RE patterns. The Apollo 11 rocks are
depleted in europium. (Figs. 4-1 – 4-4). Eu is an element half way through
the rare-earth series which may occur in the divalent as well as in the normal
stable trivalent state for the rare-earths. Divalent europium is observed in
terrestrial rocks. Eu^{+2} (radius = 1.25 Å.) is about the same size as divalent

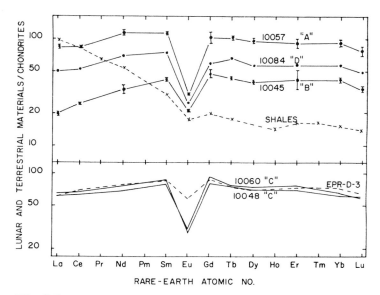

Fig. 4-4. The RE concentrations in lunar samples (solid lines), terrestrial shales (upper dashed line), and an andesite from the east Pacific rise are compared with those in a composite of nine chondritic meteorites. The RE concentrations in ppm. for the chondrites have been divided, element by element, into those for the other samples, and the resulting ratios have been plotted on a logarithmic scale against RE atomic number. After Haskin (University of Wisconsin).

strontium (Sr^{+2}, radius = 1.18 Å.) and exhibits a similar geochemical behavior, entering plagioclase and K feldspar in terrestrial rocks. This pair of elements provides an interesting example of the degree to which the chemistry of elements entering solid phases departs from that expected from their formal position in the periodic table. The strong Eu depletion is also observed in the Apollo 12 samples, including the fines, so that it is not an isolated phenomenon. Fig. 4-2 shows that Eu in the main lunar rock forming minerals is concentrated in the plagioclase feldspar, and depleted in pyroxenes and ilmenite. From these observations, many workers concluded that plagioclase separations had occurred, thus depleting the residual liquid in Eu. The total rock samples show Eu depletions by factors of 2 – 3 relative to neighboring RE (Sm-Gd). To account for this depletion by crystallization and removal of plagioclase, 60 – 90% of plagioclase removal is necessary. There is little evidence of this. Most of the chemical and mineralogical data are consistent with rapid chilling and crystallization, without wholesale separation of plagioclase. The experimental data are in conflict with the possibility both of fractional crystallization, or of melting a plagioclase-rich source.

Plagioclase does not begin to crystallize until about 30% of the liquid has crystallized. Prior removal of plagioclase means that it should be a phase occurring on the liquidus. Also, as the experimental petrologists point out, if the lava melted from material in which plagioclase remained as a residual phase, then it would also be expected to be a liquidus phase. Other elements might be expected to show depletions if extensive plagioclase separation had occurred. These include Sr and Ba. Eu^{+2} is possibly following the behavior of Sr^{+2} which is depleted relative to Ba by a factor of 3 in the lunar rocks relative to the chondritic abundances. This is a similar level to the Eu depletion. Thus both Sr and Eu may be retained selectively in the lunar interior. Alternative explanations are: (1) a previous fractionation concentrated Eu into the anorthosites, so that the highlands may be the reservoir for europium; (2) the whole moon may be depleted due to separation of Eu from the other rare earths in a high temperature reduction process. The europium problem is one of the more enigmatic problems of lunar geochemistry.

YTTRIUM

This element, (but not scandium which shows distinctly different geochemical behavior) is usually included along with the rare earth elements. It displays a similar enrichment with respect to chondritic abundances as do the RE.

THE LARGE HIGHLY CHARGED CATIONS (SEE TABLE 4-6.)

These elements (Th^{+4}, U^{+4}, Zr^{+4}, Hf^{+4}, Nb^{+5}, Ta^{+5}, Mo^{+6}, W^{+6}), because of a combination of medium to large size and high valency, do not commonly enter the lattice sites available in the common rock forming minerals.

Table 4-6. Abundances of large highly charged cations in Apollo 11 samples. Type A rocks (A); Type B rocks (B); Type C breccias (C); Type D fines (D).

		A	ref.	B	ref.	C	ref.	D	ref.
Th^{+4}	ppm.	3.4	m	1.0	m	2.6	m	2.1	m
U^{+4}	ppm.	.8	m	.25	m	.49	ave.	.54	m
Zr^{+4}	ppm.	560	h	360	h	410	h	400	a
Hf^{+4}	ppm.	19	h	11	h	11	h	10	b
Sn^{+4}	ppm.	.5	p	1	p	.3	p	.7	p
Nb^{+5}	ppm.	25	i	20	i	19	i	18	i
Ta^{+5}	ppm.	2	b	2	b	2	c	1.4	b
Mo^{+6}	ppm.	.1	o	.2	o	.2	o	.3	o
W^{+6}	ppm.	.4	b	.3	b	–	–	.25	b
Ti^{+4}	%	7.1	h, i	6.3	h, i	5.1	h, i	4.5	h, i
Th/U		4.3		4.0		5.3		3.9	
Zr/Hf		29		33		37		40	
Nb/Ta		12.5		10		9.5		12.8	

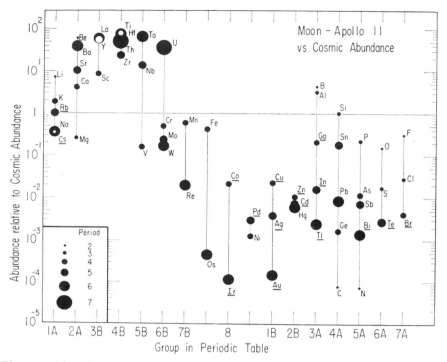

Fig. 4-5. Abundances in Apollo 11 rocks normalized to chondritic abundances.
After Ganapathy (University of Chicago).

The larger quadrivalent ions, which accompany Ti^{+4} to a limited extent in sixfold coordination in ilmenite, prefer a larger lattice site, and concentrate in the interstitial material, possibly in accessory minerals such as apatite and zircon.

As a class, these elements are abundant in the Apollo 11 rocks, being concentrated by factors of 50 – 100 over their abundances in chondritic meteorites. This enrichment is rather uniform, and occurs for many other "refractory" elements (Ba, Y, RE) which do not readily enter sixfold coordination sites in pyroxenes or olivine. These elements, dispersed in accessory minerals and in interstitial material along grain boundaries, are readily concentrated by processes of partial melting. They are strongly concentrated in the crust of the Earth and a similar strong upward concentration appears to have operated on the moon. Since the period of melting on the moon was limited apparently to a period extending over a few hundred million years between 3 and 4 billion years ago, the degree of upward concentration, if the initial abundances were chondritic, is surprising. It seems possible that the moon was enriched in the refractory elements during accretion, probably as part of the process which depleted the volatile elements. Figs. 4-5 and 4-6 show the enrichment of the refrac-

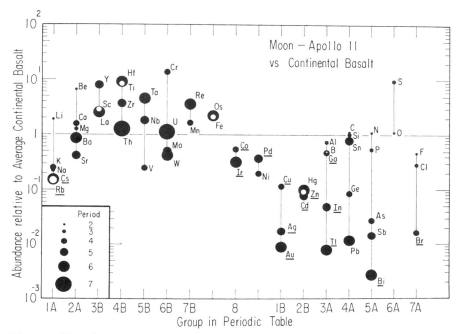

Fig. 4-6. Abundances in Apollo 11 rocks normalized to average continental basalt. After Ganapathy (University of Chicago).

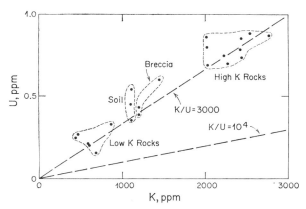

Fig. 4-7. Correlation plot of potassium versus uranium. A reference line of $K/U = 10^4$ (a typical terrestrial value) is shown. After Tera (California Institute of Technology).

tory elements relative to abundances in continental basalts, with rather constant enrichment factors over cosmic abundances of about 60. Anders (University of Chicago) attributes this enrichment to "magmatic differentiation" rather than to a primitive enrichment. Probably both factors (enrichment of minor phases during partial melting acting on material with a high content of these elements) were operating.

Thorium and uranium are of interest both because of their use in radio-active dating and because they are important sources of heat production. The high U and Th contents of the lunar rocks would produce enough heat to melt the moon. Since the shape of the moon indicates that it has been rigid for probably the past three aeons, U and Th must have been concentrated near the surface (as is the case for the Earth). This is further evidence of the efficiency of the process producing upward concentration of the elements.

Fig. 4-7 shows the K/U relationships. K/U ratios for many terrestrial rocks are constant at about 10,000. This is not the consequence of any profound geochemical coherence, but rather that both elements are strongly concentrated in residual systems by fractionation processes. The K/U ratios for chondrites are 50,000 – 80,000 and for the lunar rocks the average is about 2700. The Apollo 12 rocks show even lower ratios of about 1400 (LSPET 1970). Thus the moon, like the Earth, appears to be depleted in potassium relative to uranium and thorium, and the contribution of potassium to lunar heat production is small by comparison to that due to U and Th.

The Th/U ratios average about 4. This is similar to the typical terrestrial values for this ratio. The values for chondritic meteorites lie between 3.4 and 3.7.

In contrast to the similarity between terrestrial and lunar Th/U ratios, the Zr/Hf ratios in the lunar rocks are lower (typically 20 – 40) than ter-restrial ratios which are usually in the range 40 – 60. This ratio is not readily altered except in the later stages of fractionation of granitic rocks. Goles (University of Oregon) in an important contribution points out that this may be due to differentiation under dry conditions, and points out that some of the low-K oceanic basalts have similar ratios. Possibly the abun-dance of Hf relative to Zr in the upper crust of the Earth reflects the degree of intracrustal fractionation and is less fundamental than commonly supposed.

THE FERROMAGNESIAN ELEMENTS (SEE TABLE 4-7.)

These elements are defined as those entering sixfold coordination sites in silicate minerals, substituting in Fe^{+2} and Mg^{+2} lattice sites. The elements are divided principally into divalent and trivalent classes (although Ti^{+4} and Li^+ also fall in this group on account of size and geochemical behavior). The arrangement of the elements is in the order of crystal field site prefer-ence energies. For the transition elements, this effect is the critical factor influencing entry into the lattice sites. Some of the elements (e.g., Ni) are siderophile. The elements in this grouping show both extensive depletions and enrichments compared to chondritic meteorites or to terrestrial basalts. Thus Ni, Cu, Ga and V are strongly depleted and Cr, Sc and Ti enriched.

Table 4-7. Abundance of ferromagnesian elements in Apollo 11 samples. Type A rocks (A); Type B rocks (B); Type C breccias (C); Type D fines (D).

		A	ref.	B	ref.	C	ref.	D	ref.
Cr	ppm.	2500	ave.	1730	ave.	2100	ave.	2000	b
V	ppm.	70	h	60	h	62	h	66	h
Fe^{+3}		–	–	–	–	–	–	–	–
Sc	ppm.	86	h	87	h	67	h	60	b
Ti	%	7.1	h, i	6.3	h, i	5.1	h, i	4.5	h, i
Ni	ppm.	7	l	3	l	200	l	230	b
Co	ppm.	29	ave.	15	ave.	30	ave.	30	b
Cu	ppm.	4	c	15	c	15	c	10	b
Fe^{+2}	%	14.8	h, i	14.4	h, i	12.4	h, i	12.1	h, i
Mn	ppm.	1900	ave.	2200	ave.	2100	ave.	2000	b
Mg	%	4.6	h, i	4.2	h, i	4.7	h, i	4.8	h, i
Li	ppm.	18	j	11	j	14	j	12.5	j
Ga	ppm.	4.9	e	5.5	e	5.4	e	4.6	e
Al	%	4.6	h, i	5.5	h, i	6.7	h, i	7.3	h, i
V/Ni		10		20		.31		.29	
Cr/V		35		29		34		30	
Ni/Co		.24		.20		6.7		7.7	
Fe^{+2}/Ni		21000		48000		620		525	
Al/Ga		9400		10000		12400		15900	

The depletion in Cu and Ni may be ascribed to entry into metallic phases under the strong reducing conditions of the partial melting and crystallization of the lunar lavas. Some loss of the siderophile elements prior to accretion cannot be ruled out, lending some credence to the idea that the moon's nickel is in the Earth's core. Fe/Ni ratios in chondrites are about 20, usually between 100 – 500 in terrestrial basalts and reach about 15000 in lunar rocks. These high ratios are due to a combination of initially low Ni, and retention of Ni in residual phases during melting, probably in minor metallic phases, since the evidence for a large lunar metallic core is unconvincing. (The other siderophile elements (Au and the Pt metals) are likewise heavily depleted in the lunar samples.) The experimental work supports a pyroxene-rich interior from which the Apollo 11 basalts were derived from partial melting. This is in contrast to the large amount of olivine, a nickel-rich mineral, in the Earth's mantle. As is the case with the enrichment of the refractory elements, the depletion of the siderophile elements, points toward pre-accretion high temperature processing of the material from which the moon formed.

Cobalt, which is less siderophilic, is less depleted than Ni and is present at concentrations only a little lower than typical of terrestrial basalts. Manganese is likewise present at similar levels to terrestrial basalts.

Vanadium is depleted in the Apollo 11 rocks relative to terrestrial basaltic abundances (Fig. 4-6) by a factor of about 4. Ringwood (Australian National University) ascribes this to a crystal-chemical effect due to the

Table 4-8. Small cations in Apollo 11 samples.

		A	ref.	B	ref.	C	ref.	D	ref.
B	ppm.	.8	b	.7	b	–	–	1.0	b
Be	ppm.	3	1	1.5	1	2.0	1	1.6	1
Si	%	18.9	h, i	18.9	h, i	19.5	h, i	19.6	h, i
Si	%	18.9	r	18.7	r	19.7	r	20.2	r
Ge	ppm.	< .2	e	–	–	.4	e	.34	e

presence of vanadium in the mineral armalcolite. Armalcolite is one of the first minerals to crystallize and removal of a few percent would deplete the magma in vanadium. However, there is so little evidence of any effects of fractional crystallization that the alternative explanation that vanadium was retained in residual phases during partial melting, also suggested by Ringwood, is to be preferred.

In the Apollo 12 basalts both vanadium and nickel abundances are higher while Ti is less abundant. These differences probably reflect variations in source materials rather than in the conditions of partial melting.

The chromium abundance in the Apollo 11 basalts is one of the more notable features of their chemistry. It is about 10 times that of typical terrestrial basalts (Fig. 4-6). The significance of the high Cr content, which is about the same order of magnitude as in chondrites, lies in the extreme sensitivity of chromium to crystal fractionation processes during cooling of silicate melts. The element is rapidly depleted during basaltic crystallization and its high and rather uniform abundance, both in Type A and B rocks, indicates that near surface fractional crystallization was not a dominant process in general, nor is it possible to derive Type A-high K from Type B-low K rocks by such processes. The appearance of such large quantities of Cr in the lunar lavas contrasts with the lower partition of Cr into terrestrial volcanic rocks from high Cr source rocks in the mantle. This strong partition into the liquid phase may be due to the strongly reducing conditions. Under the more oxidizing conditions in the Earth, Cr-rich spinels may appear and retain the Cr at depth.

Scandium is also enriched in the lunar rocks, being enriched by a factor of about 10 over the cosmic abundances (Fig. 4-6). It is also depleted during fractional crystallization, although not as rapidly as Cr, but its consistently high abundance indicates little near surface fractionation in the Apollo 11 rocks. The Apollo 12 suite from Oceanus Procellarum shows more evidence of near surface fractionation with some depletion in Ni, Cr and Sc (LSPET 1970). Gallium is an element of great interest since it is somewhat volatile, and may enter metallic, sulphide or silicate phases. It is a factor of 4 lower than in terrestrial rocks and is rather constant at about 5 ppm. (It rarely varies outside the range 15 – 25 ppm. in terrestrial rocks.) The depletion of Ga is due probably to an initial depletion, along with the other volatile and chalcophile elements, and its entry into metallic phases.

In contrast to the other alkali elements, lithium is not depleted in the lunar rocks relative to terrestrial basalts. It is present at levels of 10 – 20 ppm., enriched by a factor of 5 – 10 over cosmic abundances. Although lithium is moderately volatile, its lack of depletion may be due to its entry into sixfold lattice sites and hence be contained in relatively refractory phases as a trace constituent. Certainly the heavier alkalies have been depleted apparently on the basis of volatility.

Nickel is strikingly enriched in the fine material and breccias, with typical abundances of 200 – 300 ppm. compared to the rock abundances of under 10 ppm. From a careful study of the abundances of many elements, discussed in a later section, Anders and co-workers estimate that the contribution of carbonaceous-like chondritic meteorites was about 1.9%. With an average Ni content of 1.4%, these will contribute about 250 ppm. Ni. Thus most of the nickel content in the soil is due to this source. The iron meteorite fragments which are sporadically distributed will add high local nickel contents (average Ni content of iron meteorites is 8.5%), but do not appear to contribute significantly to the total Ni content which is adequately explained by the chondritic contribution.

CHALCOPHILE ELEMENTS (SEE TABLE 4-9.)

These elements, which in terrestrial rocks enter sulfide phases, form with the alkalies a group of elements volatile at temperatures up to 1500°C. The chalcophile elements are strikingly depleted in ordinary chondrites relative to the carbonaceous chondrites. In the lunar rocks, they are generally low in abundance and are grossly depleted relative to the cosmic abundances (Figs. 4-6 and 4-8) and to the terrestrial abundances (Fig. 4-7). The basic questions are whether these elements were never accreted, were lost subsequent to accretion, or were retained in the interior during partial melting. Certainly the moon appears to be depleted rather generally in volatile elements, so that there is a strong presumption that the first alternative is correct.

Surface loss of volatiles during extrusion or meteorite impact has not found much favor with the investigators. These elements are abundant in the fines, where they have been supplied by meteorite impact. During surface extrusion of the lavas, freezing of the surface will rapidly occur and loss of volatiles will not occur. Anders (University of Chicago) points out that lead is not more strongly depleted than other much more volatile elements such as mercury, which would be more readily lost under such conditions.

Table 4-9. Abundance of chalcophile elements in Apollo 11 samples. Type A rocks (A); Type B rocks (B); Type C breccias (C); Type D fines (D).

		A	ref.	B	ref.	C	ref.	D	ref.
Tl	ppb.	.6	c	.6	c	2.8	c	2.2	c
Ag	ppb.	1.5	c	1.5	c	18	c	9	c
Hg	ppb.	5 – 13	d	.6	d	1	d	5	d
Cd	ppb.	10	c	10	c	100	c	50	h
Bi	ppb.	.3	c	.3	c	2.2	c	1.6	c
In	ppb.	3	c	3	c	5	c	< 10	c
Te	ppb.	16	c	16	c	72	c	–	–
As	ppb.	63	f	73	f	–	–	37	f
Pb	ppm.	1.7	m	.4	m	1.7	m	1.4	m
Zn	ppm.	3	f	3	f	25	c	20	c
Cu	ppm.	4	c	15	c	15	c	10	b
Ga	ppm.	4.9	e	5.5	e	5.4	e	4.6	e
Se	ppm.	.7	f	.8	f	1.6	f	.8	f
Sb	no data								

The Sr isotopic evidence does not indicate loss of Rb at the time of lava extrusion and Tatsumoto (U.S. Geological Survey) finds no evidence of lead loss. Possibly the chalcophile elements might be retained in the source regions during partial melting. However this explanation does not explain the depletion of the alkali elements, and the overall evidence favors loss of volatile elements prior to accretion.

The fine material is enriched in the chalcophile elements. Fig. 4-9 shows the excess components in the soil and breccia for the siderophile and chalcophile elements. In Fig. 4-10 Anders has compared the "extra" component in the soil with the abundances in carbonaceous chondrites. The relative concentrations show a parallel pattern to those in carbonaceous chondrites but not to those in ordinary chondrites. This evidence led Anders to propose a 1.9% addition of carbonaceous chondrite component to the soil to account for the excess chalcophile (and siderophile) elements.

THE PLATINUM GROUP ELEMENTS (SEE TABLE 4-10.)

These elements are siderophile, entering metallic phases. Exceedingly large depletions are observed for this group in the lunar rocks in comparison with cosmic abundances (Fig. 4-5) and terrestrial abundances (Fig. 4-6). The very low oxygen fugacity observed in the lunar rocks means that metallic phases will be present in at least minor amounts in the source areas and some of the depletion is due to retention of these elements in the lunar interior. Anders (University of Chicago) comments on the difference between the

Table 4-10. Abundance of Pt metals, Au and Re in Apollo 11 samples.

		A	ref.	B	ref.	C	ref.	D	ref.
Ir	ppb.	.07	c	.07	c	8	c	7	c
Pd	ppb.	< 0.5	c	< 0.5	c	< 5	c	< 5	c
Os	ppb.	< 1	g	< .4	g	< 5	g	< 14	g
Re	ppb.	< 1.5	g	< .03	g	< 3	g	< 10	g
Au	ppb.	.04	c	.04	c	3	c	2.7	b
Rh ⎫	no data								
Ru ⎬	no data								
Pt ⎭	no data								

relative abundances of the siderophile elements in terrestrial rocks and in the lunar rocks. For example, on Earth the platinum elements are depleted relative to gold, but on the moon similar depletions, relative to cosmic abundances, by factors of about 10^{-4}, are observed. These differences are considered by Anders as an objection to the fission hypothesis. If this were true, similar relative abundances of the siderophile elements would be expected in lunar and terrestrial basalts. It is an open question whether the moon as a

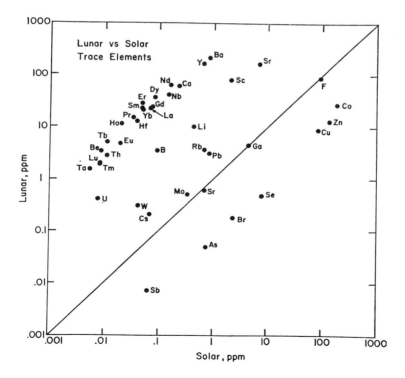

Fig. 4-8. Comparison plot of average trace element abundances for lunar rocks and soil against solar abundances. After Morrison (Cornell University).

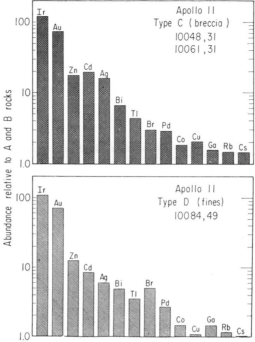

Fig. 4-9. For the first 9 elements, mean abundances in soil and breccia exceed those in Type A and B rocks by a factor greater than 2. This suggests the presence of an extraneous (meteoritic?) component. After Ganapathy (University of Chicago).

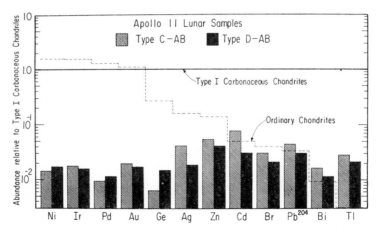

Fig. 4-10. Abundance pattern of meteoritic component, obtained by subtracting average abundances in A, B rocks from those in C and D material, and normalizing to Type I carbonaceous chondrites. Distribution is approximately flat, suggesting that meteorite component consists largely of carbonaceous-chondrite-like material, admixed in an amount of 1.9%. Ordinary chondrite material would have given a staircase pattern parallel to the dashed curve; iron meteorite material a large peak for the first four elements. After Ganapathy (University of Chicago).

whole is depleted in siderophile elements. This would imply pre-accretion separation of a metallic phase. The extreme depletion observed in the lunar basalts is probably a combination of low initial abundances, together with extreme reducing conditions, possibly coupled with the absence of water, in the source region of the lunar lavas.

The fine material shows marked enrichment by factors of 30 – 100 for the siderophile elements (notably Ir and Au) relative to the rocks. Anders (University of Chicago) explains this enrichment, along with the nickel and chalcophile elements, as due to the addition of about 1.9% of carbonaceous chondritic meteorite. There is also a small component (about 2% of the total enrichment) due to the solar wind.

The average influx rate of meteoritic and cometary material (some workers believe that carbonaceous chondrites are derived from comets) is 3.8×10^{-9} gm. per cm.^{2} per year at Tranquillity Base.

OXYGEN

Most chemical analyses do not determine oxygen directly but measure the amount of the cations present. The analysis is then expressed in terms of oxides (the elements being so weighed in classical silicate analyses). The assumption that the missing element is oxygen is less arbitrary than may appear since the main mineral phases present (silicates and minor oxides) contain oxygen as the dominant anion.

Several workers found that, using the conventional valencies for the major elements, that the summations to 100% were high. This was ascribed to various causes, e.g., presence of Ti^{+3} rather than Ti^{+4}. Direct determinations of oxygen have been made by Ehmann and Morgan (University of Kentucky) using neutron activation techniques. Si and Al were determined by the same method. They find the O content of the soil is 40.8% compared with a calculated 42.4% from the chemical analyses giving a mean O depletion of 1.6%. The *rocks* have a smaller and probably not significant depletion. The cause of the deficiency of oxygen in the soil is attributed by Ehmann and Morgan to possible reduction by hydrogen from the solar wind.

CARBON

The chemistry of this element is discussed in Chapter 5 in the section on isotopic abundances, page 178, and in the sections on Bioscience and Organic Matter, page 133.

SULFUR

The chemistry of this element is discussed in the section on sulfur isotope abundances in Chapter 5, page 144 and in Chapter 7, page 177. Most of this element appears to be present in the mineral, troilite (FeS).

HALOGENS

The abundances of fluorine (F), chlorine (Cl), bromine (Br) and iodine (I) show much variation. The ranges in composition, from Reed (Argonne National Laboratory), are as follows:

fluorine	140 – 350 ppm.
chlorine	3 – 16 ppm.
bromine	0.04 – 0.4 ppm.
iodine	0.02 – 0.6 ppm.

The ratios between the elements are much more nearly constant.

F/Cl	22
Cl/Br	51
Br/I	3

The concentrations are similar in the rocks and soils. Only about 15% of the fluorine can be accounted for as occurring in the mineral apatite. Chlorine and bromine are low in abundance, but do not appear to have been derived from the solar wind, since they are present both in rocks and fine materials at about the same concentrations. The Cl/Br ratios are low in comparison with cosmic ratios of about 400.

COMPARISON OF CHEMICAL COMPOSITION OF APOLLO 11 (TRANQUILLITY BASE) AND APOLLO 12 (OCEAN OF STORMS) SAMPLES

Preliminary chemical data have been published for the Apollo 12 samples (LSPET, 1970) and a comparison of these samples from Oceanus Procellarum with the Apollo 11 samples from Mare Tranquillitatis shows that the chemistry at the two maria sites is clearly related. Both sites show the distinctive features of high concentrations of "refractory" elements and low contents of "volatile" elements, which most clearly distinguish lunar from other materials. This overall similarity indicates that the Apollo 11 sample composition was not unique. Taken in conjunction with the Surveyor V and VI chemical data, it is suggestive of a similar chemistry for the maria basin fill.

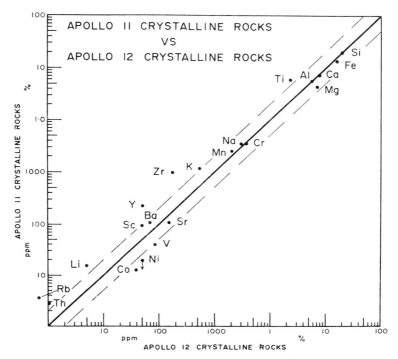

Fig. 4-11. Comparison of average composition of Apollo 11 and 12 crystalline rocks. Points lying along the 45° diagonal line indicate equal concentrations. Increasing distance from the diagonal line indicates increasing disparity in composition between the two sites. The dashed lines indicate the limits for differences by a factor of two. Elements lying to the right of the diagonal line are enriched in Apollo 11 rocks. Note the higher concentrations of Ti, K, Zr, Y, Ba, Sc, Li and Th in Apollo 11 rocks and the lower contents of Mg, V, Ni and Co. After Taylor (Australian National University).

Fig. 4-11 shows a comparison between the composition of the Apollo 11 and Apollo 12 crystalline rocks. Points lying along the 45° diagonal line indicate equality in composition. Increasing distance from the diagonal line indicates increasing disparity in composition.

In detail, there are numerous and interesting differences between the Apollo 12 and 11 rocks. These include:

1. Lower concentration of Ti both for rocks and fine material of Apollo 12. The range in composition is $0.72 - 3.4\%$ Ti $(1.2 - 5.1\%$ $TiO_2)$ compared with the range in the Apollo 11 rocks of $4.7 - 7.5\%$ Ti $(7 - 12\%$ $TiO_2)$.

2. Lower concentrations of K, Rb, Zr, Y, Li and Ba in Apollo 12.

3. Higher concentrations of Fe, Mg, Ni, Co, V and Sc in the crystalline rocks from Apollo 12. These data are consistent with the more "basic" character of the Apollo 12 rocks.

4. The significant variation in the Apollo 12 rocks is in the variation among the ferromagnesian elements. In the Apollo 11 suite there was a much wider variation in the concentration of elements such as K and Rb concentrated in residual melts. However, the unique sample 12013 represents a much more extreme composition (and probably later crystal fraction) than any of the Apollo 11 rocks.

Fig. 4-12 shows a comparison of the Apollo 11 and 12 fine material. The fine material at the Apollo 12 sites differs from that at Apollo 11 in containing about half the titanium content, more Mg and possibly higher amounts of Ba, K, Rb, Zr and Li. Thus the chemistry of the fine material is not uniform in the different maria, but reflects the local variations in the chemistry of the underlying rocks.

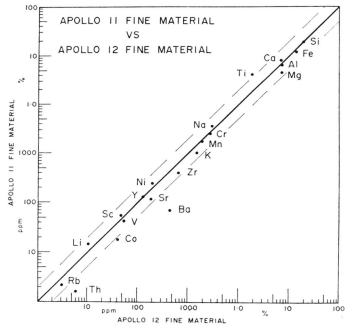

Fig. 4-12. Comparison of average composition of Apollo 11 and 12 fine material. Construction of diagram similar to Fig. 4-11. Note the higher concentration of Ti in Apollo 11 and the lower amounts of Mg, Ba, Co and Th. After Taylor (Australian National University).

APOLLO 12 ROCKS AND FINE MATERIAL

The chemistry of the Apollo 12 crystalline rocks shows differences from that of the fine material and the breccias (Fig. 4-13). The rocks are lower in Rb, K, Ba, Y, Zr, Ni and Li. Fe and Cr are higher in the rocks. Several critical element ratios are likewise distinct. K/Rb ratios average 850 in the rocks compared to 450 in the fines. The Fe/Ni ratio in the rocks (average 3000: range 2000 − 11,000) is much higher than the fine material ratios of about 600. Rb/Sr ratios are very low in the rocks (0.005), but higher (0.02) in the fines. The element abundances in the fine material thus display a generally more fractionated character than the rocks. The fine material and the breccias are generally quite similar in composition and could not have formed directly from the large crystalline rock samples, and additional components must be present. The nickel content of the breccias and fine material places an upper limit on the amount of meteoritic material contributed to the lunar surface regolith. Using an average meteoritic nickel content of 1.5%, the Ni content of the fine material represents a meteoritic contribution of the order of 1% if all the nickel were extra-lunar.

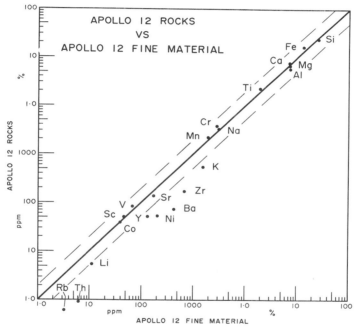

Fig. 4-13. Comparison of average composition of Apollo 12 rocks and fine material. Construction of diagram similar to Fig. 4-11. Note that the fine material is enriched in nickel (probably from meteorites) and K, Zr, Ba, Y, Li, Rb and Th, indicating a component enriched in these elements is present in the fines but not in the rocks sampled.

INTERNAL VARIATIONS IN THE APOLLO 12 ROCKS

The crystalline rocks show minor but significant internal variations in chemistry. A number of interesting geochemical trends appear when the samples are arranged in order of decreasing magnesium content. Nickel shows a striking decrease in concentration, by an order of magnitude. Chro-

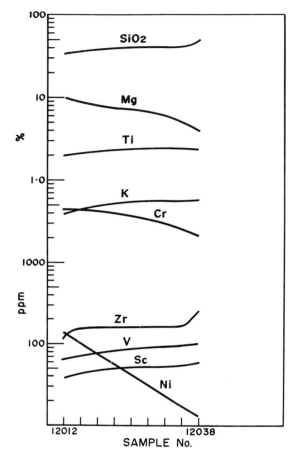

Fig. 4-14. Variation in element concentrations in Apollo 12 rocks. Samples are arranged in order of decreasing magnesium content. From "Preliminary Examination of Lunar Samples from Apollo 12." The Lunar Sample Examination Team. *Science*, Vol. 167, Fig. 10, March 6, 1970, pp. 1325-1339. Copyright 1970 by the American Association for the Advancement of Science.

mium displays a smaller relative decrease in the same direction and cobalt shows a slight decrease. Silicon increases as Mg decreases. Similar trends are shown by V, Sc, Zr, Y, K, Ba, and Ca, although the variations are small. (Fig. 4-14).

This overall geochemical behavior is consistent with the patterns observed during fractional crystallization in terrestrial igneous rocks, depleting the silicate melt in elements such as Ni and Cr which preferentially enter the early formed mineral phases, and enriching the residual melt in those elements such as Ba, K, etc., excluded from the early crystal fractions. The slight degree of enrichment of the latter elements indicates an early stage of the fractional crystallization process.

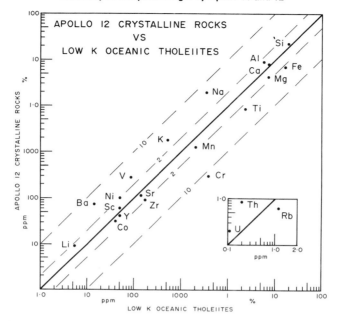

Fig. 4-15. Comparison of Apollo 12 rocks with terrestrial oceanic volcanic rocks. Construction of diagram as for Fig. 4-11. Note wide differences in composition between the two rock types.

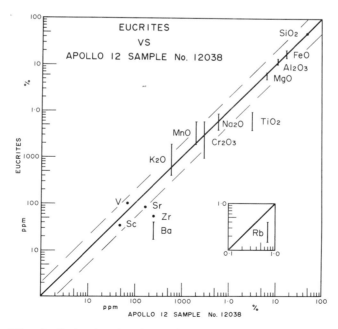

Fig. 4-16. The similarity in abundance for many elements between Apollo 12 sample 12038 and the eucrite class of basaltic achondrites. Construction of diagram as for Fig. 4-11.

Whether these rocks form a related sequence or are a heterogeneous collection of similar origins cannot be answered from the chemical evidence. Rock No. 12013 from the Apollo 12 mission is unique. It contains the highest concentration of SiO_2 (61%) yet observed in a lunar rock. The amounts of K, Rb, Ba, Zr, Y, the rare-earth element Yb, and Li are enriched by 10 – 50 times compared to the other rocks. These high concentrations are reminiscent of the terrestrial enrichment of elements in residual melts during the operation of fractional crystallization processes, and it may have crystallized from a small volume of residual melt, late in the cooling of a pool of silicate melt. Although it may represent a lunar "acidic" rock, its chemical composition is unique and does not resemble that of terrestrial granites, rhyolites or "acid" igneous rocks. Still less does it resemble tektites.

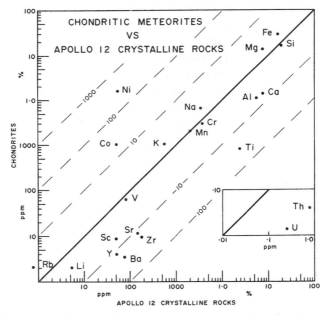

Fig. 4-17. The wide difference in composition between Apollo 12 rocks and the chondritic type of stony meteorites. Construction of diagram as for Fig. 4-11.

RELATION OF TERRESTRIAL ROCKS AND METEORITES TO APOLLO 12 ROCKS

The closest analogues among terrestrial rocks are the oceanic basaltic rocks, but the high concentrations of the refractory elements emphasize the unique chemistry of the lunar rocks. This comparison is shown in Fig. 4-15 where the differences are apparent.

The eucrite class of the basaltic achondrites are closest in composition, and sample 12038 shows many similarities in composition (Fig. 4-16). The concentration of Ti, Zr, Sr, and Ba is sufficient to distinguish them but it now seems a strong possibility that rocks of similar chemistry to the eucritic meteorites are present on the moon, in view of the variation in composition observed between and at two maria sites.

The chemistry of the Apollo 12 samples does not resemble that of chondrites (Fig. 4-17), nickel in particular being strikingly depleted. The Apollo 12 material is enriched in many elements by 1 – 2 orders of magnitude in comparison with our estimates of cosmic abundances and the maria material is clearly strongly fractionated relative to our ideas of the composition of the primitive solar nebula.

5

BIOSCIENCE AND ORGANIC MATTER

(Organic Geochemistry)

A number of laboratories examined returned lunar samples for the presence of biochemical organic compounds in the general context of the possibility of extraterrestrial life. Many of the laboratories involved had developed extremely sensitive techniques for such analyses in the course of examining other extraterrestrial samples, specifically meteorites, for traces of life. Much of the attention focused on searches for the presence of organic compounds which would indicate either fossil chemical forms or possibly prebiotic organic compounds. Thus analyses were carried out for the elemental structures of proteins, fats, carbohydrates, pigments, nucleic acid bases, hydrocarbons, organic sulfur compounds and organic polymers (Fig. 5-1) and for other data or evidence relevant to the existence of extraterrestrial organisms ranging from paleontology to microbiology. No viable organisms were detected and no evidence was obtained for fossil remains of organisms. Organic carbon was clearly present; two classes of biochemicals, amino acids and porphyrins, were tentatively detected in the lunar soil. No other biolipids were detected, nor were saturated hydrocarbons, except methane and closely related compounds. Carbon was present to an appreciable degree as inorganic carbides (the mineral cohenite). While the bulk of lunar carbon is undoubtedly indigenous to the moon, the source of the methane is believed to lie partly in the solar wind. The source of the indicated amino acids and porphyrin-like compounds cannot yet be clearly stated, but they seem more likely to be prebiotic in nature rather than biogenic. These compounds may have been indigenous to the lunar regolith or might have been introduced through the infall of meteoritic, interplanetary or interstellar, material.

TOTAL CARBON

The total carbon in the lunar samples from Apollo 11 ranged from 30 to 230 ppm. for a wide variety of samples comprising all of the major types of returned specimens. Basaltic (Type A and B) rocks contained about 67 ppm.

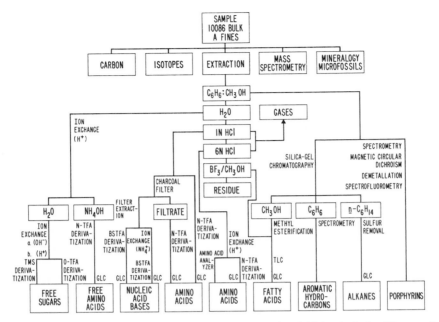

Fig. 5-1. Analytical program for organic compounds of biological significance in returned samples of lunar soil followed by NASA Ames Consortium. After Kvenvolden (NASA Ames Research Center, California).

total carbon, and the breccias had roughly 100 ppm. with a maximum, 230 ppm. Samples of lunar soil varied widely, ranging from about 100 ppm. to 350 ppm. with weighted means for two bulk soil samples at 142 and 226 ppm. The total carbon appeared to be attributable to indigenous lunar material together with meteoritic and solar wind components. In this respect it is interesting to note that the carbon content was observed to vary inversely with the size of particles in the lunar soil. For mesh sizes 60 – 140 mesh, the carbon content was determined to be 115 ppm.; for 140 – 130 mesh, 210 ppm.; and for <300 mesh, 500 ppm. (Moore, University of Arizona).

Analysis for total carbon was based on combustion methods, and the particular methods used from investigator to investigator varied somewhat. In general, the sample was heated in a stream of oxygen at 1000°C. or higher with the resulting CO_2 separated from other combustion products and estimated by gas chromatography. Spark ionization also showed the presence of carbon (Oro, University of Houston) but it appeared to give low values, e.g., 41 ppm.

The bulk of the work done on organic compounds by several groups was based on the bulk fines sample 10086 and the total carbon analyses for this sample agreed well with one another with typical values: 143, 150, 170, 168 and 157 ppm. An attempt was made to reach a material balance for the forms in which the carbon occurred (Ponnamperuma, NASA Ames Research Center, California). Extractable organic matter accounted for less than 2 ppm. and was in the form of low molecular weight hydrocarbons. In pyrolysis experiments 50 ppm. appeared as CO_2 with a residue of 60 ppm. of which 5 – 21 ppm. was carbide and an indeterminate amount was elemental carbon. The bulk of the remaining carbon was evidently due to CO. Other compounds of carbon were detected but they contributed very little to the material balance.

ORGANIC CARBON

The definition of organic carbon at the best of times is uncertain, and in the case of lunar samples it requires additional clarification. Care must be taken to point out that organic carbon, terrestrially or extraterrestrially, is not necessarily biogenic carbon. While the majority of carbon in terrestrial rocks is biogenic, the corresponding assignment for organic carbon in extra-terrestrial rocks to biogenic sources is *not* warranted. Organic carbon may be defined as carbon in compounds in which C—H bonds are abundant; C—metal bonds, largely absent; C—C bonds, abundant; C—O, C—S, C—N bonds are commonly but not necessarily present. Thus, organic compounds include hydrocarbons, C_2H_{2n+2}; organic acids, e.g., CH_3—CH_2COOH; aromatic compounds, e.g., $C_{10}H_8$; amino acids, R—$CHNH_2$—COOH, and many others.

Organic matter is difficult to determine in a rigid sense because its definition is, of necessity, vague. The principal method used in the lunar analysis was pyrolysis in an inert atmosphere with gas chromatography to detect and measure the off-gases (Johnson, NASA Ames Research Center, California). Basically the method determined volatile products which consisted primarily of C—H bonded groups, and it was calibrated on responses obtained for samples of typical organic matter including hydrocarbons, humic material, organic acids, amino acids, carbohydrates and related substances.

Fifteen different lunar samples gave values for organic carbon ranging from 10 to 126 ppm. Contamination was suspected since it was observed that the more handling particular samples received in the course of their preliminary examination, the higher were the observed contents of organic carbon. On the basis of these data for lunar samples in general, the conclusion was reached that the upper limit for indigenous lunar organic matter was only 10 ppm. The lunar fines sample which was used in all the organic studies, however, was reported to have 40 ppm. ± 8, with an operational blank value of 1 ppm., and it seems difficult in the light of the extreme care with which this sample was handled to attribute any significant portion of the observed value to contaminants. However, the possibility may exist that

C–H compounds could have been manufactured from CO and H_2O as an artifact of the experimental techniques.

CARBIDES

Carbon may exist in direct combination with metallic atoms as carbide minerals, specifically cohenite, and this has been recognized in some iron-nickel meteorite fragments in the soils; accordingly it is not surprising that the organic chemists found good evidence for carbides in the lunar soil confirming the mineralogical determinations. Acid decompositions of the lunar soil were carried out using 4.8 N. hydrochloric acid in a sealed glass ampoule heated at 98°C. for 16 hours. Methane, ethane, ethene, acetylene, propane, propene and small amounts of unidentified C_3 and C_4 hydrocarbons were detected by gas chromatography in the products of the hydrolysis, as shown in Fig. 5-2. Yields were estimated to represent an appreciable proportion of the total carbon present — from 3 to 15%. Decomposition of the lunar mineral matrix with hydrofluoric acid resulted in the evolution of methane, ethane and other gases. While a portion of the yield of gases was believed to be indigenous as such to the lunar sample, a significant proportion was attributed to the acid decomposition of carbides (Eglinton, University of Bristol, England). There was general agreement, but with few data, that the carbides probably involved iron and nickel.

METHANE

Methane exists in trace quantities in the returned lunar samples (Eglinton, University of Bristol, England) and is accompanied by smaller quantities of ethane and higher homologs. Although direct crushing of the sample under vacuum failed to reveal significant quantities of methane above background, etching of the lunar fines with hydrofluoric acid released methane in the amount of about 2 ppm. along with rare gases (argon, neon and helium), and methane was observed to be more abundant than argon. Experiments involving deuterium showed that at least a portion of the methane and ethane was present as these gases, rather than being generated from carbides. Low temperature heating of lunar fines, at 150°C., produced methane, but only at background levels.

Many experiments were carried out to pyrolyze the organic matter in the lunar soil. Vacuum pyrolysis to 900°C. produced, for example, readily detectable amounts of methane with greatest yields (1 ppm.) occurring in the temperature range from 300 to 600°C. (Burlingame, University of California). In some experiments the sample was pyrolyzed in a vessel with cold traps to collect the products prior to introduction into a mass spectrometer; in others, vaporization of volatilizable components was done directly into the ion source of a high resolution mass spectrometer.

OXIDES OF CARBON

Hydrofluoric acid treatment of the lunar soil directly yielded substantial quantities of carbon as CO: 66 ppm. in a typical analysis (Burlingame, University of California). While some CO may possibly be present in rare inclusions of gas in the mineral particles, a considerable amount of the HF-liberated CO was concluded to be present in other than gaseous form in the original lunar soil, for example as carbonyl components of the organic matter. Heating at 500°C. caused CO to be evolved in amounts of about 9 ppm. and

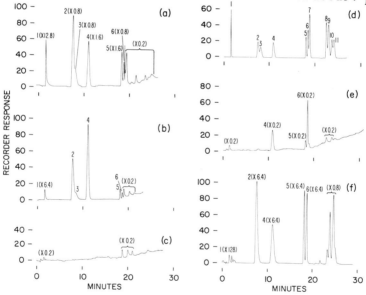

Fig. 5-2. Gas chromatograms of hydrocarbons obtained from carbides in lunar fines, with blanks and standards. Curves (a) and (b) HCl treatment of 10086-3 Bulk A fines; (c) control blank; (d) standard mixture containing about 20 μl each of (1) methane, (2) ethene, (3) acetylene, (4) ethane, (5) propene, (6) propane, (7) allene, (8) isobutane, (9) butene-1, (10) butane, (11) cis-2-butene (attenuation × 160 throughout run); (e) and (f) HCl treatment of Mighei meteorite and cohenite, Fe_3C, respectively. A 6 ft × 0.125 in. stainless steel column packed with 100-120 mesh Poropak Q was used on a Varian-Aerograph Model 1520 B instrument equipped with flame detector. Flow rate was 20 ml/min. Oven temperature initially held at 35°C for 10 min then programmed at 10°/min to 140°C where it was held. Unless otherwise indicated, peak attenuations were × 0.4 (attenuation 4, range 0.1). Each injection represented 7% of the total sample. After Chang (NASA Ames Research Center, California).

it was accompanied by <1 ppm. of CO_2. CO and CO_2 were the major pyrolytic products in all experiments especially at the higher temperature, as illustrated by a pyrolysis analysis in Fig. 5-3. In one experiment the lunar fines were demineralized with HF and the "organic" residue pyrolyzed; CO was the principal product with 18 ppm. recovered at 150°C., 13 ppm. at 500°C., and 88 ppm. at 1150°C. Subsequent studies (Burlingame, University of California) have shown that these high CO values may be erroneous.

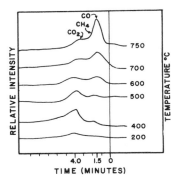

Fig. 5-3. Evolution of carbon dioxide, methane and carbon monoxide in pyrolysis of lunar fines. Sample size was 1.5 g; semicontinuous mass spectral scans of the gases were obtained for identification of peaks during the gas chromatography shown. Methane appears in the tail of the peak for carbon monoxide. After Oro (University of Houston).

ALKANE HYDROCARBONS

Saturated hydrocarbons, 0.3 to 2 ppm., (along with elemental sulfur were found by extracting lunar soil with organic solvents, e.g., mixtures of benzene and methanol (Fig. 5-4) and resolving the extract by thin layer chromatography followed by mass spectroscopy. Direct mass spectroscopy also showed the presence of hydrocarbons up to C_{10} or higher, but in most instances these were attributed to sampling contaminants (Biemann, Massachusetts Institute of Technology). Particular attention was directed to n-alkanes in the range above C_{15} by combined gas chromatography-mass spectroscopy. Sensitivities of detection were commonly 10 nanograms per compound and for the sample sizes used, detection limits of about 0.001 to 0.01 ppm. were obtained. In some instances whole extracts were examined; in others, column chromatography was used to isolate alkanes from other soluble organic matter. In no instance was evidence obtained for the presence of alkanes. In the most exhaustive analysis (Meinschein, Indiana University) a large sample (50 gm.) was extracted sequentially: first, intact; second, after being pulverized; and finally, after HF digestion. No C_{15} to C_{30} alkane was present at a concentration exceeding 0.001 ppm., and it is important to note that such analyses apply not only to normal alkanes but in addition to branched alkanes including isoprenoid hydrocarbons and a variety of other organic compounds of biogenic or prebiotic significance.

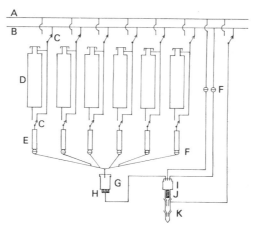

Fig. 5-4. Diagrammatic representation of closed system used in extraction of lunar fines with organic solvents. The apparatus as shown also provides for evaporation and collection of organic matter extracted from the sample. When required, a chromatographic column and fraction collector replace the collection unit shown. A. Vent manifold; B. Pressure manifold; C. Two way taps (upper Teflon, lower glass); D. Solvent reservoirs (1 1. capacity); E. Calibrated delivery volumes; F. One way taps (upper Teflon, lower glass); G. Extraction vessel; H. Glass sinter; I. Evaporation vessel; J. Magnetic valve; K. Collection vessel. After Abell (University of Bristol, England).

AROMATIC HYDROCARBONS

The as-received lunar soil sample was extracted with benzene-methanol and the extract chromatographed on silica gel (Kvenvolden, NASA Ames Research Center, California). After elution with n-hexane to remove alkanes, the column was eluted with benzene to isolate aromatic compounds. Although absorption bands were observed at 224, 274 and 280 nm (nanometer — a billionth of a meter), these were also present in the sand blank, and the presence of aromatic hydrocarbons indigenous to the lunar sample could not be inferred. In a similar manner combined gas chromatography-mass spectrometry of lunar extracts showed the presence of nanogram quantities of toluene, C_8 alkyl benzene, phenol and diphenyl which were judged to probably be contaminants although these compounds did not appear in the procedural blank. In the analysis in which thin layer analysis showed hydrocarbons (Nagy, University of Arizona), the greatest concentration of hydrocarbons appeared in the fine-grained portion of the sample and the least in the coarse-grained portion. The conclusion from those experiments is that aromatics appeared to be present in the as-received lunar samples but little confidence was placed in their being indigenous to the moon.

Heating of the sample to 400°C. failed to show the presence of a series of hetero-aromatic systems such as pyridines, furanes and thiophenes, but pyrolysis to higher temperatures produced benzene and toluene above 500°C. At still higher temperatures other alkyl benzenes and naphthalenes were observed and these were accompanied by styrenes, indenes, thiophenes and diphenyl. A number of laboratories observed aromatic compounds of the

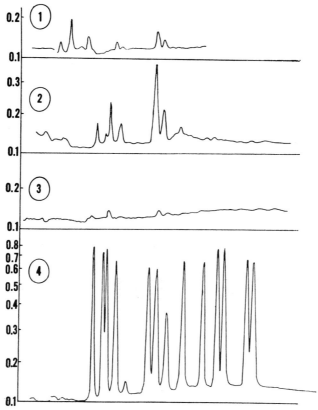

Fig. 5-5 Detection of amino acids in lunar fines, sample 10086, using ion exchange chromatography. Chromatogram no. 1 shows resolution of unhydrolyzed aqueous extract. Pair of peaks on the right correspond to retention times of glycine and alanine. Three main peaks on left are probably neither amino acids nor peptides. No. 2 is chromatogram after hydrolysis of aqueous extract. Retention times of principal peaks (left to right) correspond to aspartic acid, threonine (shoulder), serine, glutamic acid, glycine and alanine. No. 3 is chromatogram for blank analysis without a lunar sample. No. 4 is chromatogram of authentic amino acids, from left to right, aspartic acid, threonine, serine, glutamic acid, proline, glycine, alanine, cysteine/2, valine, methionine, isoleucine, leucine, tyrosine, phenylalanine (about 0.1 µg each). After Hare (Geophysical Laboratory).

foregoing types and little doubt exists as to their origin as pyrolysis products.

In summary, benzene and toluene were detected in lunar samples by several laboratories but could not be confidently accepted as indigenous compounds.

AMINO ACIDS

Considerable interest was focused on amino acids which terrestrially are the structural elements of proteins, and two laboratories (Nagy, University of Arizona; Fox, University of Miami) detected a limited number of such compounds in samples of the lunar soil. In one case, glycine and alanine were observed in direct aqueous extracts of lunar fines. To recover any bound amino acids present in the sample, the residue of the aqueous extract was subjected to conventional hydrolytic treatment and the hydrolysate examined by ion-exchange chromatography using an ultra-sensitive apparatus, with results as illustrated in Fig. 5-5. The following amino acids were detected by Fox (University of Miami):

aspartic acid	0.004 ppm.
threonine	0.001 ppm.
serine	0.006 ppm.
glutamic acid	0.008 ppm.
glycine	0.021 ppm.
alanine	0.012 ppm.

Controls and blanks were satisfactory in the sense that they contained much lower levels of amino acids, 0.0005 ppm. and exhibited different patterns of abundance. These findings were confirmed in part by Nagy (University of Arizona) who reported:

glycine	0.032 ppm.
alanine	0.036 ppm.
ethanolamine	0.022 ppm.
urea	0.065 ppm.

The indicated levels of abundance were 3 to 10 times those in the analytical background, and, as in the first case, such organic compounds were not detected in the exhaust products of a lunar retro-rocket engine. Other laboratories reported amino acids in their samples to be less than 0.001 ppm. (Ponnamperuma, NASA Ames Research Center, California), and less than 0.1 ppm. (Oro, University of Houston) using derivatization techniques for gas chromatography. Amino acids may thus be present in at least two samples of lunar soil.

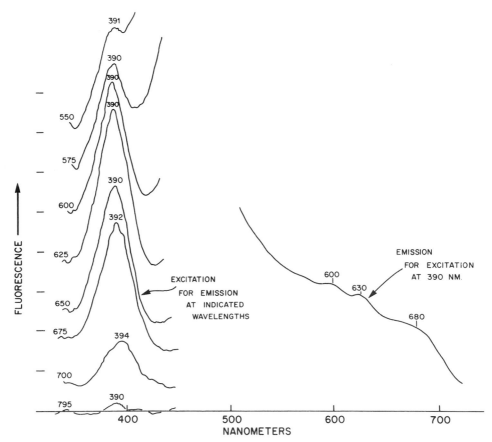

Fig. 5-6. Fluorescence detection of porphyrin-like compounds in lunar soil. Pigments detected in Apollo 11 were due to novel synthesis in rocket combustion; those in Apollo 12 evidently are indigenous to lunar soil. After Hodgson (University of Calgary, Canada).

PORPHYRINS

Porphyrins are tetrapyrrole pigments which are the molecular skeletons for the colored components of chlorophyll and hemoglobin. They are of particular interest in terms of both fossil and prebiotic biochemical structures. Tetrapyrrole pigments are normally detected and characterized by their absorption spectra, but fluorescence spectra are more sensitive and more specific for identification. Two laboratories attempted to detect porphyrins in extracts of the lunar soil. One reported that porphyrins were not detected above analytical limits of about 0.0001 ppm. (Rho, Jet Propulsion Laboratory); the other (Ponnamperuma, NASA Ames Research Center, California) reported porphyrin-like pigments at about 0.0001 ppm., well above background noise in the analysis. Similar pigments, however, were detected in the rocket exhaust along with other fluorescent pigments (Fig. 5-6), and indigenous porphyrins if present in the lunar soil were completely masked by the synthetically produced porphyrin-like pigments. An Apollo 12 sample which was evidently free of rocket pollutants, however, showed the presence of pigments which appeared to be tetrapyrroles in fluorescent behavior. These were evidently indigenous to the lunar sample and were either truly indigenous to the moon or were due to infallen meteoritic space dust. Concentration was estimated to be 0.00005 ppm. (Ponnamperuma, NASA Ames Research Center, California).

BIOLIPIDS IN GENERAL

The analyses for biolipids, in general, were much less sensitive than for porphyrin. The analytical approach in most instances was to extract the lunar soil with organic and aqueous solvents and to resolve the mixture before or after hydrolysis with thin layer, ion-exchange or gas chromatography. In some instances mass spectrometry was also used. The compounds sought are given below with the detection limits of the particular analysis (Ponnamperuma, NASA Ames Research Center, California):

fatty acids	0.01	ppm.
nucleic acid bases	0.001	ppm.
sugars (pentoses and hexoses)	0.0006	ppm.
biolipids, in general	0.005	ppm.

ORGANIC SULFUR COMPOUNDS

Elemental sulfur was estimated by thin layer chromatography (Nagy, University of Arizona) to range from 0.2 to 1.8 ppm. although some laboratories claimed that free sulfur was not present in the lunar samples. Thin layer chromatography also indicated the presence of organic sulfur compounds, and compounds of this type appeared in high resolution mass spectrometry, but these may have been formed during extraction procedures as an artifact. Hydrolysis of a lunar sample with 6 N. hydrochloric acid yielded substantial quantities of H_2S indicating about 700 ppm. of sulfide in the original material.

CARBONACEOUS MATERIAL

The specific organic compounds identified or tentatively identified accounted for very little of the total carbon present in the lunar soil, and it is believed that the bulk of the carbon exists in a nonvolatile form, either as carbide or as an undefined elemental carbon (amorphous or graphite). Scanning electron micrographs showed small cavities which could possibly have contained carbonaceous substances before they were broken open (Nagy, University of Arizona). Any organic material located in mineral enclosures would represent organic matter truly indigenous to the moon. Thus when the silicate matrix of the lunar samples was destroyed by hydrofluoric and hydrochloric acids, the amounts of carbon in the residue which may consist of highly polymeric organic matter, acid-resistant carbides and elemental carbon was between 30 and 40 ppm. The observations that substantial proportions of the total carbon evolved as CO and CO_2 rather than CH_4 on pyrolysis of the samples suggest that only a minor amount of the lunar sample nonvolatile carbon is present as complex polymers of C-H compositional type.

Organic compounds involving silicon, siloxanes, etc. appeared in analyses of lunar soils. While these were perhaps present in the lunar regolith and as such would indicate a fascinating new kind of chemistry for naturally occurring substances, current data indicate that they may be only analytical artifacts (Ponnamperuma, NASA Ames Research Center, California).

ISOTOPE ABUNDANCES FOR CARBON AND SULFUR

Carbon in the lunar soil is enriched in C^{13} relative to the PDB (Chicago) standard by about 19 $^0/_{00}$ (Kaplan, UCLA). The carbon of breccias is lighter, about ±5 $^0/_{00}$, and that of fine-grained rocks still lighter at –20 to –25 $^0/_{00}$. Meteoritic organic carbon (non-carbonate) is commonly –15 $^0/_{00}$; terrestrial organic carbon is –20 to –30 $^0/_{00}$. During pyrolysis of lunar carbonaceous material some fractions of the evolved gas were enriched in C^{13} and others depleted in C^{13} relative to the δC^{13} of the total sample. In studies on sulfur isotopes, all of the sulfur appeared to be evolved as H_2S on treatment with acid; this chemical behavior suggested the presence of troilite, and the isotopic distribution showed the same pattern as did the carbon: the lunar soil more enriched in the heavy isotope and the basaltic rocks the least enriched (Kaplan, UCLA). For a given soil sample, the smaller grain sizes are more enriched in the heavy isotope than the coarser material. The overall values for sulfur isotopes fell in the range δS^{34} = +4 to +8 $^0/_{00}$, based on meteoritic sulfur = 0 $^0/_{00}$; terrestrial sulfur in mafic igneous rocks and magmatic sulfide ores is ±2 $^0/_{00}$, and sedimentary sulfides range widely from +8 to –40 $^0/_{00}$.

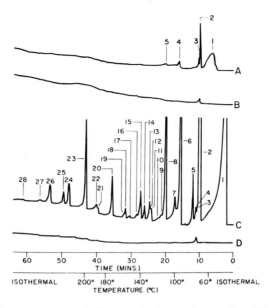

Fig. 5-7. Gas chromatogram of the pyrolysis products of a 675.8 mg powdered chip from the inside of a lunar breccia (No. 10002, 54), heated to 700°C. in He, Peak 1, CH₄; 2, CO₂ C₂H₄, and C₂H₆; 3, 4, and 5, C₅H₆, C₅H₈, and C₅H₁₀; 6 benzene; 7, thiophene; 8, toluene; 9 and 10, methyl thiophenes; 11, ethyl benzene; 12, 13 and 14, p-, m-, and o-xylenes; 15 and 18, styrene and methyl styrene; 16, 17, and 19, C₃ alkyl benzenes; 20, indene; 21 and 22, methyl indenes; 23, naphthalene; 24 and 25, methyl naphthalenes; 26, diphenyl; 27 and 28, C₂ alkyl naphthalenes. Identifications made with a Hitachi RMU-6E mass spectrometer connected to a Perkin-Elmer 226 gas chromatograph, (polyphenyl ether capillary column, 50-foot by 0.02 inch, internal diameter). After Murphy (St. Joseph's College, Connecticut).

ORGANISMS

Three thousand tests for viable organisms were carried out with nine nutrient media, at four temperatures in three different atmospheric mixtures of nitrogen, oxygen and carbon dioxide. No viable life forms were found, not even terrestrial contaminants (Oyama, NASA Ames Research Center, California).

The lunar soil failed to show the presence of microfossils that would have indicated the one-time presence of lunar life. Of interest, but of no vital significance, was an observation on a multitude of submicron-sized spheroids going down in diameter to a few hundredths of a micron, with a size distribution similar to that of sexually reproducing microorganisms. This was not to propose, however, that there were solid glass protozoa in the moon (Cloud, University of California, Santa Barbara)! Micropaleontological studies confirmed the foregoing observations with thin sections containing elongate, spheroidal, spinoise and actinomorphic structures superficially resembling terrestrial microfossils, but there was no evidence of indigenous biological activity (Schopf, UCLA), and it was agreed by all investigators that optical and electron microscope studies showed a total absence of structures that could be interpreted as biological in origin (Barghoorn, Harvard University).

SUMMARY

Carbon is present on the surface of the moon, but it must be classed as a trace element since it occurs at levels no greater than a few hundred parts per million. Of the total carbon only a very small fraction may exist as indigenous organic compounds. Most of the nonvolatile carbon is in the form of carbides or elemental carbon. Carbon also exists as low molecular weight hydrocarbons (largely methane), carbon monoxide and possibly carbon dioxide. Terrestrial rocks commonly contain polymerized organic matter and a wide variety of biolipids such as hydrocarbons, amino acids, nucleic acid bases, sugars, fats and pigments. Some of these, namely amino acids and porphyrin pigments, were probably detected in the lunar soil but the data are few and not completely confirmed. In addition, no evidence was obtained for the other biolipids and the conclusion is that there is little reason to attribute the indicated amino acids and porphyrins to extraterrestrial living organisms, but rather, if present, to prebiotic chemical synthesis in the solar system which undoubtedly is responsible for the polymeric organic matter.

6

PETROLOGY:

Experimental Studies and Origin of the Lavas

INTRODUCTION

Most of the petrological relationships established by microscopic and mineralogical studies have been discussed in the chapters on the rocks and minerals. In this chapter we discuss the experimental studies, the evidence of liquid immiscibility, and conclude with a section on the origin of the lavas.

EFFECTS OF HIGH PRESSURE ON LUNAR BASALTS

Ringwood (Australian National University) and O'Hara (Edinburgh University) have studied the behavior of lunar samples under high pressures. The pressure at the center of the moon, at a depth of 1734 km. is 47 kilobars (47,000 bars) (one bar = 10^6 dynes/cm.^{2} = 1 atmosphere = 14.15 lb./in.^{2}). This pressure is reached at depths of about 200 km. in the Earth, in the outer regions of the mantle. The phase relations are shown in Figs. 6-1 and 6-2. The most significant result is that material of lunar basalt composition transforms to a much more dense rock type, eclogite, at pressures of above 12 kilobars at 1100°C. At higher temperatures, the pressure needed to effect the transformation rises slowly, increasing at about 20 bars per degree centigrade. Extrapolation of the transformation to lower temperatures (Fig. 6-3) indicates that at zero pressure the transformation could occur at temperatures just above 500°C. Whether the transformation would occur depends on the kinetics involved.

The transition from basalt to eclogite involves changing from the mineral assemblage ilmenite-clinopyroxene-plagioclase to one composed of garnet-rutile-clinopyroxene. Thus the transition is not sharp but is smeared out over a pressure and temperature interval as the different mineral phases react. However, in comparison with terrestrial rocks, the interval is surprisingly narrow (2 kilobars at 1100°C.). The general mineral stability fields are shown on Fig. 6-3 which also shows the range of temperature distribution within

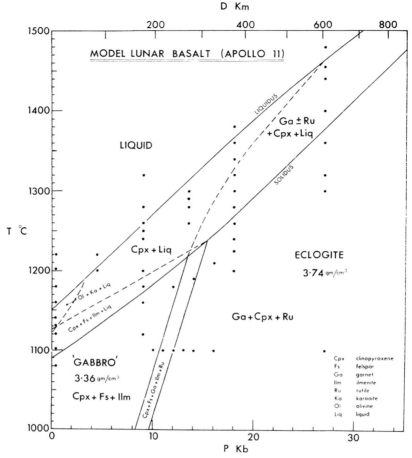

Fig. 6-1. Stability fields of mineral assemblages and melting equilibria in average Apollo 11 basalt. After Ringwood and Essene (Australian National University).

the moon, according to various workers. The low pressure at which the basalt-eclogite transition occurs (and the narrow pressure interval) are a direct consequence of the differences in chemistry of the lunar basalts, in comparison with terrestrial equivalents. Particularly critical in changing the mineral stability fields are the low content of sodium, and silicon, and the high Fe/Mg ratio.

The density of lunar eclogite is about 3.7 gm./cm.³ This high density places important constraints on the composition of the moon. If the moon has the composition of Apollo 11 basalt throughout, then the phase relations indicate that it would change to the dense phase eclogite, at depth. Figure 6-3 indicates that the temperatures in the interior are above about 750°C. at depths below 300 km. The pressure and temperature environment is thus well within the eclogite field and the long time available would ensure that equilibrium would be attained. It is thus reasonable to suppose, if the moon were composed of lunar basalt, that it would possess a central core of dense eclogite. Since the transformation occurs at low pressures, estimates of a core radius of about 1400 km. have been made, overlain by an outer 350 km. thick shell of basalt. This is an unrealistic model from many lines of evidence. From the moment of inertia studies, it appears that the moon has a uniform radial density distribution. Ringwood, O'Hara and co-workers agree that the moon cannot have the composition of Apollo 11 basalt throughout. They conclude that the basalt is derived by small degrees of partial melting deep in the interior of the moon. The nature of the parent material, the degree of partial melting and the depth at which this occurred are discussed in the next section.

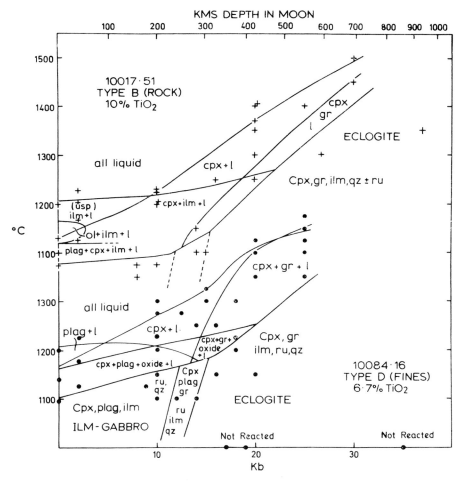

Fig. 6-2. Pressure-temperature relations for two Apollo 11 samples. After O'Hara (University of Edinburgh, Scotland).

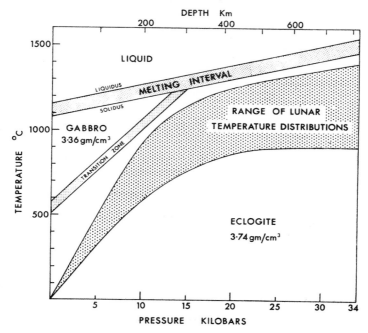

Fig. 6-3. The relation of the stability fields for gabbro, eclogite and liquid, with probable range of internal temperatures in the moon. After Ringwood and Essene (Australian National University).

MELTING BEHAVIOR OF APOLLO 11 BASALTS

The behavior of the lunar basalts during melting may be seen on Figs. 6-1, 6-2 and 6-4. The melting relationships have been studied at pressures from one atmosphere up to 30 kilobars, a pressure reached at a depth of about 700 km. within the moon.

At one atmosphere pressure, the liquidus temperature (the temperature at which melting of the various mineral phases is complete, or the temperature at which the first crystalline phase appears) lies within the range 1140 – 1220°C., as determined by various workers studying both the lunar rocks and synthetic mixtures approximating their composition. As the rock continues to crystallize, a sequence of mineral phases appears. Again the experimental sequences differ due to differing synthetic mixes and crucible compositions, but the overall picture is fairly consistent. Fe-Ti oxides (armalcolite) appear early. The first silicate to appear is olivine. Armalcolite reacts with the melt to produce ilmenite, and olivine reacts to form clinopyroxene. Finally, after about 30% of the rock has crystallized, plagioclase appears. This late appear- ance of plagioclase is a critical factor in discussing the europium depletion. The depletion in this element, which is concentrated in the plagioclase feldspar lattice, cannot be due to early crystallization and removal of plagioclase, as suggested by many workers. Akimoto (University of Tokyo) found that variation in the partial pressure of oxygen, by several orders of magnitude, (10^{-8} – 10^{-13} atm.) did not affect the order in which the minerals appeared. Where chromium was a constituent of the synthetic mixtures studied, a Cr-spinel phase was the first mineral to appear. The high content of chromium in the lunar rocks thus severely limits the amount of early crystal removal which could have occurred, and argues against near-surface fractionation as an important factor in the evolution of the Apollo 11 chemistry.

Following the appearance of plagioclase, there is abundant crystallization of the three main rock-forming minerals, ilmenite, clinopyroxene and plagioclase, until all the silicate melt is crystallized, and the "solidus" in the phase diagram is reached.

The order of crystallization in the rocks established from microscopic petrological studies is shown in Fig. 6-5. Ilmenite appears first, followed by pyroxene, plagioclase, troilite, with late crystallization of K feldspar, tridymite, cristobalite and ulvöspinel. Note that plagioclase does not appear until about 30% of the melt has crystallized, and that the accessory phases such as K feldspar, apatite and cristobalite appear very late in the cooling history of the melt.

There is abundant evidence in the natural rock textures of rapid crystallization (aided by the low viscosity). Skinner (Yale University) comments that the presence of sulfides which have crystallized from an immiscible sulfide liquid of high density ($\sim$ 5 gm./cm.³) may indicate either rapid crystallization, or late appearance of the immiscible sulfide liquid, or both. Certainly, such a dense liquid would rapidly separate, even in the low gravity field of the moon, from a silicate melt, whose density was about 3.0 gm./cm.³

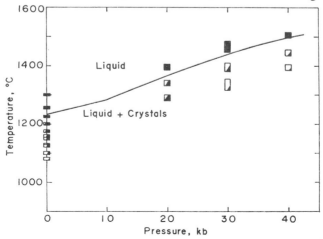

Fig. 6-4. Melting relations of a lunar rock. After Akimoto (University of Tokyo).

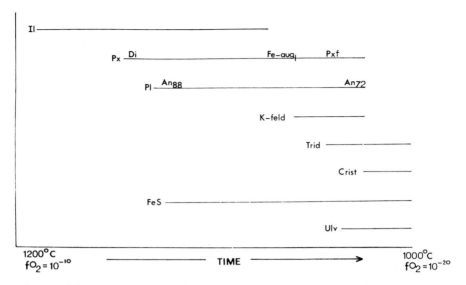

Fig. 6-5. The order of crystallization in lunar rocks, with possible temperatures and fugacities of oxygen (in atm). Il = ilmenite, Px = pyroxene, Di = diopside, Fe-aug = ferroaugite, pxf = pyroxferroite, Pl = plagioclase, K-feld = K-feldspar, Trid = tridymite, Crist = cristobalite, FeS = troilite, Ulv = ulvöspinel. After Bailey (University of Manchester, England).

MELTING BEHAVIOR AT HIGHER PRESSURES

The melting behavior up to 30 kilobars (equivalent to 700 km. depth in the moon) may be seen from Figs. 6-1 and 6-2. The minerals found in the basalts persist to pressures of about 4 kilobars. At higher pressures, the first mineral phase to appear (the so-called liquidus phase) is clinopyroxene. This persists over a very wide pressure and temperature interval, until at about 25 kilobars (equivalent to a depth of about 550 km. in the moon), garnet appears as a liquidus phase.

If the rocks with Apollo 11 chemistry crystallized in the pressure range 4 – 25 kilobars (~ 100-550 km. depths) and clinopyroxene was separated, then it would be possible to produce, by such fractional crystallization, a residual liquid rich in Ca, Al and Na, from which plagioclase could crystallize. This is one possible mechanism, according to Ringwood, of producing material similar in composition to the uplands.

SILICATE LIQUID IMMISCIBILITY; RESIDUUM; MESOSTASIS

The lunar magmas (melts) appear to have followed what might be considered a normal crystallization for most of their cooling history. This means, among other things, that early formed minerals such as ilmenite, pyroxene and plagioclase generally sequentially crystallized (with some overlap) from a magma constantly changing in composition. However, at a very late stage, perhaps when 90 – 98% of the lunar magma had crystallized, liquid immiscibility occurred — a process long suspected but never definitely proven for terrestrial rocks. In its simplest form, liquid immiscibility is a phenomenon exhibited by certain (synthetic) silicate liquids at high temperatures, wherein a melt of a specific bulk composition is unable to exist as a single homogeneous liquid. Instead the one liquid splits into two liquids which are unable to mix; the situation would be analogous to oil and water. Both silicate liquids which result would have distinctly different chemical properties, and differences in viscosity and density.

E. Roedder (U.S. Geological Survey) and P.M. Weiblen (University of Minnesota) have made an exhaustive study of the liquid immiscibility which they observed in the Tranquillity Base rocks, on the basis of unmistakable textural evidence (supported by chemical analyses) of globules of one composition found within globules of distinctly different composition. In Figs. 6-6 and 6-7 the occurrence of high silica and iron melts are illustrated; the melts, of course, have long since cooled and are represented by glass globules of each characteristic composition, in this case one high in silica and the other high in iron. Other evidence for immiscibility is also found, such as low index refraction glass inclusions in the outer margin of many late plagioclase crystals, but these are not discussed further here.

The average SiO_2 content for the lunar rocks of approximately 40% is low in comparison with terrestrial basalts, yet by the process of silicate liquid immiscibility it is possible to obtain two fractions: (a) one very high in SiO_2, K_2O and other selected elements, similar in many ways to a potassic granite, and (b) one low in SiO_2 and K_2O but very high in FeO and other elements characteristic of pyroxenite. In Table 6-1 the average chemical analyses of the two immiscible phases, determined from analysis of globules, are presented and clearly show the extreme contrast in composition of the two phases. (The reason for immiscibility is complex but is based upon bonding differences between atoms in the two liquids such that a minimum energy state is achieved.)

From Table 6-1 it is clear that one liquid (now a glass) is formed which is high Si and K, but it may also be surmised that other elements would likely be concentrated in this phase. There is very definite evidence that P, U, Zr and the rare-earth elements, as well as others, are concentrated in the late-forming, high silica glass not only by virtue of chemical analyses, but also on the basis of the fact that small quantities of many minerals containing these elements are found in this association and nowhere else in the lunar rocks. For example, in the high silica areas, apatite, fayalite, rutile, K-feld-

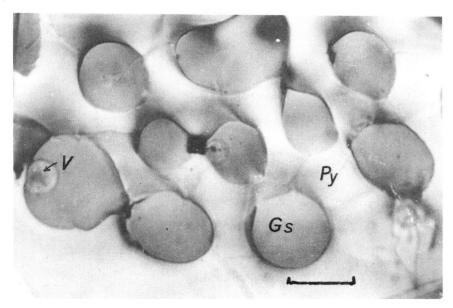

Fig. 6-6. Photomicrograph of late interstitial crystal of pyroxferroite (Py) containing blebs of clear, high-silica glass (Gs). V = vapor (shrinkage bubble or gas). Scale bar = 10 microns. Plane transmitted light. Sample 10003 (Type B). After Roedder (U.S. Geological Survey) and Weiblen (University of Minnesota).

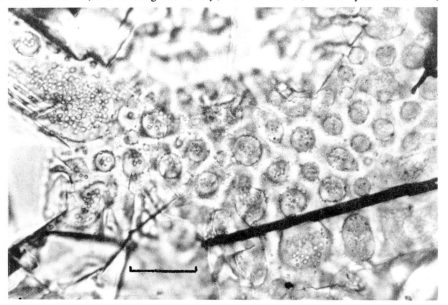

Fig. 6-7. Photomicrograph through blebs of high silica-glass embedded in a single plagioclase crystal. Each bleb contains tiny spheres of high index material believed to be high-iron glass. Scale bar = 10 microns. Plane transmitted light. Sample 10057 (Type A). After Roedder (U.S. Geological Survey) and Weiblen (University of Minnesota).

spar, quartz and other SiO_2 minerals, pyroxferroite (in part), and zirconium-bearing minerals have been identified. Because the high silica glass and minerals crystallizing within it are among the last to form, they are often referred to as late-forming or "residuum" minerals; both of these terms are used interchangeably throughout this book. Also, owing to the fact that these late-forming or residuum minerals (or globules) must occupy those areas remaining after 90 – 98% of the magma has crystallized, they must, of necessity, crystallize or solidify in between or within existing grains of early formed minerals. The technical term for interstitial material between larger mineral grains is "mesostasis."

Table 6-1. Chemical analysis (normalized to 100%) of high- and low-silica glasses resulting from silicate liquid immiscibility (in weight %). Analysis by Roedder (U.S. Geological Survey) and Weiblen (University of Minnesota).

Type	SiO_2	Al_2O_3	FeO	MgO	CaO	Na_2O	K_2O	TiO_2	Total
high-silica	76.2	11.6	2.6	0.3	1.8	0.4	6.6	0.5	100.0
low-silica	46.4	3.1	32.3	2.2	11.3	0.1	0.3	4.3	100.0

The mesostasis, generally irregular areas about 0.1 – 0.2 mm. across, occupies up to 10% of the lunar rocks and is composed of glassy or extremely fine-grained, multiphase material; it is found usually between pyroxene and plagioclase. The minerals of the residuum are extremely difficult to identify as would be expected because of their small size which has resulted from the rapidity with which the late-forming, immiscible silicate liquid probably crystallized. Although the residual (mesostasis) phases are extremely interesting both from the point of view of their unusual chemistry, rare minerals and petrologic significance, it should be realized that they represent only a very *small* proportion of the total rock. The fact that the high silica immiscible silicate is similar to some terrestrial granites should not be misconstrued to imply that there are large (or even minor) areas of granite on the moon. At this time the likelihood of abundant granite on the moon appears remote.

In any glass certain chemical elements are more soluble than if the same elements were in crystalline minerals. In the case of potassium and phosphorus, both are concentrated in the high silica glass, and in addition both are fertilizer elements. Unusually rapid growth has been reported for certain plants when they were placed on the Apollo 11 rocks after return to Earth. Even though the total abundance of potassium and phosphorus is low in the lunar rocks, the fact that they are concentrated in the residual glass, and probably in a relatively soluble form, may explain the reported fertilizer activity attributed to Apollo 11 rocks.

PETROGENESIS — ORIGIN OF THE LAVAS

The origin of the volcanic rocks which flood the great maria basins is the subject of much debate among the investigators. There is no uniformity of agreement, due mainly to the differing emphasis put on the various facts available. Thus to some geochemists, the evidence of depletion of europium is conclusive evidence for near surface removal of plagioclase feldspar, host for the element. The experimental petrologists are equally convinced that the late appearance of plagioclase during the crystallization sequence precludes this explanation. Two questions may be asked: (1) What was the source of the lavas and how were they melted? (2) What was the subsequent history of the melt prior to and during solidification?

In examining these questions, various interpretations of the information available are possible, and this is reflected in the differing origins proposed. In the following discussion, we shall adopt what appear to be the most reasonable of the alternative hypotheses. It should be remembered that the progress of scientific research lies not in the proof of theories, but their disproof, an approach which owes much to the scientific philosopher Karl Popper.

SOURCE OF THE LAVAS

Two main origins were debated: firstly, an origin from within the moon by various degrees of partial melting of parent material at depth, or, secondly, that they were derived by impact melting during the great maria basin forming events. In either case, later fractionation, for example by crystal sinking near the surface, may have altered the composition of the silicate liquid which finally crystallized to produce the Apollo 11 basalts.

PARTIAL MELTING

Various degrees of partial melting of material deep within the moon are capable of explaining the chemistry, mineralogy, the high pressure and melting studies on the lunar lavas. Both O'Hara (University of Edinburgh) and Ringwood (Australian National University) support this origin, although there are some differences in detail. One requirement is that the melt be less dense than the overall density of the moon (assuming a uniform radial density distribution) so that it will rise to the surface. Various workers calculate a density of about 3 gm./cm.^{3} for the molten lava, which crystallizes at the surface to form the Apollo 11 basalts with densities 3.3 − 3.4 gm./cm.^{3}. The experimental evidence, as shown in Figs. 6-1 and 6-2 indicates that at depths of about 200 − 500 km., the melt is in equilibrium with clinopyroxene. At shallower depths, olivine and armalcolite, the new lunar mineral, are the phases present during melting. At depths greater than 500 km., the dense phase garnet appears. Ringwood states that very small degrees of partial melting are possible, since the attainment of equilibrium between crystals and melt is independent of the relative amounts of crystals and liquid. He concludes that melting took place at depths between 200 and 500 km. (radius of moon = 1740 km.). Melting at shallow depths would leave a refractory residue of olivine and armalcolite. This would have a high density of about 3.5 gm./cm.^{3}, too dense to be acceptable as a large component of the moon. Although such a dense residue at shallow depth might at first sight explain the mascons, a chief argument against melting at shallow depths hinges on the mascons. If they are due to the volcanic activity, then they must have been emplaced in crust strong enough, and hence cool enough, to support them. If the crust was hot enough to cause partial melting, then it would be much too weak to support the mascons.

Melting at depths greater than 500 km. is also unlikely. The high pressure studies indicate that at such depths a melt of the composition of the Apollo 11 basalts would be in equilibrium with clinopyroxene and garnet. This mineral assemblage will have a density greater than 3.6 gm./cm.^{3} and corresponds to the dense rock type, eclogite. Thus, if the Apollo 11 basalts come from great depths, they have melted from a source rock denser than the overall density of the moon. The uniform distribution of density with depth precludes this. There is no evidence for an eclogite core extending to within 500 km. of the surface. For these reasons it is thought that the Apollo 11 basalts originated by partial melting of a pyroxene-type source rock between 200 and 500 km. depth.

The source of the heat is most likely to have been a combination of residual heat left over following accretion, together with some heat production due to radioactive heating. Neither source appears to be adequate on its own, but a combination must have been sufficient to raise the lunar interior to the melting point of basalt (—1200°C.) for about one billion years between 3 and 4 billion years ago. Since about that time, the interior has been too cold to produce basaltic lava flows, and the moon has remained a rigid body, supporting the mascons and its irregular shape.

IMPACT MELTING

Several workers have suggested an origin for the basalts by melting of the lunar crust or substratum during the great impacts which formed the maria basins. The fact that the density of the Apollo 11 rocks is close to that of the whole moon lends a certain initial attraction to the hypothesis.

However, there are several difficulties. The uplands are clearly of different composition, as is suggested by the Surveyor VII analysis (Table 4-1). Such a composition, or that of the "anorthosites" thought to be of highland derivation by Wood and others, could not produce the Apollo 11 rock composition, either by partial or complete melting. But perhaps the uplands represent an older lunar crust through which the giant (50 – 100 km.) objects broke, to dig the maria basins, melting the substratum.

Several points tell against this hypothesis:

1. The age relationships are discussed in Chapter 7, page 172. Both the radiometric ages and the relative maria ages, based on crater counting techniques, indicate a prolonged period of maria filling. In contrast, the impact hypothesis calls for a more or less simultaneous production of the several different maria.

2. There is fairly general accord that the Apollo 11 basalts cannot be representative of the lunar composition. As discussed on page 149, the transformation of such a composition to the dense rock type eclogite at shallow depths would mean a layered interior structure. This is not consistent with the geophysical evidence. Hence impact melting of near surface material must be followed by fractionation to produce the Apollo 11 composition. It will be shown in the next section that such near-surface fractionation is unlikely to have occurred, hence placing a severe restriction on the hypothesis. Much evidence comes from the trace element abundances to indicate that the chemistry of the Apollo 11 basalts cannot be representative of the entire moon. The uranium and thorium contents, if typical of the whole moon, would cause widespread melting at present.

The evidence that the moon has been inactive over the past 2 – 3 aeons indicates that most of the heat-producing elements have been stripped from the deep interior. The concentration levels of many other elements, (e.g., Ba, Zr, Rare Earths) are enriched in the Apollo 11 basalts by factors of 50 – 100 over cosmic abundances. These elements do not enter the common rock-forming minerals in abundance and are the first to concentrate in partial melts. Their enrichment at the lunar surface parallels similar behavior in the Earth. These elements, which are probably concentrated in interstitial phases, will be incorporated in the early fractions of partial melts.

3. Meteorites striking the lunar surface at velocities greater than several kilometers per second have a kinetic energy equivalent to several times their mass of high explosives such as TNT. When stopped, the meteorite vaporizes and intense explosion results, and a crater similar to the terrestrial bomb or shell craters is blown. Small amounts of the country rock are melted and splashed out, cooling to glass. Such processes account for the abundant glass in the soil, produced during impact of smaller meteorites. The mechanisms of melting large volumes of lava during the excavation of the maria basins

are little understood. Impacts on such a scale are outside reasonable extrapolation from terrestrial experience.

It has been suggested that in order to produce a sufficient amount of lava the rocks were near their melting temperature before impact. The extra energy provided by the impact was sufficient to raise the temperature above the melting point. However, as we have seen above, this melt must then undergo fractionation to produce the Apollo 11 composition (see next section). Furthermore, a hot surface of the moon raises many problems. The large maria-forming impacts took place at the final stages of the heavy cratering of the uplands. The surface of the moon was cool enough to support the craters and is unlikely to have been very hot.

Thus numerous difficulties beset the impact melting hypothesis.

SUBSEQUENT HISTORY OF THE MELT

Did changes in the chemical composition of the lavas occur between production of the melt and solidification as the Apollo 11 basalts? As we have seen in the previous section, the question is critical for the impact melting theory.

During the cooling and crystallization of the lava, separation of early formed mineral phases may change the composition. This may happen during the ascent of the lava to the surface, and during the spreading of the lava across the maria, as well as during the final crystallization. The extremely fluid nature of the lavas (the viscosity is in the range 5 – 10 poises, comparable to that of heavy engine oil at room temperature, and about an order of magnitude lower than terrestrial lavas) enables them to spread out widely as thin sheets. These thin flows are not conducive to much crystal setting. They cool rapidly and crystallize quickly. Whenever a deep lava lake occurs, the opportunity is present for slow cooling and crystal settling, leading to compositional changes. Such conditions will occur occasionally on the moon, perhaps best of all where the lavas are confined within large craters (e.g., in the flooded craters such as Archimedes or Plato).

Similar conditions are likely to apply in the earliest flooding of the maria basins, when extensive ponding may occur. As the basins are filled, the extreme fluidity of the lavas allows them to flow freely over the lunar surface. Even vast outpourings will only rarely form deep lakes, but instead will flood widely across the lunar surface forming the irregular seas, spreading out from the circular basins. Mare Tranquillitatis is one such, and Oceanus Procellarum, the Ocean of Storms, site of the Apollo 12 landing, is another. They are of shallow depth in comparison with the circular maria, and do

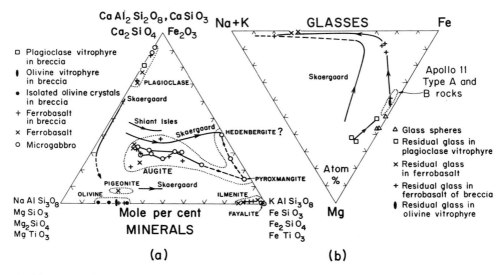

Fig. 6-8. Mineral and glass compositions from Apollo 11 rocks, with comparison trends from Skaergaard intrusion. After Smith (University of Chicago).

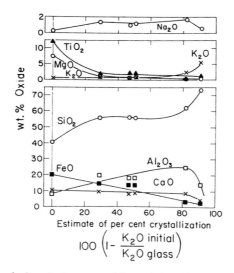

Fig. 6-9. Variation of chemical composition of Apollo 11 basalt with crystallization. After Smith (University of Chicago).

not have mascons. The restriction of the mascons to the circular maria is discussed in Chapter 8, page 197.

There is much evidence from the petrological studies that internal element fractionations occur within the rocks. Smith (University of Chicago) has deduced fractionation trends for both minerals and glasses. Figs. 6-8 and

6-9 show these trends, which resemble those of layered igneous intrusions on the earth. Although these trends are well displayed within individual minerals and rocks, yet the Apollo 11 rock suite does not show the characteristic changes in composition of a fractionated suite of rocks. The Apollo 12 rocks (LSPET, 1970) show more evidence of these effects (Fig. 4-14).

The chemistry, mineralogy and texture of the Apollo 11 rocks indicate that there has been little change in composition of the melt before final crystallization, and that the element concentrations in the present rocks closely resemble that of the initial melt. The factors that tell against the operation of near-surface fractionation include the following:

1. In terrestrial lavas, the appearance of large crystals (phenocrysts) in a matrix of small crystals or glass indicates that crystallization began well before eruption and was interrupted by rapid chilling following extrusion. Separation of early crystallizing phases is possible under these conditions. No such textures have been reported for the lunar lavas. The interrelations of the minerals indicate rapid crystallization of the main mineral phases over a limited temperature interval.

2. Chromium is an element which is rapidly depleted during fractional crystallization. Its concentration decreases dramatically in terrestrial basaltic lavas when opportunity for removal of early phases, which Cr enters, is present. In the Apollo 11 samples, Cr is present at high levels (about ten times that of typical terrestrial basalts) in both Type A and B rocks. In Apollo 12, some fractionation is apparent from the parallel decrease of Cr and Ni (Fig. 4-14). However, the general level of chromium abundances is high in both Apollo 11 and 12 rocks. Moderate degrees of fractionation would rapidly deplete the melt to levels of less than 100 ppm., which is not observed.

3. Many of the petrologists observed that the minerals showed much evidence of internal variation in composition. There is much evidence of intense melt-mineral fractionation at the microscopic level. The overall uniformity in composition of the rocks is in marked contrast, since separation of the complex minerals would produce a heterogeneous rock suite.

4. Many of the minerals present (ilmenite, sulfides and metallic iron, for example) are much denser than the melt and would readily separate, depleting the melt, in titanium, for example. The failure of these dense phases to separate (see comments by Skinner (Yale University) on page 151), indicates either very rapid crystallization, or late appearance of the phases, and, in any event, no fractionation.

5. It has been suggested that the high titanium content of the rocks might be a consequence of accumulation of crystals of ilmenite. However, there is no evidence from the rock fabric to indicate "cumulate" textures resulting from selective accumulation of crystals during cooling of silicate melts. The

evidence from the microscopic study of thin sections of rocks indicates that for much of the period of crystallization, the three main rock-forming minerals — ilmenite, pyroxene and plagioclase — were precipitating together.

6. Many of the trace elements are strongly concentrated in the Type A-high-K rocks, but the major element concentrations (including Cr) are similar in both Type A and B rocks. Hence the trace element variations are not due to fractionation of the main mineral phases, the usual cause in terrestrial rocks.

7. Strong depletion of the rare-earth element, europium, is characteristic of the lunar rocks, and would be consistent with removal of plagioclase feldspar, which is the chief host for this trace element. Various workers calculate that removal of between 50 – 90% of the feldspar would be needed to account for the observed depletion. However, plagioclase does not begin to precipitate until about 30% of the melt has already crystallized, and it then forms a complex intergrowth with ilmenite and pyroxene as the three phases precipitate together. Whatever the cause of the deficiency of europium, it does not appear to be due to near-surface fractionation.

8. The unfractionated character of the rare-earth abundance patterns indicates little near-surface fractionation.

In summary, near-surface fractionation appears to have been minimal during the crystallization of the Apollo 11 basalts. It has operated to a minor degree in the cooling of the Apollo 12 lavas. In neither case is it responsible for the major features of the chemistry.

7

AGE OF THE LUNAR ROCKS, ISOTOPE STUDIES, COSMIC RAY and SOLAR WIND EFFECTS

AGE OF THE APOLLO 11 SAMPLES

The age of the lunar rocks and fine material is one of the most important results of the scientific investigations of the lunar samples. The Preliminary Examination Team (LSPET 1969) using potassium-argon (K-Ar) techniques, (Fig. 7-1) found ages ranging from 2.7 – 3.7 billion years, or aeons.* Argon is likely to leak from rocks, and hence ages based on K-Ar techniques may give lower than the true age, or exhibit a spread due to variable loss. The LSPET (1970) age for the Apollo 12 rocks of 2.7 billion years appears to be low, for preliminary Rb-Sr ages of 3.3 billion years have been reported by Wasserburg and co-workers (California Institute of Technology). The maximum age of about 3.7 billion years for the Apollo 11 rocks led to the following comment by the Preliminary Examination Team:

> Perhaps the most exciting and profound observation made in the preliminary examination is the great age of the igneous rocks from this lunar region — it is clear that the crystallization of some Apollo 11 rocks may date back to times earlier than the oldest rocks found on Earth. (LSPET, 1969)

The subsequent scientific investigations applied most of the techniques of modern radiometric age dating to the lunar rocks. Their great age was confirmed.

The ages of the lunar rocks are important for many reasons:

1. The Apollo 11 ages from Mare Tranquillitatis date the time of filling of the maria basin.

2. Subsequent Apollo missions will enable the dates of filling of other maria basins to be established. The Apollo 12 data already indicate that this filling with lava occurs over an extended period of hundreds of millions of years. This is decisive evidence against impact produced melting as the source of the maria fill.

* Aeon: This engaging term was introduced by Urey to designate a period of one billion, a thousand million, or 10^9 years. It conjures a vision of the vast abyss of time represented by the passage of a billion years and it is used where appropriate in the text.

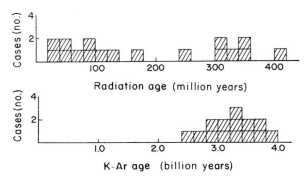

Fig. 7-1. Radiation and K-Ar ages of Apollo 11 rocks. After Funkhouser (State
University of New York).

3. The ages of the highlands, the excavation of the maria basins, and the
ages of the young ray craters will all be determined by future missions. In
this way, an absolute time scale of lunar events will be built up. It is already
possible, on the basis of detailed surface mapping to set up a relative time
scale (see Chapter 9, page 203 on the origin of the moon). Dating by radiometric methods of key selected units in this scale enables absolute ages to
be established over wide areas of the moon.

4. Finally it may be possible to calculate an age for the formation of the
moon, and hence discover its time relationship to the Earth, meteorites and
the sun. The Apollo 11 age data are the first step in this process and a wealth
of information has been accumulated.

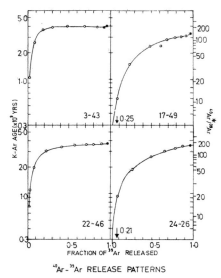

^{40}Ar-^{39}Ar RELEASE PATTERNS

Fig. 7-2. Ar^{40}-Ar^{39} release patterns from lunar rocks showing increase in apparent
K-Ar age as the more retentive sites release argon. After Turner (University of
Sheffield, England).

POTASSIUM(K)-ARGON(AR) DATING

In addition to the LSPET investigation, Wanless and co-workers (Geological Survey of Canada) determined K-Ar dates (K^{40} decays to Ar^{40} with a half-life of 12.4×10^9 years, and also to Ca^{40} by β decay). The fines and the breccias contain large amounts of "excess" Ar^{40} (see page 190). In some of the samples, this contributes 99% of the Ar^{40}. In contrast, the rocks contain only small amounts of spallation produced Ar^{40} due to cosmic radiation. Wanless estimates that only $0.1 - 0.5\%$ of the total Ar^{40} in the rocks is due to this effect, and that nearly all is due to the *in situ* decay of K^{40}. He found ages ranging from $2260 - 3370$ million years, indicating, by comparison with other methods, that some diffusive loss of argon had occurred.

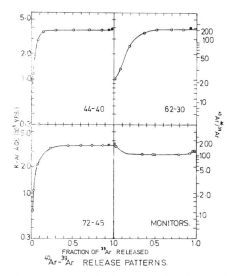

Fig. 7-3. Ar^{40}-Ar^{39} release patterns for lunar rocks. After Turner (University of Sheffield, England).

AR^{40}-AR^{39} AGES

This technique is a modification of the K-Ar technique used by Turner (University of Sheffield, England). The method depends on converting some of the K^{39} in the sample to Ar^{39} by neutron activation. The sample is then heated to release this Ar^{39} together with the Ar^{40} produced by decay of K^{40}. Thus both potassium and argon are effectively measured by the same analytical technique. In a sample which has quantitatively retained argon, both Ar^{39} and Ar^{40} will be in the same lattice sites and will be released in fixed proportions, and an age can be calculated. If argon has migrated within the rock, or if it has been lost or gained, variable Ar^{39}/Ar^{40} ratios will result. During heating of the sample to release the argon, that from the more readily outgassed sites is released first, and the Ar^{40}/Ar^{39} ratio will decrease as the more retentive sites release argon. The argon released at higher temperatures is considered to come from potassium lattice sites, and the age calculated from the ratios, to approach the true age.

Figs. 7-2 and 7-3 illustrate the apparent age increase as argon from the more retentive sites is released. Eventually a plateau of Ar^{40}/Ar^{39} ratios is reached, indicating a maximum age. From Turner's data, all the lunar rocks appear to have lost argon by variable amounts, from 7 to 48%. The spread in "high temperature" Ar^{40}/Ar^{39} ages is from 3.5 – 3.9 aeons and the average of 3.7 billion years agrees with Rb-Sr ages. Turner regards this spread of 400 million years as real, with the Type B-low K rocks giving higher ages ($\frown$ 3.8 billion years) compared to the Type A-high K rocks with ages of 3.6 billion years. This is additional evidence that two separate rock units have been sampled.

RUBIDIUM(Rb)-STRONTIUM(Sr) AGES

Rb-Sr* dating techniques have many advantages, including a simple decay scheme of parent to daughter involving weak β decay without lattice disruption, non-gaseous daughter product, and ready retention of daughter isotope in the parent crystal lattice site, due to generally similar geochemical behavior of the two elements. The method measures the time which has elapsed since Rb-Sr fractionation took place. At least two rock samples with differing Rb-Sr ratios are needed to determine this age, and they must have been cogenetic. In the case of the lunar rock samples, which are scattered from random meteorite impact craters, there is no *prima facie* case that they are from the same rock unit, or have an identical age of formation. Individual minerals within each rock formed at the same time and hence meet the requirements for establishing a meaningful age. Fig. 7-4 shows the rock data in the conventional plot of Sr^{87}/Sr^{86} vs. Rb^{87}/Sr^{86}. Two groups corresponding to Type A-high K-high-Rb and to Type B-low K-low Rb are apparent. Although an isochron could be drawn through these data, the ages so calculated are subject to the basic uncertainty that the rocks may be of differing ages.

Fig. 7-5 gives a similar plot of the data, illustrating the separation of the two groups and the displacement of the fines sample from a simple mixing line between the two groups. The approach using separated mineral fractions is shown in Figs. 7-6 and 7-7. These give ages ranging from 3.6 – 3.8 aeons.

---

* Rb^{-87} decays to Sr^{87} by β decay with a half-life usually given as 5.0×10^9 years. There is some uncertainty in the decay constant, but the various workers use similar values.

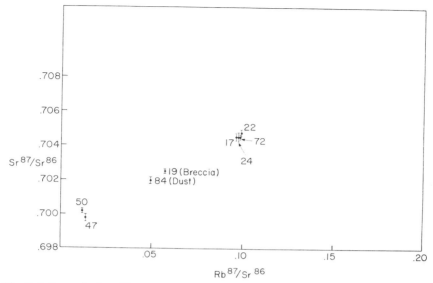

Fig. 7-4. Sr evolution diagram for whole rock samples. After Gopalan (U.C.L.A.).

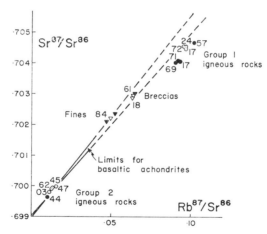

Fig. 7-5. Sr^{87} evolution diagram for lunar rocks. After Compston (Australian National University).

As was the case for the Ar^{40}/Ar^{39} ages, differences in the ages appear for the two rock types although in this case the relative groupings are reversed, with the high K rocks giving the older ages.

A striking feature of the Rb-Sr age studies is the low initial Sr^{87}/Sr^{86} ratio (the Type A-high K rocks contain slightly higher initial ratios than the Type B-low K rocks). In comparison with the cosmic Rb/Sr ratios, Rb was fractionated from Sr very early in the history of the solar system at about 4.6 aeons, and the source material of the lunar lavas has not been in a

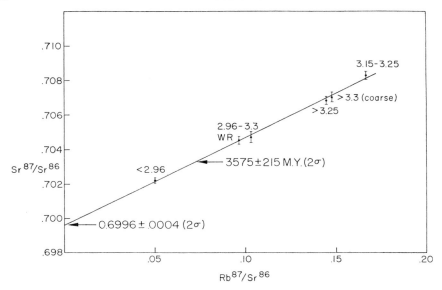

Fig. 7-6. Sr evolution diagram for various density fractions from rock 10017. After Gopalan (U.C.L.A.).

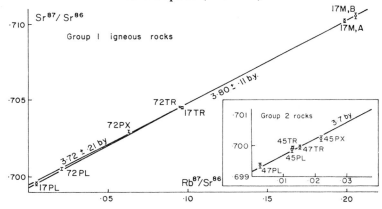

Fig. 7-7. Sr⁸⁷ evolution diagram for minerals separated from rocks. TR = total rock, Pl = plagioclase, Px = pyroxene, M = mesostasis. After Compston (Australian National University).

rubidium-rich environment since that time. According to Hurley and Pinson (Massachusetts Institute of Technology), the Rb/Sr ratio of the lunar source materials could not have exceeded about 0.006 since very early in the history of the solar system. The chondritic ratio is about 0.24, a factor of 40 greater, while estimates for the total Earth Rb/Sr ratio are about 0.03. The evidence from the Sr isotopes that the very low Rb/Sr ratio came into existence at about 4.6 aeons and not at the time of volcanism (at about 3.7 aeons) provides independent evidence for early loss of volatile elements, rather than evaporative losses at the time of eruption of the lavas.

Rb-Sr AGES OF FINE MATERIAL

Several workers have commented on the apparent old "age" of the fine material. The consensus is that the regolith has been derived mainly from local sources in Mare Tranquillitatis, with a minor (5 – 15%) component derived from elsewhere on the moon. Thus the fine material is a *mixture* of different components of differing ages and therefore bulk samples have no meaningful or unique age.

A "model age" may be calculated from the observed average Sr isotopic abundances in the fines. If an initial ratio equivalent to the basaltic achondrites (BABI) is assumed, the "age" so calculated for the fines is 4.6 aeons. Since this age is close to the assumed age of the condensation of the solar nebula it has been widely discussed. Clearly the fine material is mainly composed of local debris of the high-K and low-K rocks with ages of about 3.7 aeons. In order to account for the excess in radiogenic Sr^{87} in the fines, another component, labelled "magic" by Wasserburg, must be present. This may be the anorthositic fragments of possible highland derivation. Wasserburg suggests from the chemistry of the fines that they, and the breccia, contain a component with K/Rb and K/Cs ratios lower than the rocks and with probable higher Rb and Cs concentrations.

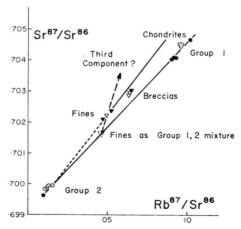

Fig. 7-8. Sr^{87} evolution diagram showing fines and breccias as mixtures of group 1 and group 2 rocks plus a smaller third component of high Sr^{87}/Sr^{86}. After Compston (Australian National University).

The 2% chondritic component in the soil cannot account for the excess radiogenic Sr^{87}. Fig. 7-8 illustrates how the apparent 4.6 billion year age arises. This diagram shows that the Sr^{87}/Sr^{86} ratios are displaced from the simple mixing line of the high K and Rb-low K and Rb rocks. The meteorite component can provide only a minor displacement, as indicated, and another component rich in radiogenic Sr^{87} is needed. The effect is to displace the Sr isotopic ratios for the fines to a position which can be assigned a model age of 4.6 aeons if an initial ratio is assumed.

The implication that a source of more radiogenic strontium exists on the moon raises interesting questions: Was there an early upward and outward concentration of Rb and the other elements which accompany it, very early in the history of the moon? The migration of Rb would be followed by Th, U, K, the rare-earths, Zr, Hf, and all the elements typically concentrated in the outer layers and crust of the Earth. If the moon has had a similar outward concentration, as discussed in the section on origin, this is of great significance for our views of planetary development.

URANIUM(U)-THORIUM(Th)-LEAD(Pb) AGES

The radioactive decays of uranium and thorium to yield daughter lead isotopes are much more complex than the K-Ar or Rb-Sr decay schemes. Th^{232} decays to Pb^{208}, emitting 6α and 4β particles, with a half-life of 13.9 billion years. U^{235} which comprises 0.72% of natural uranium, decays to Pb^{207} emitting 7α and 4β particles, with a half-life of 0.71 billion years. U^{238}, the principal isotope of uranium, comprising 99.28% of the element, decays to Pb^{206}, emitting 8α and 6β particles, with a half-life of 4.51 billion years, close to the accepted age of the meteorites and the Earth. The remaining lead isotope, Pb^{204} is non-radiogenic, and serves as an index of the amount of common lead present. Because of the length and complexity of the decay schemes, and the complex geochemical behavior of the three elements, the great potential of the lead method is not always realized. However, the lead isotope data have provided critical fingerprints for the lunar samples.

The total lead concentration is very low in the moon. The element was not detected by LSPET (1969) at 2 ppm. and ranges from 0.4 – 1.7 ppm. in the rocks and fine material (Table 4-4). This is low in comparison with average crustal lead concentrations of 15 ppm. and with the carbonaceous chondrite values of 3 – 4 ppm. The low abundance of lead parallels that of the other volatile elements and indicates loss of such elements at or before accretion of the moon. The comparatively high uranium and thorium contents mean that a major portion of the lunar lead is radiogenic in origin, so that the amount of common lead is very low. Thus contamination by terrestrial lead can be a serious problem.

The ratio U^{238}/Pb^{204}, frequently referred to as μ, is very distinct for terrestrial and lunar rocks. It is commonly in the range 5 – 10 for terrestrial rocks, and rarely exceeds 30. The mean value is about 9. In contrast, in the lunar rocks, the present day values (the ratio is usually so quoted) range from 200 – 1400. Assuming an age of 4.6×10^9 years for the moon, the initial ratio at accretion would be about 80. This ratio is one of the most distinctive indexes of lunar geochemistry. It serves, for example, to make a lunar origin for tektites highly improbable, for they display the terrestrial values of the ratio.

LEAD ROCK AGES

Tatsumoto (U.S. Geological Survey) obtained rock ages in the range 3.4 – 3.8 billion years, in general agreement with the Rb-Sr ages. Silver (California Institute of Technology) reports higher lead ages for the rocks, ranging from 4.1 – 4.2 billion years. Some of the disagreement between the various interpretations of the lead isotope data stems from the corrections applied for the amount of contamination by terrestrial lead. Silver concludes that essentially all the Pb^{204} in the lunar leads is due to terrestrial contamination. These discrepancies can only be resolved by further work to establish the true levels of Pb^{204} in the lunar samples.

LEAD DATA FOR THE FINE MATERIAL

The fine material contains about 1.4 ppm. lead, 0.5 ppm. uranium and 2 ppm. Th. The U^{238}/Pb^{204} ratio, μ, is about 240 and the lead is thus highly radiogenic, mainly derived by decay of U and Th. As is the case for the strontium age data, an apparent "age" of about 4.6 aeons can be calculated from the lead isotope data. Since the fines are composed mainly of fragments of igneous rocks with ages of 3.7 billion years, derived from the bedrock, the announcement of the apparent older "ages" at the Houston conference caused much speculation.

Wasserburg and co-workers (California Institute of Technology) postulate that an extra "magic" component is required to explain the "model ages" of 4.6 billion years given both by the Rb-Sr and the Th-U-Pb isotopic data. Silver also agrees that "an additional component of lead with higher Pb^{207}/Pb^{206} ratios than the composite value must be present in the fines." On the basis of his estimate of an age for the rocks of 4.1 – 4.2 billion years, he calculates that the excess leads are derived from material with an age of nearly 5 billion years. He concludes that the minimum age for the moon is *4.95 aeons!* This is several hundred million years older than the commonly accepted ages of 4.5 – 4.7 billion years for the age of the Earth and meteorites, and the inferred condensation of the solar nebula. The other students of the lead isotope data do not agree with this interpretation. Alternative explanations are possible. Compston and co-workers (Australian National University) have proposed a model involving multistage fractionation histories and migration of lead or uranium, to explain the apparent anomaly of the old regolith ages. Further testing of these models is needed.

FURTHER SIGNIFICANCE OF LEAD ISOTOPE DATA

Several other pertinent conclusions may be made from a study of the lead data:

a. Fission hypothesis. The isotopic ratios argue strongly against fission of the moon from the Earth. The U/Pb fractionation (and Rb-Sr fractionation) took place at about 4.6 aeons very close to the age of formation of the Earth. Hence fission would have to occur at this time and not later as in many variants of the fission hypothesis. Many other chemical difficulties beset the fission hypothesis. (See Chapter 9 on the origin of the moon.)

b. Meteoritic contribution. The low amount of Pb^{204} in the lunar fines and breccias restricts the amount of carbonaceous chondrites (which contain about 3 – 4 ppm. Pb) which can be added to the regolith to less than 2%.

c. Tektites. Tektites contain typical terrestrial lead isotope ratios and these are grossly dissimilar to lunar lead (see page 40).
Wetherill (University of California at Los Angeles) notes that the lead isotope ratios in the fines are not from a rare or unique sample, but include lead from many sources, including possibly the highlands. Lunar lead is thus in general predicted to be highly radiogenic, making a lunar origin for tektites improbable, a conclusion already reached on geochemical grounds.

SIGNIFICANCE OF ROCK AGES
FOR SOURCE OF MARIA BASIN MATERIAL

Although many entertaining hypotheses had been advanced about the nature of the maria fill (e.g., dust, sedimentary rocks, asphalt lakes) the Apollo 11 rocks are now known to be clearly igneous and volcanic, (page 7) analogous to terrestrial flood lavas such as the Columbia River Basalts or the Deccan Traps, (although considerably more fluid, as noted in Chapter 8). Two rival hypotheses were available to explain the source of this material. Either the lavas were formed deep within the moon by partial or selective melting, as is the case for terrestrial lavas, and were erupted onto the surface, or they were derived by fusion of pre-existing surface rocks during the very large impact events which formed the maria basins. Relevant evidence about this problem can be gained from a study of the composition of the lavas themselves (see Chapter 6, page 157 on petrogenesis) but a decisive and simple test can distinguish between these two hypotheses. The argument is due mainly to Professor Harold Urey (University of California) and runs as follows: The basins now filled with mare material were created by impact of large objects, and resembled Mare Orientale. Debris from these impacts is scattered across the face of the moon. Such debris from the Mare Imbrium collision was first detected by the U.S. geologist, G. K. Gilbert, in 1893. The Apollo 13 mission was scheduled to land on some of this outthrown debris at Fra Mauro.

However, there is no sign of this impact produced debris lying on the surface of the neighboring Mare Serenitatis. Thus this mare must be more recent than Mare Imbrium. However, the converse is also true. There is no outthrown debris from the collision which produced the Serenitatis basin lying on the broad and smooth lava surfaces of Mare Imbrium. Thus, if the lavas filling the maria were produced by impact, the two events must have occurred at the same time.

This conclusion applies generally across the moon. None of the maria surfaces have debris on them from any of the great maria basin collisions. Thus, if the lavas filling the basins were produced by the impacts which dug the basins, all the events must have occurred at the same time. In this way, the collisional debris can sink from sight in the liquid lava lakes.

The other hypothesis provides for flooding of the maria basins long after they were formed. The impact produced debris is covered up by successive flows derived from the interior of the moon. This sequence of events was strongly advocated by astrogeologists, on the basis of the apparent differences in ages as shown, for example, by the differing abundances of craters on the maria surfaces. The age data from Apollo 11 was suggestive but not decisive in deciding between these two viewpoints. Their great age of 3.7 billion years was sufficiently ancient to provide some support for the impact melting theory. The Apollo 12 rocks provided a decisive answer. Their age is several hundred million years younger than those from Mare Tranquillitatis, indicating at least two widely separated epochs of maria filling and probably a long continued history of such processes. Such a long time interval is inconsistent with the stratigraphic requirements for simultaneous or near simultaneous maria filling by impact produced lavas. It indicates that the lavas which filled the maria basins, and which spilled over into adjoining regions, came over long intervals from the interior of the moon, in an analogous fashion to terrestrial lava flows.

ISOTOPIC ABUNDANCES

Relative isotopic abundance measurements have been made by several investigators. There are two principal reasons for this work. The first is to look for isotope abundance anomalies between the Earth and the moon, particularly for the heavier elements, and the second is to study the variations in the isotopic ratios for those lighter elements (e.g., carbon, oxygen, sulfur) which are subject to fractionation in the Earth due to geological processes (e.g., crystallization from a melt).

ISOTOPIC HOMOGENEITY IN THE SOLAR NEBULA

Was the solar nebula isotopically homogeneous? The data for the Earth and the meteorites indicate that they were formed from elements with similar stable isotope abundance ratios. The capture hypothesis for the origin of the moon implies that it was formed elsewhere in the solar system. Thus it might provide us with samples from a region far removed from where the Earth or the meteorites formed. In any event, it gives another source of information on the homogeneity or otherwise of the solar nebula.

The possibility is always present that a late injection of r-process nuclides (see Chapter 4, page 99) (produced from a nearby supernova) may have occurred shortly before, or during condensation of the solar nebula. Such a cause has been suggested as a triggering mechanism to initiate condensation. The possibility, although remote, of finding material from outside the solar system (in addition to galactic cosmic ray effects) is a further reason for the investigation. Such material would be expected to differ in at least some stable isotope ratios, because of the probable different evolutionary paths of element synthesis in differing parts of the galaxy.

Fields and co-workers (Argonne National Laboratory) looked for the transuranic elements. None were found. In particular, they searched for evidence of plutonium and curium. Pu^{244} has a half-life of 83 million years and Cm^{247} has a half-life of 16 million years. The absence of these nuclides argues against nearby (within one light year or less) supernovae explosions within the past one billion years.

Tatsumoto and Fields found that the U^{238}/U^{235} ratio "is exactly the same as that of terrestrial material." Wanless and co-workers looked at the following isotope ratios: Li^7/Li^6, K^{39}/K^{41}, Rb^{85}/Rb^{87}, Sr^{84}/Sr^{86}, Sr^{86}/Sr^{88} and U^{238}/U^{235}. These ratios agreed with terrestrial and meteoritic values. No isotopes of thorium other than Th^{232} were observed. The evidence from these nuclides indicates that the material from which the moon formed was isotopically similar to that forming the Earth and the meteorites.

LIGHT ISOTOPE FRACTIONATION

A number of lighter isotope ratios (e.g., O^{18}/O^{16}, S^{32}/S^{34}, C^{12}/C^{13}) are fractionated during geological processes and much useful information, relevant, for example, to crystallization temperatures, has been obtained. Similar studies have been made on the lunar rocks and fine material.

Epstein and Taylor (California Institute of Technology) measured the Si^{30}/Si^{28} ratio and found that it was similar in lunar and terrestrial rocks. It is subject to slight fractionation during geological processes.

OXYGEN ISOTOPES

The O^{18}/O^{16} ratios were measured by several workers. The data are customarily expressed as deviations from a standard sample, in parts per 1000.

$$\delta\,O^{18} = \left(\frac{(O^{18}/O^{16})\,\text{sample}}{(O^{18}/O^{16})\,\text{std. ocean water}} - 1 \right) 1000$$

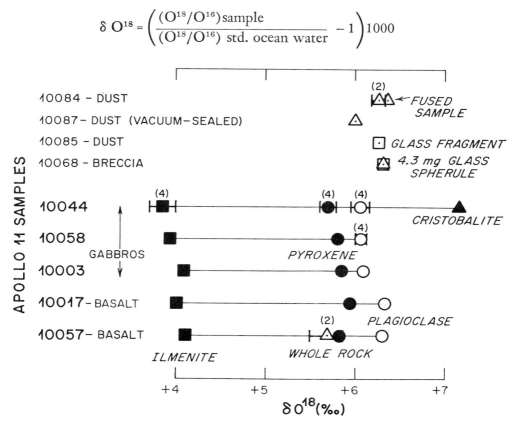

Fig. 7-9. $\delta\,O^{18}$ values for minerals and rocks from the Sea of Tranquility. After Taylor and Epstein (California Institute of Technology).

Fig. 7-9 gives the range on δ O¹⁸ values for lunar rocks and minerals. Fig. 7-10 shows the comparison of δ O¹⁸ values for meteorites, terrestrial mafic and ultramafic rocks, and lunar samples.

No significant differences exist in the ratios between the lunar rocks, terrestrial basaltic and ultramafic rocks, and chondritic meteorites. The achondrites and stony-irons show very different ratios. This is of interest because

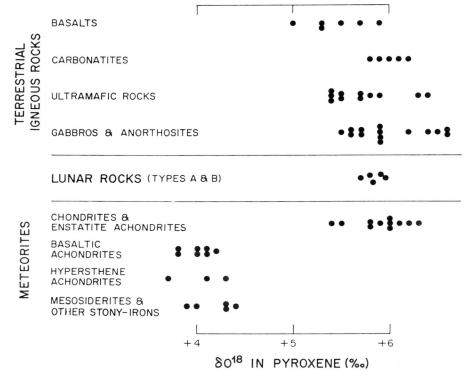

Fig. 7-10. Comparison of δ O¹⁸ values of pyroxenes from the Apollo 11 lunar rocks with those from terrestrial rocks and meteorites. After Taylor and Epstein (California Institute of Technology).

the achondrites show many mineralogical and some chemical similarities with the lunar rocks. Taylor and Epstein suggest that the achondrites are derived from a separate oxygen isotope reservoir compared to the Earth, moon and chondrites.

The breccias and dust show slight δ O¹⁸ enrichment (0.3 – 0.7 per mil) compared to the rocks. It is suggested that O¹⁸ rich components are added to the regolith. The carbonaceous chondrite component cannot add sufficient excess O¹⁸. Possibly the excess O¹⁸ comes from the same source as the excess radiogenic strontium and lead. The solar wind may also be richer in O¹⁸.

CRYSTALLIZATION TEMPERATURE

The uniformity of O^{18}/O^{16} ratios in all the lunar rocks indicates that equilibrium was attained rapidly during crystallization. As in terrestrial rocks and meteorites, the $\delta\,O^{18}$ values for the minerals increase in the sequence:

	$\delta\,O^{18}$
ilmenite	$3.85 - 4.12$
clinopyroxene	$5.67 - 5.95$
plagioclase	$6.06 - 6.33$
cristobalite	7.16

The $\delta\,O^{18}$ values for the minerals from different rocks are very similar, and there is no evidence of oxygen isotope exchange or equilibration during cooling following crystallization at temperatures estimated between 1120°C. and 1200°C. This effect is attributed to the very low water content of the lunar rocks.

From the petrological studies we know that the rocks crystallized rapidly, and that the minerals are often inhomogeneous. Nevertheless there is no sign of isotopic zoning in the minerals.

TEKTITES

These have typical $\delta\,O^{18}$ values of $+9 - +11.5$ per mil. Taylor and Epstein showed that the O^{18}/O^{16} values of tektites were consistent with derivation from a mixture of a high silica igneous component (quartz?) and a lower silica component formed in presence of aqueous solutions. They conclude that the possibility of finding such material in the moon is remote. Even if SiO_2 rich rocks exist they are unlikely to have $\delta\,O^{18}$ values as high as 9 if the lunar cristobalite values of about 7 are typical. Taylor and Epstein conclude that it is a reasonable inference that "high O^{18} rocks that are suitable tektite parent materials are rare or non-existent on the lunar surface."

SULFUR ISOTOPES

Fig. 7-11 shows the distribution of sulfur isotopes in meteorites, lunar and terrestrial rocks, expressed as $\delta\,S^{34}$ values.

$$\delta\,S^{34}\,{}^{0}/_{00} = \left(\frac{S^{34}/S^{32}\ \text{sample} - S^{34}/S^{32}\ \text{std.}}{S^{34}/S^{32}\ \text{std.}} \right) 1000$$

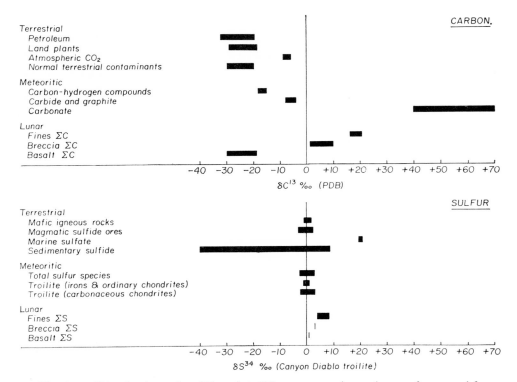

Fig. 7-11. Distribution of δC^{13} and δS^{34} among various phases of terrestrial, meteoritic and lunar components. After Kaplan (U.C.L.A.).

Std. = FeS (troilite) from Canyon Diablo iron meteorite. All sulfur is present as FeS. The concentration range is from 650-2300 ppm. which is rather more than usually observed in terrestrial basalts. No elemental sulfur or sulfate has been detected. S^{34} is enriched in the fines and Kaplan (University of California) suggests that this is due mainly to selective production of H_2S^{32} by solar wind proton bombardment. This is lost from the surface and thus S^{34} builds up. The excess total sulfur in the fines is attributed mainly to contributions from carbonaceous chondrites and the solar wind.

CARBON ISOTOPES

The C^{12}/C^{13} ratios have also been studied by Kaplan, Friedman and co-workers. Fig. 7-11 shows the variation expressed as δC^{13} values.

$$\delta C^{13}\ {}^0/_{00} = \left(\frac{C^{13}/C^{12}\ \text{sample} - C^{13}/C^{12}\ \text{std. limestone}}{C^{13}/C^{12}\ \text{std. limestone}} \right) 1000$$

The lunar rocks are rather similar to the normal terrestrial contaminants. The breccias and fines are enriched in C^{13}. Kaplan (University of California) suggests that the excess carbon in the fines is derived from carbonaceous chondrites and the solar wind. The lunar rocks contribute about 70 ppm. carbon and the fines are in the 100-200 ppm. range. Kaplan calculates that with the solar wind and carbonaceous chondrites contribution, the total carbon should be in the range $250 - 400$ ppm. He suggests, analogous to the case of sulfur, loss of CH_4, formed by solar proton bombardment, from the surface. Selective formation and loss of C^{12} enriched CH_4 accounts for the C^{13} enrichment in the soil.

This proposal of solar wind "erosion" of the surface could be tested by comparison of samples from polar and sunlit regions of the moon — a project for post-Apollo visits!

HYDROGEN

Epstein, Taylor, Hintenberger, Friedman and co-workers have investigated the hydrogen/deuterium ratio.

Lunar hydrogen is very depleted in deuterium relative to terrestrial water standards. Epstein and Taylor suggest that even the small amount of deuterium detected may be due to terrestrial water contamination. They conclude that:

> the implications of the presence of even small amounts of water on the moon are so important that it is imperative that valid criteria for its presence on the moon be used. We believe that such criteria are still lacking.

They estimate that the lunar hydrogen contains not more than 10 ppm. deuterium. They conclude that the largest fraction of hydrogen in the fines is derived from the solar wind.

COSMIC-RAY BOMBARDMENT OF THE LUNAR SURFACE

The moon's surface is much superior to meteorites as a recorder of exposure to cosmic radiation. It has been in its present orbit for a long time, whereas the orbits of meteorites are uncertain,* extending probably inside the orbit of Venus and out to the asteroidal belt. They thus possess inherent limitations both in time and space since, for example, they may have been exposed to a widely varying flux of solar cosmic rays.

* The orbits of two meteorites have been determined since they were photographically recorded during entry. Both indicate an elliptical orbit extending to the asteroidal belt. These data help to dispose of the myth that meteorites come from beyond the solar system, an old suggestion rendered unlikely by a mass of chemical and isotopic evidence.

Meteorites also suffer from much surface ablation loss during entry so that the record of low energy cosmic radiation, preserved near the original surface, is largely lost. It should be noted that the lunar surface has 2π geometry for exposure to cosmic radiation, compared with 4π geometry for meteorites. The lunar *rocks* are thus free of most of the difficulties associated with the interpretation of cosmic ray effects in meteorites.

A variety of effects are produced by the cosmic ray bombardment of the lunar surface. Two main sources of cosmic radiation are present: (1) the high energy, so called "galactic" cosmic rays which come from outside the solar system; they typically have energies in the range 1 – 10 billion electron volts (BeV)/nucleon and (2) the lower energy radiation from the sun, mainly associated with solar flare effects, producing particles with energies in the 10 – 100 million electron volts (MeV)/nucleon range. These particles are mainly protons and α particles, and they are much less penetrating. Their range in rocks is of the order of millimeters. A great deal of information has been gathered from the study of the effects of this radiation, which seems to have persisted for long periods of time without major changes. The radioactive nuclides produced yield historical information. The other main products (tracks due to nuclear particles and rare gases) give an integrated record over the whole exposure time. We now consider these studies in detail.

These various fields have been developed by different investigators. The radiogenic nuclides (except for the rare gases) are dealt with first, followed by the studies of tracks due to passage of nuclear particles. The rare gases constitute a separate study since they are produced by a variety of processes such as trapping of solar wind particles, natural fission and radiogenic decay in addition to the cosmic ray bombardment. They are dealt with separately following the fission track section.

RADIOGENIC NUCLIDES (EXCEPT RARE GASES)

The surface layers record and preserve the effects of the low energy solar flare particles (10 – 100 MeV./nucleon) while comparison with the deeper layers gives information about the effects of the higher energy (1 – 10 BeV/ nucleon) particles on the lunar rocks. In addition information about cosmic ray flux may be obtained from the record preserved in the lunar rocks and fine material.

A wide variety of radiogenic nuclides has been identified. A typical list of these is given in Table 7-1. They vary from Co^{56} with a half-life of 77 days to Be^{10} with a half-life of 2.5 million years.

Table 7-1. Typical radiogenic nuclides produced by cosmic ray action on rock 10017 and fine sample 10084. Note the decrease in activity with depth especially for Fe^{55} and Co^{56}. The values given are in dpm./kg. (disintegrations per minute per kilogram) and are subject to an uncertainty of 10–20 %. Adapted after Shrelldraff (University of California).

Nuclide	Half-life	Rock Depth from Surface				
		0 – 4 mm.	4 – 12 mm.	12 – 30 mm.	60 mm.	Bulk fines
Be^{10}	2.5×10^6 yr.	14.0		15.8	–	16.4
Na^{22}	2.6 yr.	81	43	37	31	51
Al^{26}	7.4×10^5 yr.	133	74	66	65	107
Cl^{36}	3×10^5 yr.	< 33	16.0	17.4	–	16.0
V^{49}	330 days	–	–	–	–	8.9
Mn^{53}	2×10^6 yr.	94	43	50	48	46
Mn^{54}	312 days	36	39	10	36	29
Fe^{55}	2.5 yr.	445	96	94	98	216
Co^{56}	77 days	125	< 16	< 8	–	40
Co^{57}	270 days	5.8	< 1.5	< 2.3	–	< 1.6
Ni^{59}	8×10^4 yr.	< 3		–	–	3.3

The activities versus depth values are given in Table 7-1. These show that Na^{22}, Al^{26}, Mn^{53} and especially Fe^{55} and Co^{56} are strongly enriched in the first 4 mm., and are derived in part from solar flare activity. The long half-lives of Al^{26} (740,000 years) and Mn^{53} (2 million years) provide evidence for the continuation of solar flare activity for periods of the order of a hundred thousand to one million years. The short-lived species, which include Co^{56}, Co^{57}, Mn^{54}, Fe^{55} and Na^{22} have abundances consistent with production from known recent events. Two of these were the solar flares of November 18, 1968, and April 12, 1969. The production of the radionuclides depends on the composition of the target. Thus Na^{22} is produced mainly from aluminium with some contributions from magnesium and silicon. Al^{26} is likewise mainly produced from aluminium and silicon in the rocks.

NUCLEAR PARTICLE TRACK STUDIES

A variety of tracks due to natural radiation damage (e.g., Fig. 7-12) exist in lunar materials and these have been extensively studied. The tracks may be formed by several processes:

a. Heavy primary cosmic rays. Tracks due to bombardment by heavy cosmic ray particles appear to be mainly formed by iron group nuclei. Most workers report that more tracks appear in feldspar than in pyroxene, but this appears to be due to differences in the reaction to acid etching (which reveals the tracks) than to any inherent difference in registration threshold. (Fig. 7-13).

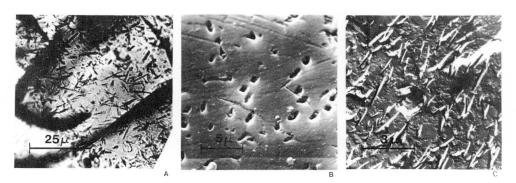

Fig. 7-12. Etched fossil tracks in feldspar as seen with different types of instruments: (A) in the optical microscope tracks appear as long dark lines; (B) in the stereo-scan electron microscope the tracks show up as deep, geometrically-shaped holes; (C) plastic replicas viewed with a transmission electron microscope prove that the holes seen in the stereo-scan at high track densities are not superficial surface pits. After Crozaz (Washington University).

Fig. 7-13. Electron microscope replica of etched cosmic ray tracks in an augite crystal etched for 1½ minutes. The larger dimension of the photograph measures 8μ. Many of the track replicas were bent in the process of extraction. After Fleischer (General Electric Co.).

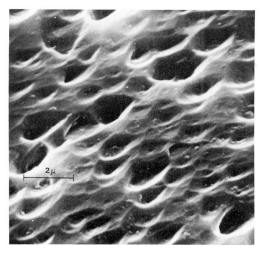

Fig. 7-14. Scanning electron microscope picture of etched spallation recoil tracks in an annealed feldspar. After Crozaz (Washington University).

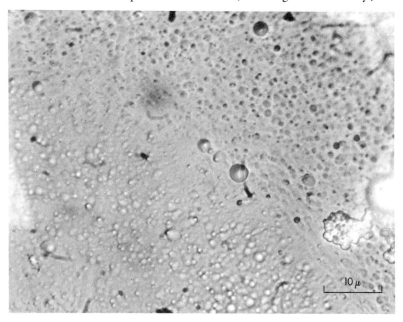

Fig. 7-15. The tiny dots are probable spallation recoil tracks induced in glass spherule 10005, 7.8, 1, 2 by cosmic ray bombardment. The source of the larger tracks is unidentified. After Fleischer (General Electric Co.).

b. Recoil nuclei from spallation reactions. Fission tracks occur due both to spontaneous fission of U^{238} and induced fission during irradiation. The tracks are isotropic in contrast to the cosmic ray tracks which are anisotropic (Fig. 7-14).

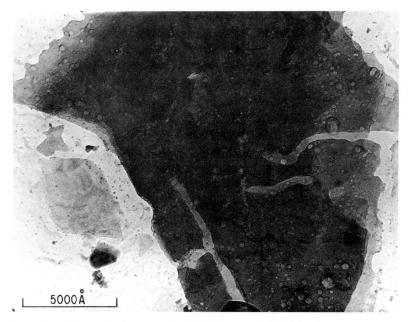

5000 Å

Fig. 7-16. Possible etched solar wind tracks from heavy (mass > 200) nuclei. After Fleischer (General Electric Co.).

c. Nuclear fission. Spallation recoil tracks: many short (<2 micron) tracks due to high energy protons are observed. (Fig. 7-15).

d. Heavy solar wind ions. Some tracks in the extreme surface layers (e.g., rock 10017) are attributed to heavy solar wind nuclei with mass about 200. A Pb nucleus at solar wind velocity (about 300 – 500 km. per second) has energy equivalent to that of recoil nuclei in the U and Th α decay chains. (Fig. 7-16).

TRACK DENSITY vs. DEPTH

The density versus depth information from nuclear tracks is useful in measuring the flux of low energy particles, stopped near the surface, in identifying the former position of rocks and also in calculating the rate of erosion of lunar rocks. Examples of the variation of track density with depth are given in Fig. 7-17. The near-surface regions are dominated by tracks due to solar flare particles, while the tracks in the interiors of the lunar rocks are mainly due to "galactic" cosmic rays. Tracks due to the latter cause dominate at depths greater than 0.5 cm. The excess tracks observed near the surface have up to a factor of 50 times the track density observed in the interior. These excess tracks have both a steep density profile and a short track length (∼ 1 micron) indicating a low energy source.

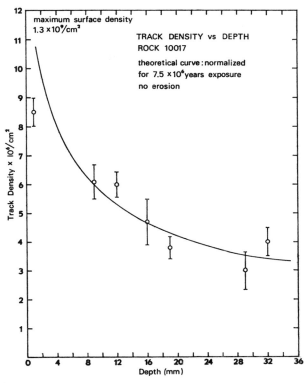

Fig. 7-17. Track density vs. depth for feldspars from rock 10017. The solid line shows a theoretical fit to the data for galactic cosmic rays. After Crozaz (Washington University).

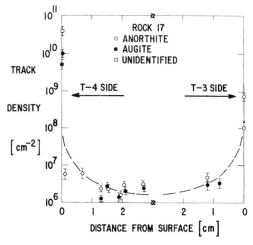

Fig. 7-18. Track densities vs. depth from the two surfaces of rock 10017. High values on both sides show that the rock has been turned over at least once. After Fleischer (General Electric Co.).

RATES OF EROSION FROM NUCLEAR TRACK DENSITIES

Shoemaker (California Institute of Technology) on geological grounds estimated an erosion rate of $1 - 2 \times 10^{-7}$ cm. per year of lunar rocks by micrometeorites. If the cosmic ray energy spectrum is known, then the profile of the fission track densities provides an excellent method for estimating the rate of erosion. Erosion of the rocks has been discussed in the section dealing with the regolith (see p. 33). Certainly some erosion occurs by "chipping." The many small pits occurring on the rocks provide evidence of this. They do not appear to saturate the present surface.

There is some disagreement among fission track workers on the estimated rates of erosion. Walker (Washington University) arrives at a figure of 10^{-8} cm./year for rocks 10003 and 10017. Fleischer (General Electric Co.) Price and O'Sullivan (University of California) calculate an erosion rate of 10^{-8} cm./year for rocks 10003 and 10017. Fleischer (General Electric Co.) considers that the rate is $100 - 10,000$ times slower, quoting a range from 10^{-9} to 10^{-11} cm./year.

SURFACE RESIDENCE TIMES

Track ages of the rocks give the time of residence in the upper few centimeters while the spallation ages give the time the sample was in the upper 100 cm. of soil. Hence the track ages are always less than or equal to the spallation ages. It is clear that tumbling or rolling over of the rocks has occurred. Fig. 7-18 shows track densities decreasing inward from two surfaces of rock 10017. A detailed history has been established for this rock and this is quoted as probably typical of the fate of rocks in the regolith.

a. Rock crystallized at ⌐ 3600 million years.

b. At 3600 – 500 million years before present, the rock was buried deeply enough not to be affected by cosmic radiation.

c. At 500 – 5.7 million years, the rock was buried to depths of 15 –100 cm. beneath the surface.

d. At 5.7 – 2.85 million years, the rock was on the surface.

e. At 2.85 million years, it was flipped over to the position in which it was picked up.

This sequence is not uniquely determined and possibly represents the integrated time spent in the various positions so that the rate of tumbling may be greater. The evidence is consistent with a history of excavation of rocks from lava flows beneath the surface by meteorite impact, followed by "gardening" as part of the regolith.

In this connection, the core tube samples from Apollo 11 show no correlation of track density with depth and indicate thorough stirring of the soil to a depth of at least 40 cm.

Surface residence times varying from 80,000 to about 60 million years have been established for time spent in the top 10 cm. of soil. Thus, if a "rolling stone" model is adopted implying multiple burial and exposure, it becomes difficult to calculate a unique erosion rate for the rocks. Undoubtedly, complex histories for individual rocks account for some of the reported discrepancies in ages.

Finally, the nuclear track densities in spherules indicate a rather uniform surface effect. Thus it appears that the small grains have been tumbled over a long period of time. This casts doubt on the observation by Frondel and others that the small pits found randomly on spherule surfaces formed during free flight. They may equally well have occurred during turnover at the surface of the regolith.

RARE GASES

The rare gases — helium, neon, argon, krypton and xenon — are so-called because they are strongly depleted on the Earth. They were probably never accreted, for the heavier ones could not be lost from the Earth at its present size. They are quite abundant cosmically and were present in the original solar nebula in amounts comparable to neighboring nonvolatile elements. Once trapped in rocks, they remain intact, except for loss by diffusion. They accordingly preserve the record of the processes which formed them or altered their isotopic composition.

There is no evidence in the lunar rocks or soil of rare gases which might be residual from a primitive atmosphere. However, large quantities of rare gases were found, particularly in the lunar fines. There are several sources for the gases.

1. Trapping of gases from the solar wind.*

2. Trapped solar flare particles.

3. Gases produced by reactions induced in rocks by cosmic ray bombardment (e.g., He^3, Ne^{21}, Ar^{38}, Xe^{131}).

4. Gases produced by fissionogenic processes (e.g., Xe isotopes from fission of U^{238}) in rocks.

5. Radioactive decay of elements present in rocks (e.g., Ar^{40} from K^{40}). (See page 165.)

---

* Solar wind: the solar wind in the neighborhood of the Earth under normal conditions consists mainly of ionized hydrogen moving from the sun with velocities in the range 300 – 500 km. per second. The average density is about 10 ions per cm.^{3} The particles have energies in the kilovolt range, much less energetic than the "cosmic rays" associated with solar flares.

Many of these sources were distinguished by such techniques as stepwise heating of samples, or etching of grains to study variation with depth, followed by mass spectrometric analysis of the released gases. The interpretation of the rare gas data provides information about

1. surface exposure ages,
2. crystallization of rocks,
3. solar processes.

The most interesting single result was the occurrence in the fines and breccias of very large amounts of trapped gases, mainly derived from the solar wind. Most of this gas is within about one micron of the grain surface. Even this indicates that there has been some diffusion into the grains, since, for example, the penetration depth of He^4 from the solar wind does not exceed 0.05 micron; and the entire solar wind component should be within 0.1 micron of the surface.

The overall abundance ratios for helium/neon/argon/krypton/xenon indicate that the lighter noble gases have been lost by diffusion relative to the heavier ones. Compared to krypton and xenon, about 10% of the helium, 20% of the neon and 50% of the argon have been retained by the grains in the fines. When the appropriate corrections are made for this loss by diffusion, the isotope ratios of the rare gases in the solar wind are obtained. These are close to the estimates of their abundance in the sun (except that xenon may be higher), and so to their "cosmic" abundances (See page 99). Thus the solar wind may be a very good sample of the "cosmic" element abundances.

Within the interior of the grains, where the solar wind does not penetrate, the rare gases produced by spallation reactions have been studied. These reactions are induced by the solar flare and galactic cosmic ray bombardment, and the amounts of the noble gases so produced are very much less than those derived from the solar wind. The Ne^{20}/Ne^{22} and Ne^{22}/Ne^{21} ratios are similar to those in gas-rich meteorites. The high Ne^{20}/Ne^{22} ratios are possibly due to generation of Ne^{20} from Na^{23} by solar flare activity by reactions such as Na^{23} ($p\alpha$) Ne^{20}. The isotope ratios produced by the spallation reactions are typically about unity. The cosmogenic Ne, Ar, Kr and Xe are similar to the abundances found in Ca-rich achondrites (possibly of lunar origin). Xe^{131} is higher in the lunar samples probably due to the production of this isotope by spallation reaction on barium or the rare-earth elements, which are more abundant in the lunar rocks than in the achondrites. No evidence was discovered for an excess of Xe^{129} produced by decay of extinct I^{129} (half-life = 16 million years). It is clear that the breccias have many of the characteristics of gas-rich meteorites and this indicates that they may have a similar origin. This would involve their formation on the surface of a large body, exposure to cosmic radiation and lithification by shock following meteorite impacts.

COSMIC RAY EXPOSURE AGES

All the rocks contain noble gases produced by spallation reactions. The relative isotopic abundances reflect the chemistry of the sample and the absolute amounts indicate the period during which the sample was exposed to cosmic radiation. Absolute ages can be calculated, making various assumptions about cosmic ray flux and production rate of cosmogenic nuclides. Typically 2π geometry is assumed, and a production rate of 1.0×10^{-8} cm.^{3}/ 10^6 year for He^3. The cosmic ray exposure ages for the rocks in general give the time that the rock has lain on the surface since it was excavated by meteorite impact. Several different ages * may be calculated. The $Ar^{38}/Ar^{37}+$ Ar^{39} is a typical example. High energy bombardment by galactic cosmic rays of Fe, Ti and Ca in the lunar samples produces the rare gases Ar^{37} (half-life = 35 days) and Ar^{39} (half-life = 269 years). Typical reactions are K^{39} (n,p) Ar^{39}, Ca^{42} (n,a) Ar^{39} and Ca^{40} (n,a) Ar^{37}. From the similarity of the Ar^{39} production in meteorites and lunar samples, the intensity of high energy (>200 MeV./nucleon) radiation in the vicinity of the moon is about the same as that experienced by meteorites, at least for the past 400 years or so. There appears also to have been a high rate of production of Ar^{39} due to the reaction K^{39} (n,p) Ar^{39} implying a strong flux of low energy (down to 50 MeV./nucleon) protons.

An exposure age may be calculated from the ratio of nonradiogenic Ar^{38} to the radioactive species Ar^{37} and Ar^{39}. An age of 110 million years has been calculated for rock 10057. This compares with an age based on the abundance of He^3 of 52 million years. The age difference is thought to be due to the preferential loss of light He relative to the heavier argon. The relative exposure ages are related to the rate of "gardening" ** of the regolith.

In general the Ar^{38}/Ar^{37} and Ar^{39} ages are in excess of the He^3/H^3 ages, indicating loss of the more volatile He^3. The breccia ages are about an order of magnitude older than the whole rock ages. Probably this is due to the inheritance of an old soil age since the breccias were apparently formed from fine material close to the surface.

---

* e.g. ages based on He^3/H^3, Ne^{21}/Ne^{22}, $Ar^{38}/Ar^{37} + Ar^{39}$, Kr^{82}/Kr^{81} ratios.
**This picturesque term was apparently first used by David Parkin in 1965 to describe the turning over and stirring of the regolith (Shrelldraff, University of California).

The cosmic ray exposure ages vary by about a factor of ten for different rocks, typical values being from 50 – 500 million years. These values are consistent with the concept of "gardening" of the regolith by meteorite impact processes.

THE ARGON^{40} ANOMALY

Ar^{40} results from the decay of K^{40} (See page 165). The primordial ratio of Ar^{40} to stable Ar^{36} is very low (10^{-3}). The amount of Ar^{40} generated from K^{40} indicates whole rock ages of 3.5 billion years. However, the *fines* contain about 100 times as much radiogenic argon as would be produced *in situ*. Clearly some enrichment mechanism has been operative to enrich Ar^{40} in the soil. One suggestion is that some Ar^{40} atoms, resulting from the K^{40} decay, leak from the lunar surface and are ionized by solar radiation. Following ionization, the particles are then subject to rapid acceleration by the magnetic fields associated with the solar wind and strike the lunar surface with energies of 100 eV. – 1000 eV. within a few seconds. At low energies, they are neutralized but not trapped and hence recycled. Ions with impact energies > I KeV. are trapped in the fines, thus building up an excess of Ar^{40}.

8

PHYSICAL PROPERTIES

Seismology, Heat Flow, Magnetism, Density, Viscosity, and the Mascons

INTRODUCTION

In this chapter, we discuss the significance of the various measurements of physical properties made on the moon or on the lunar rocks. We begin with a discussion of the seismic signals and the information they give about the interior of the moon. This is followed by a short discussion of heat flow. Actual measurements will be made on later Apollo missions. The magnetic properties of the rocks are noted, with a discussion of the question of whether the moon had, or was exposed to, an ancient magnetic field. Sections on density and viscosity follow. These properties are significant in understanding the nature of the excess mass concentrations or *mascons* which underlie the circular maria. The chapter concludes with a discussion of the nature of mascons, about which much relevant evidence has been gathered from the Apollo rocks.

THE LUNAR INTERIOR — SEISMIC EVIDENCE

Information about the internal structure of the moon and possible seismic or tectonic activity can be obtained, as on the Earth, by observations of seismic events. The Apollo 11 mission carried a passive seismic experiment package (PSEP) (Fig. 8-1) which has deployed on the surface, 17 meters south of the lunar module footpad. It operated for 21 Earth days. The Apollo 12 mission deployed another seismometer, placed about 140 meters away from the LM in order to cut down seismic noise produced by the LM. Fig. 8-2 shows the seismic signal when Armstrong ascended the ladder of the landing module.

Critical differences exist between terrestrial seismic records and the signals from the lunar seismometers. First is the very low background noise level, well below that of Earth-based seismometers. Before the Apollo 11 mission, three theories were debated:

1. The noise level would be high due to diurnal temperature variations causing thermal stress and spallation.

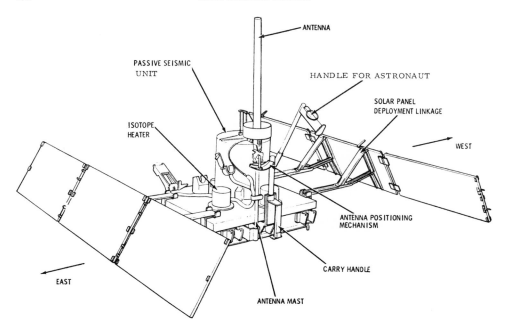

Fig. 8-1. Diagram of lunar seismometer. After Latham (Columbia University).

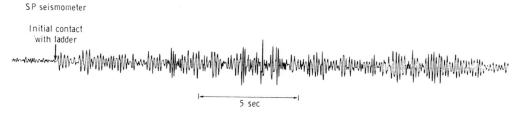

Fig. 8-2. Signal recorded when astronaut Armstrong ascended the ladder of the lunar landing module. After Latham (Columbia University).

2. The noise level would be high due to numerous meteorite impacts.

3. The absence of apparent large tectonic features, oceans and atmosphere would produce a low noise level.

This last view now appears to be correct.

A number of signals were recorded during the 21-day operation. Possible explanations for the signals received are (a) venting gases from the LM, (b) thermal stress relief from the LM and PSEP structures, (c) meteorite impacts, (d) rock slides on steep slopes and moonquakes. The first two mechanisms do not appear to be important. Meteorite impact is considered by Latham (Columbia University) to be an important source of signals, and he leaves open the question of existence of moonquakes.

However, the most intriguing feature of the lunar seismic signals is their long duration and lack of discrete phases (Fig. 8-3). In terrestrial seismograms, the relative times of arrival of these phases provide much valuable information about internal structure. The signal recorded by the impact of the Apollo 12 LM ascent stage is typical and shows (Fig. 8-3) a slowly emergent beginning in contrast to the sharp pulse of terrestrial seismograms. It builds slowly to a maximum and gradually decreases in amplitude. There appears to be much wave scattering.

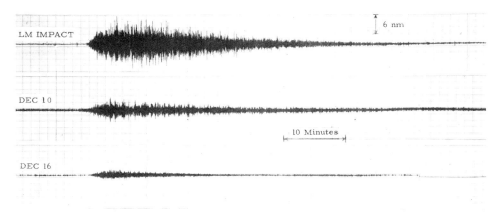

Fig. 8-3. Seismic signals received from the LM impact and from natural sources on December 10 and December 16, 1969. After Latham (Columbia University).

The unexpectedly long duration of the signals is either due to the source mechanisms being prolonged or it is a propagation effect. Possible ways of producing an extended source signal could include:

1. rock slides,
2. secondary ejecta impacts, in the case of meteorite impact,
3. collapse of "fairy castle" type structures or other fragile structures.

None of these seem very likely and Latham concludes that the extended length of the signals is due to very low attenuation in the lunar interior.

These conditions in the lunar interior, a very low attenuation * and a large degree of wave scattering, are mutually exclusive in terrestrial experience and may be unique to the moon. It indicates that the internal structure of the moon is radically different from that of the typical concentric layered crustal structure of the Earth's outer few hundred kilometers.

* This corresponds to high values of the seismic parameter Q which has typical values in the range $10-300$ for the Earth, but is an order of magnitude higher $(3000-5000)$ for the moon.

Kanamori (University of Tokyo) has made direct measurements of the velocity of P and S seismic waves in Apollo 11 rock samples. This material has a high attenuation (low Q) at low pressures. At higher pressures, higher values of Q are found. However, it is a reasonable assumption based on petrological and geochemical evidence that the lunar interior, with apparently high Q values, does not consist of material equivalent to the lavas filling the mare.

Latham (Columbia University) suggests that the lunar interior, in addition to possessing a low attenuation (high Q) for seismic waves, is also heterogeneous and might resemble a set of cold blocks of differing composition in welded contact, at least in the outer 20 km. or so, underlain by a rigid interior. If this view is correct, it favors the hypothesis that the lunar uplands represent the original accreted material and that the moon accreted at rather low temperatures.

LUNAR HEAT FLOW

No heat flow experiments were carried out on Apollo 11 or 12. One was scheduled for Apollo 13, (Langseth et al., Science, Vol. 168, p. 211) and will be performed on the later Apollo missions.

The heat flow data will provide an important parameter in our understanding of the moon. Contributions to the observed heat flow will result from energy due to the initial accretion and that generated by subsequent radioactive decay of potassium, uranium and thorium. Since the moon is smaller than the Earth (1/80 mass) it will have lost a greater proportion of its initial heat. Hence lunar heat flow measurements will give more information about the distribution of K, U and Th throughout the moon than do similar measurements on the Earth. On the other hand, the restriction of measurements to shallow probes (a 3 meter penetration is planned) will lead to measurements being made entirely within the regolith. The heterogeneous nature of the regolith and the probable irregular contact with bedrock may lead to local disturbances of the heat flow. Ness et al. (J. Geophys. Research Vol. 72, p. 5769, 1967), inferred that temperatures throughout the moon were less than 1000°C. although other data indicate that mean melting temperatures may occur at depths greater than 500 km.

However, there may now be considerable near surface concentration of U and Th. Certainly the interior would be molten if the moon had the high concentrations of these elements revealed in the surface rocks (typically 500 ppm. K; 1 ppm. U; 3 ppm. Th). The heat flow experiment will make a marked contribution toward our understanding of the lunar interior and the distribution of the radiogenic heat producing elements (K, U and Th) throughout the moon.

MAGNETIC PROPERTIES

The origin of the Earth's magnetic field is generally ascribed to the presence of a conducting fluid iron-nickel core.

The moon is known to have only a very weak magnetic field at present. The general field, measured by the Explorer satellites, is less than 5 gamma.* The present magnetic field strength of the Earth is 60,000 gamma at the equator. The Apollo 12 magnetometer measured a local field of 30 gamma. However, the field may have been stronger in the past, with the implication of a fluid core. Alternatively, the moon may have been much closer to the Earth when the Apollo 11 and 12 rocks crystallized. The present field of the Earth at the Roche limit ** is about 4000 gamma.

The major magnetic minerals are iron (ferromagnetic) ilmenite (antiferromagnetic) and pyroxene (paramagnetic) and the magnetic properties of the lunar samples are due to these. This is in contrast to terrestrial materials where magnetite and hematite make the most important contributions. Troilite does not apparently make any magnetic contribution and hence must be stochiometric (FeS) since any departure from stochiometry renders it ferromagnetic. This is confirmed by the detailed mineralogical studies.

The most significant result is that the breccias appear to possess a stable remnant magnetism, somehow acquired on the lunar surface. One suggestion is that this magnetization is shock induced, acquired during the formation of the breccias by meteoritic impact. Runcorn (University of Newcastle-upon-Tyne) suggests that the rocks acquired their magnetism in an ancient field of internal origin of about 1000 gamma. This may have been the strength of the lunar field 3.7×10^9 years ago, or the magnetism may have been acquired in the Earth's magnetic field if the moon was closer to the Earth at that time. Nagata (University of Tokyo) notes that the stability of the remnant magnetism of the breccias extends over a wide range, and that this is related to their mechanism of formation by meteorite impact.

Clearly the magnetic properties raise more questions than they answer but the consensus is that the rocks were exposed to a field of about 1000 gamma at the time of their formation.

DENSITY OF LUNAR ROCKS

The density of the lunar basalts is in the range $3.3 - 3.4$ gm./cm.^{3} which is close to the overall density of the moon (3.34 gm./cm.^{3}). This result caused much speculation when first announced by LSPET (1969). This situation

* one gamma = 10^{-5} Oersted, the CGS unit of magnetic field strength.
** The Roche limit is the limit of closest approach of a body to the Earth before breakup due to gravitational forces occurs.

is in great contrast to that for the Earth, where the overall density is 5.52 gm./cm.^{3}; the continental crustal rocks have densities typically about 2.6 – 2.8 gm./cm.^{3} and the oceanic crustal rocks have densities about 2.9 – 3.0 gm./cm.^{3} It is clear that the moon does not have a uniform surface and that the upland rocks are less dense. The calculated density from the Surveyor VII analysis is 3.0 gm./cm.^{3}, significantly less than that for the maria.

Are the maria rocks representative of the interior? If they were derived by impact melting then they could be expected to be representative of the surface material. In other sections we have seen that the relative age relationships for the maria make impact melting unlikely to be the major origin of the maria basin fill. From information on the moment of inertia, the moon appears to be rather uniform in density throughout. Although the density of the lunar basalts would appear at first glance to be consistent with impact melting, both the density differences from the highlands and the age differences among the maria pose difficulties. Further difficulties appear from the trace element abundances and the experimental work. The density of the silicate melt from which the rocks crystallized on cooling has been estimated at 3.0 gm./cm.^{3}

LUNAR LAVA VISCOSITY

The viscosity of the liquid lunar lavas, before crystallization occurs, is an important property. One of the difficulties in accepting a volcanic origin for the material filling the maria basins had been that the lavas would not be fluid enough to cover such extensive areas as Mare Imbrium so smoothly. This was a reasonable objection on the basis of terrestrial experience. As the lunar photography (e.g., Ranger and Orbiter pictures) became more detailed in the past five years, the rarity of individual flow fronts and the remarkable smoothness and the large scale of the wrinkle ridges of the maria became more evident. On the Earth, basalts cover immense areas of Washington and Oregon (the Columbia River flows), India (Deccan Traps), Brazil (Parana basalts) and other areas. However, these are not on the scale of the floods of material on the lunar surface.

This problem was resolved by measurements of the viscosity of synthetic mixtures of the same composition as the lunar lavas. Weill, Murase and McBirney at the University of Oregon found that the viscosity was very low, at least an order of magnitude less than that of terrestrial basalts. A typical value for the lunar lava viscosity is 10 poises at 1400°C. (The poise is the cgs unit of viscosity. One poise = 1 dyne sec./cm.^{2}.) This value is comparable to the viscosity of heavy motor oil at room temperature. This low viscosity is a consequence of the chemical composition, most notably due to the lower SiO₂ content (40%) in comparison with terrestrial basalts (close to 50% SiO₂), and to the high iron and titanium contents. This low viscosity will permit the lunar lavas to flow faster and farther than their terrestrial counterparts (even though they have higher densities) resulting in very thin, extensive flows. Thus the widespread flooding of the lunar surface by lavas is accounted for.

Also, even though they are close to the surface and cooling rapidly, the low viscosity of the lunar basalts apparently permitted rapid growth of coarse crystals, whereas higher viscosity terrestrial basalts have much finer-grained textures. It has been pointed out by Weill (University of Oregon) that an upper crust on a lunar lava might form quickly, but the main mass of liquid would continue to move under this crust. This would promote the formation of large lava tubes which, upon collapse, might explain the sinuous rilles in the maria, variously attributed to rivers and other unlikely lunar mechanisms. They are clearly cut by flowing liquids. The low viscosity of the lunar lavas will enable them to reach high velocities on low slopes and cause their flow to be turbulent. Thus they may flow in channels reminiscent of river channels, a comparison often remarked of the sinuous rilles.

MASCONS

The Apollo 11 samples provided useful insights into the possible origin of the mascons. This term is applied to the large positive near surface gravity anomalies characteristic of most of the circular maria (but not the irregular maria). The mascons, first reported by Muller and Sjogren (*Science*, Vol. 161, p. 680, 1968) have caused much speculation. Such gravity anomalies due to excess mass occur on the Earth over elevated areas, and negative anomalies, due to deficiency of mass per unit area, occur, for example, at the sites of the great ocean trenches. On the moon, in contrast, the positive gravity anomalies, denoting excess mass per unit area, are detected within the low-lying regions. The largest anomalies are 220 milligals, under Mare Imbrium and Mare Serenitatis. (One milligal is 1/1000 of the cgs unit of gravity, the gal. The normal value for gravity for the Earth is 980 gals.) Smaller positive anomalies exist under the following maria: Crisium, Nectaris, Humorum, Humboltianum, Orientale, Smythii, and under Sinus Aestuum and Grimaldi, together with two unnamed mascons. Sinus Iridum, the Bay of Rainbows on the coast of the Sea of Rains (Mare Imbrium) is distinctive in possessing a negative anomaly of −90 milligals.

Many suggestions have been made about the origin of the mascons. Central to the problem is the strength of the outer layers of the moon. The moon has supported its irregular shape (the axis pointing toward the Earth is 1 km.

longer than the other axes) for a long period despite tidal stresses. This implies that the moon has been cold, but is consistent with small amounts of partial melting in the interior. One suggestion is that the mascons are the remnants of the colliding objects (large meteorites, asteroids or primitive Earth satellites) which produced the great maria basins by impact.

O'Hara (University of Edinburgh) has suggested that the mascons are due to the accumulation of dense iron-titanium oxides on the bottom of large lava lakes, during cooling and crystallization of the lunar basalts. This is a possible explanation, but encounters the difficulties that there is little evidence of near surface fractionation or sinking of such phases (see Chapter 6, page 159). Possibly such a mechanism might operate where the lavas are ponded, as in the flooded craters. Such ponding might also occur during the first stages of filling of the impact basins.

Ringwood (Australian National University) suggests that the mascons are due mainly to the transformation of the lunar basalts to the denser rock, eclogite, at the base of the circular maria. This transformation, at shallow depths and low temperatures (see Fig. 6-3) depends critically on the kinetics of the reactions. Gabbros may be intruded beneath the mare basins, causing excess mass concentrations. Objections have been raised to volcanic explanations for mascons on the grounds that excess mass per unit area cannot result simply from transfer upwards of material. However, with only small degrees of partial melting in the interior, it is possible to segregate the lavas from wider areas than their surface outcrop. There are two reasons for the concentration of lavas initially at the sites of the circular maria. The basins are low lying and so tend to fill first. Secondly, the molten lava rising from the interior will be chanelled toward the circular maria by the large zones of broken rock and rubble underlying them.

Baldwin (in *The Measure of the Moon,* University of Chicago Press, 1963) has estimated that the depth of crushing and brecciation of rock beneath an impact crater 10 miles in diameter extends to a depth of about 3 miles. Although it is difficult to extrapolate accurately to the large mare basin structures, the depth of breccia beneath, for example, Mare Serenitatis could extend to 200 km. (The original dimensions of the basin before lava filling are 700 km. diameter, and 14 km. deep.)

Thus the paradox arises that the circular maria basins will be initially sites of mass deficiency, or negative gravity anomalies. Sinus Iridum may be still in this condition. The rising molten lavas will first fill the rubble zone either with a mass of minor intrusions or possible larger coherent masses of gabbro. Subsequently, the basins themselves will fill up, with some bottom accumulation of early dense crystal phases if the lavas are ponded. Much of the deeper gabbro may transform to eclogite. Alternatively, the mass of the volcanic pile emplaced in the less dense "crustal" material (anorthosite?) may be sufficient to produce the gravity excess.

Finally, the flooding of the irregular maria occurs. This surface flooding is much shallower than that in the circular maria and there are no mascons in these areas.

9

ORIGIN OF THE MOON

INTRODUCTION

The wealth of scientific data which has accumulated from the study of the Apollo 11 rocks provides new insights into the origin of the moon. The question is of ancient lineage. The moon has had a profound effect on human affairs, mainly in mystical and religious connotations. It is an interesting speculation that our history could have been different if the great concentric ring structures of Mare Orientale (900 km. diameter) were centered like a bull's eye on the visible face, instead of being, except for one outer ridge, out of sight from the Earth. Our primitive religions could have had mainly a lunar basis dominated by one-eyed gods. If a marker is needed, the time of emergence of Homo Sapiens as a distinct species could well be placed as that moment when the origin of the moon was first pondered. This question has not been without danger. Anaxagoras was banished from Athens on a charge of impiety for suggesting that the moon was not the goddess Artemis (sister of Apollo) but a stone. Galileo first saw the lunar craters in 1610 but his critics refused to look through his telescope. Subsequently, it was generally thought that the craters were due to volcanic action. Procter, in his book, *The Moon* (1873), apparently was the first to suggest meteorite impact as an origin for the large craters.

This view was vigorously defended in 1893 by Gilbert, one of the leading students of terrestrial landscapes. Ironically, he thought that the Arizona crater was not of meteoritic origin. He first recognized the great Imbrium collision and suggested that the great maria basins were formed by giant collisions, a point emphasized by Urey, Baldwin and Shoemaker. The impact versus volcanic debate for the origin of the lunar craters has recently been resolved in favor of an impact origin for most features. As a result of the study of the surface features of the moon by Earth-based telescopes, the Ranger and Orbiter unmanned spacecraft, the Surveyor unmanned soft landings and the Apollo manned landings, we have a good picture of the geological * relationships of the various formations. Radiometric dating of the

---

* The term *geology*, although usually thought of as the study of the planet Earth, may, on a strict etymological definition, be applied to the study of earth, or solid materials, without restriction to this planet.

Apollo 11 and 12 rocks has enabled the beginnings of an absolute time scale in terms of millions of years to be attached to the relative sequence of events on the moon. The present state of this scale is shown in Table 9-1. In comparison with the Earth, the principal events are old. Nearly all geological activity on our planet has occurred since 3.3 billion years.

The origin and relative ages of the surface features of the moon are thus relatively well understood. We now turn to the question of the origin of the moon itself. A multitude of theories have been advanced, but they fall into three general groups:

a. fission from the Earth,
b. capture by the Earth,
c. formation along with the Earth as a double planet.

In the following sections, we discuss the constraints imposed on these theories by the new data from Apollo 11 and 12. No attempt is made to give an account of the host of rival theories proposed. Most of these now have to be evaluated in the light of the investigations discussed in this book.

It is clear that the chemical data provide critical boundary conditions. The full import of the chemistry was first demonstrated by Urey in his book, *The Planets* (Yale University Press, 1952). This work was a milestone in our understanding of the origin of the solar system, comparable to the appearance of the Laplace hypothesis in *Exposition du système du monde* in 1796. The constraints imposed by the new data are now discussed.

FISSION HYPOTHESES

These stem from the suggestion in 1878 by George Darwin that the moon was separated from the Earth by the action of tidal forces. Jefferies, in the first edition of his book, *The Earth* (1929), showed that it was highly improbable that the tides would become high enough. Interest remained alive because the theory provided a ready explanation for the density of the moon which could be made to match the uncompressed density of the upper mantle. It is a necessary requirement of the theory that the Earth's core had already separated before fission. The theory leads to interesting geochemical consequences, which many of the investigators have remarked. The separation of the metallic core is expected to deplete the mantle in many of the siderophile elements that preferentially enter the metal. However, the Earth's mantle and crust contain moderately high amounts of elements, such as nickel, indicating the equilibrium was not fully attained. The extreme depletion of the lunar lavas in these elements is more marked than in most terrestrial basaltic rocks. In many other ways, the Apollo basalts show chem-

Table 9-1. Lunar Time Scale.

Event	Period of Lunar Time	Absolute Age (Billions of years or aeons)
Formation of young ray craters (e.g., Copernicus)	Copernican	
Formation of older craters with rays no longer visible (e.g., Eratosthenes)	Eratosthenian	
Flooding of maria basins and some older craters by lavas (Archimedean Epoch)	Imbrium	3.3 – 3.8
Formation of maria basins by large impacts (Apenninian Epoch) Heavy cratering of uplands	Pre-Imbrium	
Formation of upland surface		
Accretion of moon	–	4.6 ?

ical differences from their terrestrial analogues. These distinctions have been pointed out through the text. If the lunar interior was similar to the mantle of the Earth, then it is reasonable to suppose that lavas on the moon would be similar to those erupted on the Earth. The most reasonable comparison is with the composition of the voluminous basaltic volcanic rocks of the ocean floors. These comparisons have been made in the section on chemistry, and the differences are profound (Fig. 4-15). Other terrestrial basalts are even further removed in composition. These great distinctions in composition between the chemistry of the lunar basalts and their terrestrial analogues are strong evidence that the lunar interior is not similar in chemical composition to the mantle of the Earth. This is a formidable, and possibly fatal, objection to the fission hypothesis.

CAPTURE HYPOTHESES

This has enjoyed much popularity, but removes the origin of the moon to a remote part of the solar system. When the iron abundance in the sun was thought to be lower, it was possible that the low density of the moon indicated that it was a primitive object. This was a principal attraction of the hypothesis, with the possibility that the lunar samples might be representative of the primitive solar nebula. However, the chemistry of the Apollo samples reveals that they are strongly fractionated relative to the composition of the carbonaceous chondrites, or to the "cosmic" element abundances. Even though the lunar lavas are probably derived by small degrees of partial melting from the interior, and so are not representative of the composition of the whole moon, yet it is clear from the trace element chemistry that they cannot be melted from material of "cosmic" composition. The extreme deficiencies of the siderophile and volatile elements, (Figs. 4-5 and 4-8) and the enrichment of refractory elements, in comparison with terrestrial basalts, (Figs. 4-6 and 4-15) indicate that the interior of the moon is further removed from primitive compositions than the interior of the Earth.

Capture of the moon is still possible since the lunar composition may have arisen elsewhere by extreme chemical processing of the primitive nebula. However, it is now necessary to invoke extra assumptions and special conditions. Simpler explanations appear to be available. We shall have to search further afield for samples representative of the primitive solar nebula. It is possible that sampling of comets by space probes would provide this.

DOUBLE PLANET HYPOTHESES

The accretion or condensation of the moon as a sister planet to the Earth has been less popular than the other hypotheses, since in its simplest form it fails to explain the low density of the moon in comparison with the Earth. If both bodies condensed from the same portion of the solar nebula at the same time, then there is no *a priori* reason to expect that one body will be 1.6 times denser than the other. To overcome this difficulty in the hypothesis some form of chemical fractionation has been introduced. Thus, if metal and silicate fractions were present, the metal phase could be accreted preferentially into the Earth. However, we have seen that the lunar silicates are not the same as those in the terrestrial mantle, so that some additional selective fractionation of silicates is needed to account for these chemical differences. It is clear from the Apollo 11 and 12 data that revision of this hypothesis is necessary to account for both the density and the chemical differences between Earth and moon.

Ringwood (Australian National University) and Opik (Ireland) have suggested a modification of the double planet theory, referred to as the *precipitation hypothesis*, to account for many of the observations. This model proposes that the moon was formed by accretion from a ring of planetismals which formed around the Earth following condensation of the planet. This ring of planetismals arises in the following manner, as a consequence of the final stages of accretion. It is assumed that the Earth began to condense from cold solar nebula material, equivalent in composition to the Type I carbonaceous chondrites. This accretion took place in a short period of time (less than one million years). As the radius of the growing Earth increases, so does the gravitational energy of infall. By making suitable assumptions about the time of accretion, the surface temperature of the Earth can approach 2000°C. in the final stages, when all incoming material is vaporized. The primitive Earth develops a massive atmosphere, mainly of hydrogen and carbon monoxide, resulting from the reduction of iron from oxide to metal, but containing perhaps 10 – 20% of volatilized silicates. These condense and form a "sediment ring" around the Earth. The gases and the more volatile components are driven away mainly by early intense solar radiation, leaving behind the refractory components, from which a metallic phase may have already been separated. Thus, material depleted in the volatile and siderophile elements and enriched in the refractory elements is left. Opik has discussed the condensation of the moon from such a sediment ring. As the moon increases in size, larger and larger objects are swept up due to the increasing gravitational attraction. The heavy cratering of the uplands may represent this stage. Finally, the larger (50 – 100 km.) objects are captured and produce the giant maria basins by impact. Thus the moon is formed. Initial heating of the lunar interior during accretion is reinforced by that due to radioactive decay of uranium, thorium and potassium. The internal temperature rises to the melting point of the lunar basalts about half a billion years after accretion. The lava floods continue for perhaps half a billion years until the interior cools down. For the past three billion years the moon has been relatively inactive, and the major process has been the slow meteorite bombardment of the surface, producing occasional young ray craters such as Copernicus, Kepler and Tycho.

Discussions of the formation of the lunar uplands, which are probably different in composition to the interior, must await sample return from future Apollo missions.

GLOSSARY

ACCESSORY MINERAL. A term applied to a mineral occurring in small amounts in a rock.

ACCRETION. A term applied to the growth of planets from smaller fragments or dust.

ACHONDRITE. Stony meteorite lacking nickel-iron and chondrules.

AEON. One billion years ($=10^9$ years).

AGGLOMERATE. A rock composed of fragments of various sizes, shapes and degree of angularity.

ALKALI ELEMENT. A general term applied to the univalent metals Li, Na, K, Rb and Cs.

ALKANE HYDROCARBON. Hydrocarbon saturated with hydrogen atoms.

AMINO ACID. Organic compound comprising both acid and basic functional groups; the unit constituents of proteins.

AN. Abbreviation for anorthite.

ANGSTROM (Å). A unit of length, 10^{-8} cm.; commonly used in crystallography and mineralogy.

ANION. A negatively charged ion (for example, O^{-2}, F^{-1}).

ANORTHITE (An). $CaAl_2Si_2O_8$, the most calcic member of the plagioclase (feldspar) series of minerals.

ANORTHOSITE. A coarse-grained igneous rock made up almost entirely of plagioclase feldspar.

APATITE. $Ca_5(PO_4)_3(F,Cl)$; a mineral.

ARMALCOLITE. $(Mg_{0.5}Fe_{0.5})Ti_2O_5$; a mineral only known from the moon.

AROMATIC HYDROCARBON. Hydrocarbons undersaturated in hydrogen comprising benzene, C_6H_6, and related compounds.

ARTIFACT. Compound inadvertently synthesized, commonly in the course of a chemical analysis.

ATMOSPHERE. Unit of pressure ($=1.013$ bars).

AUGITE. A member of the clinopyroxene group of minerals which are the most abundant minerals on the moon; usually black or dark green in color.

BAR. The international unit of pressure (one bar $= 0.987$ atmosphere).

BASALT. A fine-grained, dark colored igneous rock composed primarily of plagioclase (feldspar) and pyroxene; usually other minerals such as olivine, ilmenite, etc. are present.

BASALTIC ACHONDRITE. Calcium-rich stony meteorites, lacking chondrules and nickel-iron, showing some similarities to terrestrial and lunar basalts; eucrites and howardites are types of basaltic achondrites.

BEDROCK. Any continuous solid rock whether exposed on the surface or overlain by loose soil.

BIOCHEMICAL. Organic compounds directly relevant to life processes.

BIOGENIC. From living organisms.

BIOLIPIDS. Organic compounds from living matter, soluble in organic solvents.

BRECCIA. A rock made up of angular, coarse fragments of other rocks, embedded in a fine-grained matrix.

BOTRYOIDAL. Having the shape of a bunch of grapes.

CARBIDE. A compound of an element, usually a metal, with carbon.

CARBONACEOUS CHONDRITES. A class of meteorites containing up to 5% organic matter generally believed to have formed by inorganic processes; this type of meteorite is considered the most "primitive" in the solar system.

CARBONACEOUS MATERIAL. Substance predominantly composed of carbon, with complex molecular structure involving hydrogen, oxygen, nitrogen, and related elements.

CATION. A positively charged ion (for example, Na^{+1}, Ti^{+4}).

CHALCOPHILE ELEMENT. An element tending to concentrate in sulfide minerals.

CHONDRITE. The most abundant class of stony meteorite characterized by the presence of chondrules.

CHONDRULE. Small, rounded body in meteorites (generally less than 1 mm. in diameter), commonly composed of olivine and/or orthopyroxene.

CHROMITE. $FeCr_2O_4$; a mineral.

CLEAVAGE. The tendency of a mineral to split along smooth planes, parallel to crystal faces or directions.

CLINOPYROXENE. Minerals of the pyroxene group, such as augite and pigeonite, which crystallize in the monoclinic system.

COGENETIC. Formed at the same time.

COORDINATION NUMBER. The number of anions (usually oxygen) which surround a cation in a crystalline solid.

CORONA. The outer tenuous atmosphere of the sun.

COSMIC ELEMENT ABUNDANCES. The abundances of the chemical elements in the solar nebula before formation of the sun, planets and meteorites.

COSMIC RADIATION. (a) High energy "galactic" radiation (1-10 BeV/nucleon) coming from outside the solar system; (b) Lower energy radiation (10-100 MeV/nucleon) derived mainly from solar flares.

COSMOCHEMISTRY. The study of the abundance and distribution of elements in the universe.

CRATER. A bowl-shaped depression caused by volcanic eruptions, meteorite impact, etc.

CRISTOBALITE. A variety of SiO_2 that forms at high temperatures; a mineral.

CRYSTALLINE. (a) Rocks composed of well-defined minerals; (b) Minerals which have a definite internal structure.

DENDRITIC. Branching, or tree-like, structure found in some minerals.

DEVITRIFICATION. Process whereby glassy material converts to different minerals.

DIFFERENTIATION. See magmatic differentiation.

DIVALENT. An element with a double charge (e.g., Ca^{+2}).

DUMBBELL. A shape characterized by two spheres connected by a short "bar."

DUST. Lunar dust is the extremely fine-grained powdery material which coats lunar rocks and fines; it is a component of the fines (soils), but is not synonymous with fines (soils).

ECLOGITE. A dense rock consisting of garnet and pyroxene, similar in chemical composition to basalt.

EJECTA. Material blown out of a volcano or meteorite impact center.

ELECTRON MICROSCOPE. A type of microscope using electrons instead of light, and capable of extremely high magnification of many types of specimens (including rocks and minerals).

ELECTRON PROBE. A modern instrument capable of performing chemical analyses on extreme small areas (as small as one micron).

ELECTRON VOLT (eV). The energy acquired by a particle carrying unit electronic change moving through a potential difference of one volt.

KeV = one thousand eV.

MeV = one million eV.

BeV = one billion eV.

END-MEMBER. One or more (chemical) compounds used in the interpretation of a more complex mineral or mineral group.

EROSION. The process(es) by which loosened rock material is carried away.

EUCRITE. A type of basaltic achondrite (qv).

EUHEDRAL. Well-formed crystals exhibiting crystal faces.

EXSOLUTION. At high temperatures, pairs or groups of minerals will be in solid solution (as one phase), but upon cooling one or more mineral phases may separate out; unmixing.

EXTRA TERRESTRIAL. Beyond the Earth.

EXTRUSIVE. A rock solidifying on the Earth's (or moon's) surface (generally rapidly), as in the case of lava.

FELDSPAR. A group of related minerals (e.g., plagioclase, potassium feldspar), which are abundant on Earth and moon.

FERRIMAGNETISM. Magnetism exhibited by ferrites and other mixed oxides.

FERROMAGNETIC. Possessing magnetic properties similar to those of iron (paramagnetic substances with a magnetic permeability much greater than one).

FINES. Lunar material arbitrarily defined as less than 1 cm. in diameter; synonymous with "soils."

FISSIOGENIC PROCESSES. Production of nuclides by natural fission of heavier species (e.g., uranium).

FISSION TRACK. A narrow continuous trail of damage produced by passage of a fission fragment through solid material.

FRACTIONAL CRYSTALLIZATION. Formation and separation of mineral phases of varying composition during crystallization of a silicate melt or magma, resulting in a continuous change of composition of the magma.

FRACTIONATION. The separation of chemical elements from an initially homogeneous state into different phases or systems.

GABBRO. A coarse-grained, dark igneous rock made up chiefly of plagioclase (usually labradorite) and pyroxene. Other minerals often present include olivine, apatite, ilmenite, etc.

GARDENING. The process of turning over the lunar soil or regolith by meteorite bombardment.

GAS CHROMATOGRAPHY. Process for analyzing and separating components of a gaseous or volatile liquid mixture, based on transit times through a packed bed of powder.

GEOCHEMISTRY. The study of the abundance, distribution and migration of chemical elements in various parts of the Earth and moon.

GLASS. A natural material which has been cooled extremely rapidly so that minerals were unable to form; a supercooled liquid. In lunar material, glass is found as spheres in the soils, and in selected portions of rocks which otherwise contain minerals.

GRANITE. An igneous rock composed chiefly of quartz and alkali feldspar.

GRANULAR. A rock texture in which the mineral grains are nearly equidimensional.

GROUNDMASS. The fine-grained rock material between larger mineral grains; used interchangeably with matrix.

HALF-LIFE. The time interval during which a number of atoms of a radioactive nuclide decay to one half of that number.

HALOGENS. A general term applied to the elements F, Cl, Br and I (group VIIb of the periodic table).

HAND SPECIMEN. A piece of rock large enough to hold and examine without a microscope.

HEXAGONAL. A type of crystal arrangement in which crystals have 3 equal axes at 120° and lying in one plane, and a fourth unequal axis perpendicular to the other three.

HOWARDITE. A type of basaltic achondrite (qv).

HYDROCARBON. Compound consisting solely of carbon and hydrogen.

HYDROTHERMAL ALTERATION. Changes in rocks resulting from action of hot emanations high in water content.

IGNEOUS. Applied to rocks or processes involving the solidification of hot, molten material.

ILMENITE. $FeTiO_3$; most abundant opaque lunar mineral.

IMMISCIBLE. When two or more liquids (or solids) cannot be mixed, as in the case of oil and water.

IMPACT. The wearing away of rocks by the effect of definite blows; in the case of the lunar rocks, impact is generally related to meteorites of all sizes.

IMPACT MELTING. The process by which country rock is melted by the impact of a meteorite or comet.

INDIGENOUS. Present naturally.

INDURATED. Hardened; rocks may be hardened by heat, pressure, cementation, etc.

INTERSTITIAL. Mineral matter which crystallizes in interstices (generally late-forming).

INTRUSIVE. A rock solidifying (generally slowly) below the surface.

INVOLATILE ELEMENT. See refractory element.

IONIC RADIUS. The effective radius of ionized atoms in crystalline solids; ionic radii commonly lie between 0.4 – 1.5 Angstrom units.

IRON METEORITE. A class of meteorite composed chiefly of iron or iron-nickel.

IRON-NICKEL. (Fe-Ni); a mineral.

ISOCHRON. A line on a diagram passing through plots of samples with the same age but differing isotope ratios.

ISOTOPES. Atoms of a specific element which differ in number of neutrons in the nucleus; this results in different atomic weight, and very slightly differing chemical properties (for example, U^{235} and U^{238}).

KILOBAR (Kb or Kbar). 1000 bars; a unit of pressure approximately equal to 1000 atmospheres.

LATTICE SITE. The position occupied by an atom in a crystalline solid.

LAMELLAE. Thin plates or layers of one mineral in another mineral.

LAVA. Fluid rock which emanates from the interior of the Earth (or moon) from volcanoes, etc.; upon solidification forms an extrusive igneous rock (see magma).

LAYERED IGNEOUS INTRUSION. A body of plutonic igneous rock which has formed layers of different minerals during solidification; it is divisible into a succession of extensive sheets lying one above the other.

LIQUIDUS. The line or surface in a phase diagram above which the system is completely liquid.

LITHIFICATION. The process of converting loose material into hardened rock.

LITHOPHILE ELEMENT. An element tending to concentrate in oxygen-containing compounds, particularly silicates.

LOW K OCEANIC THOLEIITE. See oceanic theoleiite.

LSPET. Lunar Sample Preliminary Examination Team.

MAGMA. The term applied to molten rock as long as it is below the surface of the Earth (or moon) which, upon solidification, becomes an intrusive igneous rock; when extruded onto the surface, this material is called lava.

MAGMATIC DIFFERENTIATION. The production of rocks of differing chemical composition during cooling and crystallization of a silicate melt or magma by processes such as removal of early formed mineral phases.

MANTLE. The solid region of the Earth extending from the base of the crust (10 – 50 km. depth) to the top of the core (2900 km depth); principal constituents are iron, magnesium, silicon and oxygen, occurring as mineral phases of increasing density with depth.

MARE (PL. MARIA). A sea; a term used to describe those dark, generally flat areas of the moon formerly thought to be seas. Apollo 11 and 12 missions to the moon landed on maria.

MASCON. Regions of excess mass concentrations per unit area, identified by positive gravity anomalies, on the lunar surface.

MASKELYNITE. Feldspar converted to glass by shock effects due to meteorite impact.

MASS SPECTROMETER. Instrument for measuring mass of atoms or molecules.

MATRIX. The fine-grained material in which larger mineral or rock fragments are embedded; often used interchangeably with groundmass.

MELT. The hot, molten material from which igneous rocks solidify.

MESOSTASIS. The interstitial, generally fine-grained material, between larger mineral grains in a rock; may be used synonymously with matrix and groundmass.

METAMORPHIC. Applied to rocks or processes involving change, whether this be due to heat, pressure or chemical action.

METASTABLE. A mineral form (or assemblage) which is not the most stable form (or assemblage) at a particular temperature and pressure and tends to convert to a more stable form (or assemblage).

METEORITE. A metallic or stony (silicate) body that has fallen on Earth or the moon from outer space.

METHANE. The simplest hydrocarbon, CH_4.

MINERAL. A naturally occurring, solid substance with a characteristic chemical composition (generally inorganic), which usually has a definite internal arrangement of atoms.

MINERALOGY. The science dealing with the identification, chemical composition, classification and origin of minerals.

MOMENT OF INERTIA. A measure of the effect of relative distribution of mass within a rotating body $= \Sigma(mr^2)$.

MONOCLINIC. A type of crystal arrangement in which the crystals have three unequal axes, two of which are inclined to each other, and a third is perpendicular to the others.

MU $= \mu$. The ratio U^{238}/Pb^{204}.

NANOGRAM (ng). One-billionth of a gram.

NASA. National Aeronautics and Space Administration.

NEUMANN LINES. Characteristic structure found in certain types of iron meteorites.

NOBLE GASES. The rare gases, helium, neon, argon, krypton, xenon and radon.

NUCLEON. Sub-atomic nuclear particles (mainly protons and neutrons).

NUCLIDES. Atoms characterized by the number of protons (Z) and neutrons (N). The mass number (A) = N + Z; isotopes are nuclides with same number of protons (Z) but differing numbers of neutrons (N); isobars have same mass number (A) but different numbers of protons (Z) and neutrons (N).

OCEANIC THOLEIITE. Basaltic lavas characterized by very low concentrations of potassium and related elements; probably the most common lava erupted at the mid-ocean ridges.

OERSTED. The cgs unit of magnetic intensity.

OIL IMMERSION. A microscopic technique designed to obtain very high magnifications.

OLIVINE. $(Mg,Fe)_2SiO_4$; a mineral.

OPAQUE. A mineral which does not transmit light in thin section.

OPHITIC. A rock texture which is composed of elongated feldspar crystals embedded in pyroxene or olivine.

ORDER OF MAGNITUDE. Commonly used term for a factor of ten.

ORGANIC COMPOUND. Compound composed largely of carbon and hydrogen; sometimes with nitrogen, oxygen and sulfur.

ORGANOGENIC. Scientific colloquialism referring to elements commonly involved in biochemical substances.

ORTHORHOMBIC. A type of crystal arrangement in which the crystal forms have three unequal axes at right angles to each other.

OXIDIZING ENVIRONMENT. An environment in which oxygen is available for chemical reactions.

PARAMAGNETISM. In a magnetic field, paramagnetic substances align with the field (the magnetic permeability is greater than one); ferromagnetism is an extreme example of paramagnetism.

PERIDOTITE. An igneous rock characterized by pyroxene and olivine (but no feldspar).

PETROGRAPHY. The science concerned with the systematic description and classification of rocks.

PETROLOGY. The science of rocks; includes identification, chemical composition, classification, origin, etc.

PHENOCRYST. A large, conspicuous crystal in igneous rocks, surrounded by a fine-grained groundmass.

PHOTOMICROGRAPH. An enlarged photograph of a microscopic object taken by a camera attached to a microscope.

PHOTOSPHERE. An outer layer of the sun, about 350 km. thick, which is the source of most solar radiation.

PIGEONITE. $(Mg,Fe,Ca,Al,Ti)_2Si_2O_6$; a mineral.

PLACER. A concentration of gravels, sand and occasionally heavy (or valuable) minerals, derived from weathered and eroded rocks.

PLAGIOCLASE. A sub-group (or series) of the feldspar group of minerals.

PLUMOSE. A radiating arrangement of crystals.

PLUTONIC. A term applied to igneous rocks which have crystallized at depth, usually with coarsely crystalline texture.

POIKILITIC. Essentially synonymous with poikioblastic.

POIKIOBLASTIC. A rock texture in which small, granular crystals occur irregularly scattered in a larger crystal of another mineral.

POISE. cgs unit of viscosity (= 1 dyne sec/cm.^{2}).

POLYMERIZED ORGANIC MATTER. Organic matter, the unit molecules of which have become chemically bonded to one another to form a plastic-like substance.

PORPHYRIN. Organic compound comprising carbon, nitrogen and hydrogen, basically $C_{20}H_{14}N_4$ and higher homologues.

PPM. parts per million — 1 ppm = .0001%; 10 ppm = .001%; 100 ppm = .01%; 1000 ppm. = .1%.

PREBIOTIC. Precursor to the evolution of life.

PRE-CAMBRIAN (Precambrian). All rocks formed before Cambrian time; older than about 600,000,000 years.

PRINCIPAL INVESTIGATOR (P.I.). A leader of a group of scientists approved by NASA to study a piece (or pieces) of moon material.

PROTEIN. Ubiquitous components of all living tissue; polymers of amino acids; composed of carbon, hydrogen, nitrogen, oxygen and sulfur.

PYROLYSIS. Heating under controlled conditions such as inert atmosphere to prevent oxidation, commonly to 1000°C.

PYROXENE. A closely-related group of minerals which includes augite, pigeonite, etc.; the most abundant mineral at Tranquillity Base.

PYROXENOIDS. A group of related minerals (e.g., wollastonite, rhodonite) similar to pyroxenes, but with slightly different crystal structure.

PYROXFERROITE. $Ca_{0.15}Fe_{0.85}SiO_3$; a mineral known only from the moon.

RADIOACTIVE ISOTOPE. An isotope which is capable of changing spontaneously into another element.

RADIOGENIC ISOTOPE. An isotope produced by the decay of a radioactive isotope.

RADIOGENIC LEAD. Lead isotopes formed by radioactive decay of uranium and thorium (Pb^{206} from U^{238}; Pb^{207} from U^{235}; Pb^{208} from Th^{232}).

RARE-EARTH (RE OR REE). A collective term for elements with atomic number 57-71, which includes La, Ce, etc.

RARE GASES. The noble gases, helium, neon, argon, krypton, xenon, and radon.

REDUCING ENVIRONMENT. An environment in which oxygen is not available for chemical reactions.

REFRACTIVE INDEX. An optical property of minerals (and other materials) related to the velocity of light.

REFRACTORY (INVOLATILE) ELEMENT. An element whose oxides (e.g., ZrO_2) have boiling points above 2500°C.

REGOLITH. Loose surface material, composed of rock fragments and soil, which overlies consolidated bedrock.

RESIDUAL LIQUID. The material remaining after most of a magma has crystallized; it is sometimes characterized by abundance of volatile constitutents.

RESIDUUM. Late-forming minerals, generally very fine-grained and difficult to identify.

ROCK. Naturally occurring, solid matter covering a large and essential portion of the Earth or moon; usually an aggregate composed of more than one type of mineral.

r-PROCESS NUCLIDES. Those nuclides produced under conditions of intense neutron flux in supernovae explosions.

RUTILE. TiO_2; a mineral.

SCANNING ELECTRON MICROSCOPE. A modern instrument capable of obtaining extremely high magnification simultaneously with great depth of focus.

SIDEROPHILE ELEMENT. An element tending to be concentrated in metallic iron.

SILICA TETRAHEDRON. The basic configuration of silicate structures, where four oxygen atoms and one silicon are arranged in a compact pyramidal figure with the silicon atom in the center of the structure; the silica tetrahedron is the most important building block of minerals.

SILICATE. A mineral (or compound) whose crystal structure contains SiO_4 tetrahedra, in any one of several possible arrangements.

SINTERED. Similar to a cinder.

SOIL. Fine-grained lunar material arbitrarily defined as less than 1 cm. in diameter; synonymous with "fines."

SOIL MECHANICS. The science of the mechanical and physical properties of soils.

SOLAR NEBULA. The primitive disk shaped cloud of dust and gas from which all bodies in the solar system originated.

SOLAR WIND. The stream of charged particles (mainly ionized hydrogen) moving outward from the sun with velocities in the range 300 − 500 km./sec.

SOLID SOLUTION. Substitution of one element (or compound) for another element (or compound) in a mineral.

SOLIDUS. The line or surface in a phase diagram below which the system is completely solid.

SOLVUS. A curved line or surface in a phase diagram separating a solid solution field from a field of two or more solid phases.

SPALLED. Broken or chipped surfaces, usually in layers parallel to a surface.

SPECIFIC GRAVITY. The ratio of the mass of a body to a mass of an equal volume of water at a specific temperature; a characteristic physical property used in the study of minerals.

SPINEL-GROUP. General term for several minerals (e.g., chromite, magnetite) with chemical, physical and structural properties similar to spinel; general formula is AB_2O_4.

STABLE ISOTOPE. An isotope which will not change into another (radiogenic) isotope.

STOICHICMETRIC. Applied to minerals whose composition is close to an ideal formula.

STONY METEORITE. A class of meteorite composed chiefly of silicate minerals such as pyroxene, olivine, etc.

SUBOPHITIC. Similar to ophitic texture, but the size difference between the feldspar and pyroxene crystals is not so great.

TEKTITES. Small glassy objects of wide geographic distribution formed by splashing of melted terrestrial country rock during meteorite, asteroid or cometary impacts.

TERRESTRIAL. Earth(ly).

TETRAHEDRON. See silica tetrahedron.

TEXTURE. The arrangement, shape and size of grains composing a rock.

THERMOLUMINESCENCE. An emission of light exhibited by minerals when heated.

THIN SECTION. A rock or mineral fragment ground extremely thin (0.03 mm); under these conditions many minerals (except those classed as opaque) are transparent under the microscope where they can be studied.

Trace element. An element found in very low (trace) amounts; generally less than 0.1%.

Tranquillity Base. Landing site of the Apollo 11 mission.

Triclinic. A type of crystal arrangement in which the crystals have three unequal axes, all of which intersect at oblique angles.

Tridymite. A variety of SiO_2; a mineral.

Trivalent. An element with a triple charge (e.g., Al^{+3}).

Troilite. FeS; a mineral.

Twinning. A common phenomenon exhibited by some minerals, in which apparent single crystals are actually composites of several parts, which are related to each other in a definite crystallographic manner.

Ulvöspinel. Fe_2TiO_4; a mineral.

Vesicle (vesicular). Bubble-shaped, smooth-walled cavity, usually produced by expansion of vapor (gas) in a magma.

Viable. Able to live.

Vitrification. Process of being converted to glass.

Volatile element. An element volatile at temperatures below 1500°C.

Volatiles. Those elements or compounds (e.g., H_2O, F, Cl, OH) which are commonly concentrated in the residuum of a melt, and have low boiling points.

Volcanism. All processes related to the formation of lava flows, volcanic rock and volcanoes.

Vug (vuggy). Small, irregular shaped, rough-walled cavity in a rock.

Weathering. The process(es) by which rocks are worn away, to eventually form soil.

Zoning. Variations in composition in a mineral grain; may be detected by chemical analyses, or observed in a microscope by changes in color, etc.

CONVERSION FACTORS

Length

kilometer (km.)	= 0.6214 miles (mi.)
mile (mi.)	= 1.6094 kilometers (km.)
meter (m.)	= 100 centimeters (cm.)
	= 39.37 inches (in.)
	= 3.281 feet (ft.)
	= 1.0936 yards (yd.)
centimeter (cm.)	= 1/100 of a meter
	= 0.394 inches (in.)
millimeter (mm.)	= 1/1000 of a meter (m.)
	= 1/10 of a centimeter (cm.)
	= 0.03937 inches (in.)
inch (in.)	= 2.54 centimeters (cm.)
	= 25.4 millimeters (mm.)
micron (μ)	= 1/1000 of a millimeter (mm.)
	= one-millionth of a meter

Mass

kilogram (kg.)	= 1000 grams (gm.)
	= 2.205 pounds (lb.)
pound (lb.)	= 0.454 kilogram (kg.)
gram (gm.)	= 1/1000 of a kilogram (kg.)
	= 0.035 ounce (oz.)
ounce (oz.)	= 28.35 grams (gm.)
milligram (mg.)	= 1/1000 of a gram (gm.)
microgram (μg.)	= one-millionth of a gram (gm.)
nanogram (ng.)	= one-billionth of a gram (gm.)

Units of Concentration

parts per million (ppm):	1 ppm = 0.0001%
	10 ppm = 0.001%
	100 ppm = 0.01%
	1000 ppm = 0.1%
parts per billion (ppb):	1 ppb = 0.0000001% (=0.001 ppm)
	10 ppb = 0.000001% (= 0.01 ppm)
	100 ppb = 0.00001% (= 0.1 ppm)
	1000 ppb = 0.0001% (= 1 ppm)

Mean diameter	=	3476 km
Mean diameter	=	.27 (Earth = 1.0)
Mass	=	.012 (Earth =1.0)
Density	=	3.34 gm/cm^3
Surface gravity	=	.165 (Earth = 1.0)
Velocity of escape	=	2.4 km/sec

CHEMICAL SYMBOLS AND ELEMENTS

Ac .... Actinium	He .... Helium	Pt .... Platinum
Ag .... Silver	Hf .... Hafnium	Pu .... Plutonium
Al .... Aluminum	Hg .... Mercury	Ra .... Radium
Ar .... Argon	Ho .... Holmium	Rb .... Rubidium
As .... Arsenic	I .... Iodine	Re .... Rhenium
At .... Astatine	In .... Indium	Rh .... Rhodium
Au .... Gold	Ir .... Iridium	Rn .... Radon
B .... Boron	K .... Potassium	Ru .... Ruthenium
Ba .... Barium	Kr .... Krypton	S .... Sulfur
Be .... Beryllium	La .... Lanthanum	Sb .... Antimony
Bi .... Bismuth	Li .... Lithium	Sc .... Scandium
Br .... Bromine	Lu .... Lutetium	Se .... Selenium
C .... Carbon	Mg .... Magnesium	Si .... Silicon
Ca .... Calcium	Mn .... Manganese	Sm .... Samarium
Cd .... Cadmium	Mo ...... Molybdenum	Sn .... Tin
Ce .... Cerium	N .... Nitrogen	Sr .... Strontium
Cl .... Chlorine	Na .... Sodium	Ta .... Tantalum
Cm .... Curium	Nb .... Niobium	Tb .... Terbium
Co .... Cobalt	Nd .... Neodymium	Tc ...... Technetium
Cr .... Chromium	Ne .... Neon	Te .... Tellurium
Cs .... Cesium	Ni .... Nickel	Th .... Thorium
Cu .... Copper	Np .... Neptunium	Ti .... Titanium
Dy .... Dysprosium	O .... Oxygen	Tl .... Thallium
Er .... Erbium	Os .... Osmium	Tm .... Thulium
Eu .... Europium	P .... Phosphorus	U .... Uranium
F .... Fluorine	Pa .... Protactinium	V .... Vanadium
Fe .... Iron	Pb .... Lead	W .... Tungsten
Fr .... Francium	Pd .... Palladium	Xe .... Xenon
Ga .... Gallium	Pm .... Promethium	Y .... Yttrium
Gd .... Gadolinium	Po .... Polonium	Yb .... Ytterbium
Ge .... Germanium	Pr .... Praseodymium	Zn .... Zinc
H .... Hydrogen		Zr .... Zirconium

SUBJECT INDEX